'Tis the Season to
CROCHET ™

The Needlecraft Shop

EDITOR Bobbie Matela
ART DIRECTOR Brad Snow
PUBLISHING SERVICES MANAGER Brenda Gallmeyer

ASSOCIATE EDITORS Mary Ann Frits, Kathy Wesley
ASSISTANT ART DIRECTOR Nick Pierce
COPY SUPERVISOR Michelle Beck
COPY EDITORS Mary O'Donnell,
Judy Weatherford
TECHNICAL ARTIST Leigh Maley

GRAPHIC ARTS SUPERVISOR Ronda Bechinski
BOOK DESIGN Brad Snow
GRAPHIC ARTISTS Jessi Butler,
Minette Collins Smith
PRODUCTION ASSISTANTS Cheryl Kempf, Marj Morgan,
Judy Neuenschwander

PHOTOGRAPHY Tammy Christian,
Don Clark, Matthew Owen,
Jackie Schaffel

PHOTO STYLISTS Tammy Nussbaum,
Tammy M. Smith

PUBLISHING DIRECTOR David McKee
MARKETING DIRECTOR Dan Fink
EDITORIAL DIRECTOR Gary Richardson

Copyright © 2006 The Needlecraft Shop
Berne, IN 46711

PRINTED IN THE UNITED STATES OF AMERICA
FIRST PRINTING 2006, China
LIBRARY OF CONGRESS NUMBER 2005933354
HARDCOVER ISBN-10: 1-57367-234-3
HARDCOVER ISBN-13: 978-1-57367-234-4
SOFTCOVER ISBN-10: 1-57367-235-1
SOFTCOVER ISBN-13: 978-1-57367-235-1

Every effort has been made to ensure the accuracy and completeness of
the instructions in this book. However, we cannot be responsible for human
error or for the results when using materials other than those specified in the
instructions, or for variations in individual work.

2 3 4 5 6 7 8 9

'Tis the Season
Every Month of the Year!

Over the years you've probably made many of your Christmas gifts for family and friends. By creating your gifts and decorations throughout the year, you can actually have time for baking cookies and planning parties as the holidays arrive. If you've ever been rushing to finish a crocheted gift on Christmas Eve you'll appreciate what I mean.

In this book we have included many beautiful decorations and timely gift projects that will make the holidays special.

Our **Wonderland Decorations** chapter is filled with fabulous ideas for trimming trees and fashioning mantel displays.

See our **Splendid Tabletops** projects to find ideas for setting the stage for your dinner or party festivities.

Send **Handsome Greetings** with cards, gift trims and bottle covers that show your spirit of giving.

Create a warm, welcoming look **Throughout the House** with afghans, throws and colorful accessories.

Find **Special Wearables & Quick Gifts** that will please your loved ones, including sweaters, hats, scarves, mittens, necklaces, stocking stuffers and even a dog coat.

With jolly wishes,

Bobbie Matela

Mary Ann Frits

Wonderland Decorations

Splendid Tabletops

Handsome Greetings

Throughout the House

Special Wearables & Quick Gifts

Wonderland Decorations

*Create a beautiful holiday setting with crocheted
decorations, stockings on the fireplace, a wreath,
shelf sitters, a tree skirt and garland.*

Perky Penguins

DESIGNS BY JENNINE KOREJKO

SKILL LEVEL ▰▰▱▱
EASY

FINISHED SIZE
4 inches tall

MATERIALS
Medium (worsted)
  weight yarn:
    8 oz/560 yds/224g black *(A)*
    2 oz/140 yds/56g white *(B)*
    1 oz/70 yds/28g yellow *(C)*
    small amount of red *(D)*, blue
      (E), green *(F)*, gray *(G)*,
      orange *(H)*, turquoise *(I)*,
      light yellow *(J)*, tan *(K)*, rose
      (L), pink *(M)*, purple *(N)*
Size E/4/3.5mm crochet
  hook or size needed to
  obtain gauge
Small amount of black embroi-
  dery floss
Tapestry needle
Stitch markers
½ yd ¼-inch-wide white satin ribbon
Polyester fiberfill
Small weight or plastic beans
  (optional)

GAUGE
5 sc = 1 inch

Instructions

BASIC PENGUIN

BODY & HEAD
Note: Body and Head are worked in continuous rnds. Do not join; mark beg of rnds.

Rnd 1 (RS): Starting at bottom of body with A, ch 2; 6 sc in 2nd ch from hook.

Rnd 2: 2 sc in each sc. *(12 sc)*

Rnd 3: [Sc in next sc, 2 sc in next sc] 6 times. *(18 sc)*

Rnd 4: [Sc in next 2 sc, 2 sc in next sc] 6 times. *(24 sc)*

Rnd 5: [Sc in next 3 sc, 2 sc in next sc] 6 times. *(30 sc)*

Rnd 6: Sc in each sc.

Rnds 7–10: Rep rnd 6.

*Note: For **sc dec,** draw up lp in each of 2 sts indicated, yo and draw through all 3 lps on hook.*

Rnd 11: Sc in next 3 sc, **sc dec** *(see Note)* in next 2 sc; *sc in next 3 sc, sc dec in next 2 sc; rep from * 4 times. *(24 sc)*

Rnds 12 & 13: Rep rnd 6.

Rnd 14: [Sc in next 2 sc, sc dec] 6 times. *(18 sc)*

Rnd 15: [Sc in next sc, sc dec] 6 times. *(12 sc)*

Rnd 16: 2 sc in each sc. *(24 sc)*

Rnd 17: Rep rnd 6.

Rnd 18: [Sc in next 3 sc, 2 sc in next sc] 6 times. *(30 sc)*

Rnds 19 & 20: Rep rnd 6.

Rnd 21: [Sc in next 3 sc, sc dec] 6 times. *(24 sc)*

Rnd 22: Rep rnd 6.

Rnd 23: [Sc in next 2 sc, sc dec] 6 times. *(18 sc)*

Rnd 24: [Sc in next sc, sc dec] 6 times. *(12 sc)*

Note: If using weight or beans, place in bottom of Body. Stuff firmly with fiberfill.

Rnd 25: [Sc dec] 6 times. *(6 sc)*

Rnd 26: [Sk next sc, sl st in next sc] 3 times.

Fasten off and weave in ends.

WING
Make 2.
Note: Wing is worked in joined rows.

Row 1 (RS): With A and leaving a 8-inch end for sewing, ch 5; 3 dc in 4th ch from hook *(beg 3 sk chs count as a dc)*; 4 dc in next ch; join with a sl st in 3rd ch of beg 3 sk chs, turn.

Row 2: Ch 3 *(counts as a dc on this and following rows)*, dc in same ch as joining and in next 3 dc, 2 dc in next dc; dc in next 3 dc; join in 3rd ch of beg ch-3, turn.

Row 3: Ch 2, keeping last lp of each dc on hook, dc in next 4 dc, yo and draw through all 5 lps on hook; ch 1, keeping last lp of each dc on hook, dc in next 5 dc, yo and draw through all 6 lps on hook; ch 1; join in 2nd ch of beg ch-2.

Fasten off and weave in end not left for sewing.

BELLY
Row 1 (RS): With B, ch 5; sc in 2nd ch from hook and in next 3 chs, turn. *(4 sc)*

Row 2: Ch 1, 2 sc in first sc; sc in next 2 sc, 2 sc in next sc, turn. *(6 sc)*

Row 3: Ch 1, 2 sc in first sc; sc in next 4 sc, 2 sc in next sc, turn. *(8 sc)*

Row 4: Ch 1, 2 sc in first sc; sc in next 6 sc, 2 sc in next sc, turn. *(10 sc)*

Row 5: Ch 1, sc in each sc, turn.

Row 6: Rep row 5.

Row 7: Ch 1, sc dec in first 2 sc; sc in next 6 sc, sc dec in next 2 sc, turn. *(8 sc)*

Row 8: Ch 1, sc dec; sc in next 4 sc, sc dec. *(6 sc)*

Fasten off, leaving an 8-inch end for sewing. Weave in other end.

FACE

Row 1 (RS): With B, ch 4; 2 sc in 2nd ch from hook, sc in next ch, 2 sc in next ch, turn. *(5 sc)*

Row 2: Ch 1, 2 sc in first sc; sc in next 3 sc, 2 sc in next sc, turn. *(7 sc)*

Row 3: Ch 1, 2 sc in first sc; sc in next 5 sc, 2 sc in next sc, turn. *(9 sc)*

Row 4: Ch 1, sc in each sc, turn.

Row 5: Ch 1, sc dec; sc in next sc, ch 1, sl st in next 3 sc, ch 1, sc in next sc; sc dec.

Fasten off, leaving an 8-inch end for sewing. Weave in other end.

BEAK

With C and leaving an 8-inch end for sewing, ch 4; sl st in 2nd ch from hook, sc in next ch, in next ch work (hdc, ch 1, sl st, ch 1, hdc); working in unused lps on opposite side of beg ch, sc in next lp, sl st in next lp and in beg sk ch.

Fasten off and weave in end not left for sewing.

FOOT
Make 2.

Row 1 (RS): With C, ch 2; sc in 2nd ch from hook, turn.

Row 2: Ch 1, sc in first sc, turn.

Row 3: Rep row 2.

Row 4: Ch 1, hdc in first sc, ch 2, sl st in 2nd ch from hook—*picot made*; dc in same sc, picot; hdc in same sc; picot; ch 1, sl st in same sc.

Fasten off, leaving an 8-inch end for sewing. Weave in other end.

FINISHING

Step 1: Referring to photo for placement and using ends left for sewing, sew Wings to side of Body. Sew Face to Head, Belly to Body, and Feet to bottom of Body.

Step 2: Sew Beak to Face.

Step 3: Referring to photo for placement and with embroidery floss, make 2 French knots *(see Fig. 1)* for eyes, and straight sts *(see Fig. 2)* for eyebrows and nostrils.

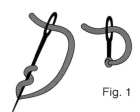

Fig. 1

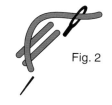

Fig. 2

WINTER GIRL PENGUIN

PENGUIN

Work same as Basic Penguin on pages 8 and 9 through Finishing.

SCARF

With D, ch 43, working in back bumps only, hdc in 5th ch from hook *(beg 4 sk chs count as a ch-1 sp, a hdc and a ch-1 sp)*; *ch 1, sk next ch, hdc in next ch; rep from * 18 times. *(21 hdc)*

Fasten off and weave in ends.

FRINGE

For fringe, cut 1½-inch strands of D; use 1 strand for each knot. Tie 3 knots in each end of scarf. Trim ends even.

BOW

Rnd 1 (RS): With D, ch 2; sc in 2nd ch from hook, turn.

Rnd 2: Ch 3, in first sc work (3 dc, ch 3, sl st); working in unused lp on opposite side of beg ch, in lp work (sl st, ch 3, 3 dc, ch 3, sl st); join in first ch of turning ch-3.

Fasten off, leaving an 8-inch end for sewing. Weave in other end.

FINISHING

Step 1: Sew Bow to top of Penguin's Head.

Step 2: Tie Scarf around Penguin's neck.

CANDY CANE PENGUIN

PENGUIN
Work same as Basic Penguin on pages 8 and 9 through Finishing.

SCARF
With E, work same as Scarf for Winter Girl Penguin.

CANDY CANE
Note: Candy Cane is worked in continuous rnds. Do not join; mark beg of rnds.

Rnd 1 (RS): With D, ch 2; sc in 2nd ch from hook; change to B by drawing lp through; drop D.

Note: Rnds 2–9 are worked in **back lps**—*see Stitch Guide—only.*

Rnd 2: Sc in next 3 sc; change to D; drop B.

Rnds 3–8: Rep rnd 2, alternating D and B.

Rnd 9: Sc in next 3 sc; join in first sc.

Fasten off and weave in all ends.

FINISHING
Step 1: Tack top of Candy Cane to form curve. Referring to photo for placement, sew to Penguin's Wing.

Step 2: Tie Scarf around Penguin's neck.

PENGUIN WITH WREATH

PENGUIN
Work same as Basic Penguin on pages 8 and 9 through Finishing.

WREATH
Rnd 1 (RS): With F, ch 9; join to form ring; ch 2, tr in same ch as joining; ch 1; *in next ch work (sl st, ch 2, tr, ch 1); rep from * 7 times; join in base of beg ch-2.

Rnd 2: Sl st in next ch of beg ch-2 and in next tr, ch 1; * sl st in next tr, ch 1; rep from * 7 times;

join in 2nd sl st of beg 2 sl sts.

Fasten off, leaving an 8-inch end for sewing. Weave in other end.

EAR MUFFS
Ear Piece
Make 2.
With H, ch 3, sl st in 3rd ch from hook, [ch 2, sl st in same ch] 7 times.

Fasten off, leaving an 8-inch end. Weave in other end.

Band
Join G in first ch-2 sp on 1 Ear Piece; ch 14; join in first ch-2 sp on 2nd Ear Piece.

Fasten off and weave in ends.

FINISHING
Step 1: Tack Ear Piece to each side of Head.

Step 2: Sew Wreath to 1 Wing.

Step 3: Cut 9-inch length of white

ribbon. Tie ribbon in bow at bottom of Wreath. Trim ends.

PENGUIN BABY BOY

PENGUIN
Work same as Basic Penguin on pages 8 and 9 through Finishing.

BIB
Row 1 (RS): With I, ch 8; sc in 2nd ch from hook and in each rem ch, turn. *(7 sc)*

Row 2: Ch 1, 2 sc in first sc; sc in next 5 sc, 2 sc in next sc, turn. *(9 sc)*

Row 3: Ch 1, sc in each sc, turn.

Rows 4 & 5: Rep row 3.

Edging & Ties
Working along next side in sps formed by edge sc, sl st in next 5 sps; working in unused lps of beg ch, sl st in each lp; working across next side in sps formed by edge sc, sl st in next 5 sps, ch 13—*tie made*; join in first sl st.

Fasten off and weave in ends.

LOLLIPOP
Candy Top
With J, ch 4; 13 dc in 4th ch from hook *(beg 3 sk chs counts as a dc)*; join in first ch of beg 3 sk chs. Fasten off.

Stick
Join K in joining sl st of Candy Top; ch 10, sl st in back lp of each ch; join in joining sl st.

Fasten off and weave in all ends.

FINISHING
Step 1: Referring to photo for placement, sew Lollipop to Penguin's Wing.

Step 2: Slip Bib around Penguin's neck.

PENGUIN BABY GIRL

PENGUIN
Work same as Basic Penguin on pages 8 and 9 through Finishing.

BOW
With L, work same as Bow for Winter Girl Penguin.

BIB
Row 1 (RS): With M, ch 8; sc in 2nd ch from hook and in each rem ch, turn.

Row 2: Ch 1, sc in each sc, turn.

Row 3: Ch 1, 2 sc in first sc; sc in next 5 sc, 2 sc in next sc, turn. *(9 sc)*

Row 4: Ch 1, sc in each sc, turn.

Note: *For **sc dec**, draw up lp in each of 2 sts indicated, yo and draw through all 3 lps on hook.*

Row 5: Ch 1, **sc dec** *(see Note)* in first 2 sc; sc in next 5 sc, sc dec in next 2 sc. *(7 sc)*

Edging & Ties
Working along next side in sps formed by edge sc, sl st in next sp; [ch 2, sl st in next sp] 4 times;

ch 2; working in unused lps of beg ch, sl st in next lp; *ch 2, sl st in next lp; rep from * across; ch 2; working along next side in sps formed by edge sc, sl st in next sp; [ch 2, sl st in next sp] 4 times; ch 13—*tie made;* join in first sl st.

Fasten off and weave in ends.

FINISHING
Step 1: Sew Bow to top of Penguin's Head.

Step 2: Slip Bib around Penguin's neck.

SANTA PENGUIN

PENGUIN
Work same as Basic Penguin on pages 8 and 9 through Finishing.

VEST
Row 1 (RS): With D, ch 19; hdc in 3rd ch from hook *(beg 2 sk chs count as a hdc)* and in next 15 chs, 2 hdc in next ch, turn. *(19 hdc)*

Row 2: Ch 2 *(counts as a hdc on this and following rows),* hdc in first hdc and in next 2 hdc, ch 3, sk next 2 hdc, hdc in next hdc, 2 hdc in next hdc; [hdc in next 2 hdc, 2 hdc in next hdc] twice; hdc in next hdc, ch 3, sk next 2 hdc, hdc in next 2 hdc, 2 hdc in 2nd ch of beg 2 sk chs, turn. *(20 hdc)*

Row 3: Ch 2, hdc in first hdc and in next 3 hdc, 4 hdc in next ch-3 sp; hdc in next 12 hdc, 4 hdc in next ch-3 sp; hdc in next 3 hdc, 2 hdc in 2nd ch of turning ch-2, turn. *(30 hdc)*

Row 4: Ch 2, hdc in first hdc and in next 28 hdc, 2 hdc in 2nd ch of turning ch-2. *(32 hdc)*

Fasten off and weave in ends.

HAT
Rnd 1 (RS): With D, ch 3; 2 hdc in 3rd ch from hook *(beg 2 sk chs count as a hdc);* join in 2nd ch of beg 2 sk chs. *(3 hdc)*

Rnd 2: Ch 2 *(counts as a hdc on this and following rnds),* hdc in same ch as joining; 2 hdc in each of next 2 hdc; join in 2nd ch of beg ch-2. *(6 hdc)*

Rnd 3: Ch 2, hdc in same ch as joining and in next hdc; [2 hdc in next hdc, hdc in next hdc] twice; join in 2nd ch of beg ch-2. *(9 hdc)*

Rnd 4: Ch 2, hdc in same ch as joining; [hdc in next hdc, 2 hdc in next hdc] 4 times; join in 2nd ch of beg ch-2. *(14 hdc)*

Rnd 5: Ch 2, hdc in each hdc; join in 2nd ch of beg ch-2.

Rnd 6: Ch 2, hdc in same ch as joining and in next hdc, [2 hdc in next hdc, hdc in next hdc] 6 times; join in 2nd ch of beg ch-2.

Fasten off, leaving an 8-inch end for sewing. Weave in other end.

Trim
Hold piece with RS facing you and rnd 6 at top; join B in **back lp** *(see Stitch Guide)* of first hdc;

ch 1, sc in same lp and in back lp of each rem hdc; join in first sc.

Fasten off and weave in ends.

Pompom
Cut 1 (3-inch) strand and 10 (1-inch) strands of B. Lay 1-inch strands across 3-inch strand and tie knot in center. Fluff and trim to desired shape and fullness.

FINISHING
Step 1. Sew Pompon to top of Hat. Sew Hat to top of Penguin's Head.

Step 2. Place Vest on Penguin.

PENGUIN WITH GIFT

PENGUIN
Work same as Basic Penguin on pages 8 and 9 through Finishing.

GIFT BOX
Center
Row 1 (RS): With H and leaving an 8-inch end, ch 5; sc in 2nd ch from hook and in each rem ch, turn. *(4 sc)*

Row 2: Ch 1, sc in each sc, turn.

Row 3: Rep row 2.

Row 4: Working in **front lps** *(see Stitch Guide)* only, sc in each sc, turn.

Rows 5–10: [Work rows 2–4] twice.

Row 11: Rep row 2.

Row 12: Sc in each sc.

First Side
Row 1 (RS): Ch 1, working along next side in sps formed by edge sc, sc in next 3 sps, turn, leave rem rows unworked.

Row 2: Ch 1, sc in each sc, turn.

Row 3: Ch 1, sc in each sc.

Fasten off, leaving an 8-inch end for sewing.

2nd Side
Hold Center with RS facing you and opposite long edge at top; join H in edge sc of row 12.

Row 1 (RS): Ch 1, working in sps formed by edge sc, sc in same sp and in next 2 sps, turn, leave rem rows unworked.

Row 2: Ch 1, sc in each sc, turn.

Row 3: Ch 1, sc in each sc.

Fasten off, leaving an 8-inch end for sewing.

Weave in ends not left for sewing.

Assembly
Fold beg ch row to row 12; sew tog, carefully matching sts; fold in each side and sew in place. Stuff lightly before closing.

FINISHING
Step 1: Tack Gift Box to Penguin's Wings.

Step 2: Tie ribbon in bow and trim ends. Tack to top of Gift Box.

PENGUIN DE-LIGHTS

PENGUIN
Work same as Basic Penguin on pages 8 and 9 through Finishing.

SCARF
With N, work same as Scarf for Winter Girl Penguin.

CHRISTMAS LIGHTS
Strand
With G and leaving an 8-inch end for sewing, ch 25. Fasten off, leaving an 8-inch end for sewing.

Bulbs
Join N in 3rd ch of Strand; ch 2, sl st in 2nd ch from hook and in same ch as joining.

Fasten off and weave in ends.

Rep with L, C, F, and H for rem Bulbs, skipping 5 chs between each Bulb.

FINISHING
Step 1: Tack Christmas Lights to Penguin's Wings.

Step 2: Tie Scarf around Penguin's neck. 🍂

Christmas Ornament Trims

DESIGNS BY SUE PENROD

SKILL LEVEL ■■□□
EASY

FINISHED SIZE
8¼ inches long

MATERIALS
Aunt Lydia's Classic Crochet size 10 crochet cotton (350 yds per ball):
- 1 ball each #421 goldenrod (A), #494 victory red (B), #484 myrtle green (C)

or

J.&P. Coats Royale Metallic Crochet size 10 crochet cotton (100 yds per ball):
- 1 ball #90G gold/gold (A)

Aunt Lydia's Classic Crochet size 10 crochet cotton (300 yds per ball):
- 1 ball each #420 cream (B), #661 frosty green (C)

Size B/1/2.25mm crochet hook or size needed to obtain gauge
2½-inch glass ornament
Tapestry needle
White craft glue
Small container (for mixing stiffening solution)
Piece of cardboard
Plastic wrap
Straight pins

GAUGE
8 sc = 1 inch

Instructions

PICOT STRAND
With A, [ch 5, ch 3, sl st in first ch from hook—*picot made*] 9 times; ch 2.

Fasten off and weave in ends. Set aside.

FLOWER
Make 9.
With B, ch 6; in 6th ch from hook work [sl st, ch 5] 5 times; sl st in same ch—*petals made*.

Fasten off and weave in ends.

ASSEMBLY
Slip center of 1 Flower over first picot of Picot Strand. Pull ch end to close Flower around picot; tie ends in knot. Trim ends. Position petals so that 2 opposite petals lay over Picot Strand.

EDGING
Join C with a sl st in first ch of Picot Strand; ch 4, sk first petal on first Flower; *sc in next petal, ch 4, sl st in first ch—*picot made*; ch 1, sc in next flower petal, ch 4, sk first petal on next Flower; rep from * 7 times; sc in next petal, picot; ch 1, sc in next flower petal, ch 4, sl st in last ch on Picot Strand, ch 4; working in petals on opposite side of Flowers, sk next petal; *sc in next petal, picot; ch 1, sc in next flower petal, ch 4, sk first petal on next Flower; rep from * 7 times; sc in next petal, picot; ch 1, sc in next flower petal, ch 4, sl st in same ch on Picot Strand as joining sl st made.

Fasten off and weave in ends.

FINISHING
Step 1: Make stiffening mixture of 60 percent white glue and 40 percent water. Mix well in small container such as paper cup. Cover cardboard with plastic wrap.

Step 2: Place trim in mixture to saturate.

Step 3: Remove trim from mixture and place flat on plastic-covered cardboard, shaping as necessary. Let dry.

Step 4: Glue trim around center of ornament, overlapping ends. ❧

Colorful Garland & Ornaments

GARLAND
DESIGN BY
DONNA COLLINSWORTH

SKILL LEVEL EASY

FINISHED SIZE
1½ inches x desired length

MATERIALS
Caron Glimmer super bulky
   (super chunky) weight yarn
   (1¾ oz/49 yds/50g per skein):
      1 skein each #0009 willow
      (A), #0015 iris (B), #0004
      carnation (C), #0008 apple
      (D), #0005 red (E), #0007
      mango (F)
Size G/6/4mm crochet hook or
   size needed to obtain gauge
Tapestry needle

GAUGE
Round bead: 1 inch long

Long bead: 1¾ inches long.

Instructions

Note: *Instructions are written for 12 inches of garland.*

ROUND BEAD
Make 1 each of B, C, D, E & F.

Rnd 1 (RS): Ch 2; 10 sc in 2nd ch from hook; join with a sl st in first sc, turn.

Rnd 2: Ch 1, sc in each sc; join in first sc, turn.

Rnds 3 & 4: Rep rnd 2.

Rnd 5: Sk first sc, sc in next sc,

[sk next sc, sc next sc] 4 times; join in first sc. (5 sc)

Fasten off and weave in ends.

LONG BEAD
Make 4.
Rnd 1 (RS): With A, ch 2; 6 sc in 2nd ch from hook; join with a sl st in first sc, turn.

Rnd 2: Ch 1, sc in each sc; join in first sc, turn.

Rnds 3–5: Rep rnd 2.

Rnd 6: Sk first sc, sc in next sc, [sk next sc, sc next sc] 4 times; join in first sc. (3 sc)

Fasten off and weave in ends.

ASSEMBLY
Insert hook through center of 1 Round Bead and draw A through; insert hook through center of 1 Long Bead and draw A strand through; continuing in same manner, string remaining Beads in desired sequence, alternating Round and Long Beads. Draw 8 inches of A strand through last bead. Fold end in half and knot forming ending lp. Rep on opposite end, cutting A 8 inches from first Bead.

ORNAMENTS
DESIGN BY MELODY MACDUFFEE

SKILL LEVEL ◖◗◻◻ EASY

FINISHED SIZE
3 inches in diameter

MATERIALS
For Version 1
Red Heart Classic medium
   (worsted) weight yarn (3½
   oz/190 yds/99g per skein):
      1 skein each #230 yellow
      (A), #849 olympic blue
      (B), #254 pumpkin (C)
Size H/8/5mm crochet hook or
   size needed to obtain gauge
3-inch plastic foam ball
Tapestry needle

For Version 2 (4 MEDIUM)
Red Heart Classic medium
   (worsted) weight yarn (3½
   oz/190 yds/99g per skein):
      1 skein each #596 purple
      (A), #755 pale rose (B),
      #912 cherry red (C)
Size H/8/5mm crochet hook or
   size needed to obtain gauge
3-inch plastic foam ball
Tapestry needle

For Version 3 (4 MEDIUM)
Red Heart Classic medium
   (worsted) weight yarn (3½
   oz/190 yds/99g per skein):
      1 skein each #912 cherry red
      (A), #230 yellow (B), #676
      emerald green (C)
Size H/8/5mm crochet hook or
   size needed to obtain gauge
3-inch plastic foam ball
Tapestry needle

GAUGE
Rnds 1 and 2 = 2 inches

Instructions

ORNAMENT
Rnd 1 (RS): With A, ch 5, join with a sl st to form ring; 8 sc in

sk sc on working rnd behind dc] 7 times; join in back lp of first sc. *(32 sc)*

Rnd 5: Ch 1, sc in same lp as joining and in back lp of each rem sc; join in first sc. Fasten off.

Rnd 6: Join C in back lp of first sc; ch 1, sc in same lp and in back lp of next sc, 2 dc in front lp of next st 3 rows below, sk next 2 sc on working rnd behind dc, [sc in back lp of next 2 sc, 2 dc in front lp of next st 3 rows below, sk next 2 sc on working rnd behind dc] 7 times; join in back lp of first sc.

Rnd 7: Rep rnd 5.

Rnd 8: Join A in back lp of first sc; ch 1, sc in same lp and in back lp of next sc, dc in front lp of next 2 dc 3 rows below, sk next 2 sts on working rnd behind dc, [sc in back lp of next 2 sts, dc in front lp of next 2 dc 3 rows below, sk next 2 sts on working rnd behind dc] 7 times; join in first sc.

Rnd 9: Rep rnd 5.

Rnds 10 & 11: With B, rep rnds 8 and 9.

Rnds 12 & 13: With C, rep rnds 8 and 9.

Rnds 14 & 15: With A, rep rnds 8 and 9.

Insert plastic foam ball.

Note: *For **dc dec,** [yo, insert hook in front lp of st indicated, yo, draw lp through, yo, draw through 2 lps on hook] twice; yo and draw through all 3 lps on hook.*

Rnd 16: Join B in back lp of first sc; ch 1, sc in same lp and in back lp of next sc, **dc dec** *(see Note)* in front lps of next 2 dc 3 rows below; sk next 2 sts on working rnd behind dc dec; [sc in back lp of next 2 sts, dc dec in front lps of next 2 dc 3 rows below, sk next 2 sts on working rnd behind dc dec] 7 times; join in first sc. *(24 sts)*

Note: *For **sc dec,** draw up lp in each of 2 sts indicated, yo and draw through all 3 lps on hook.*

Rnd 17: Ch 1, sc in same sc as joining; **sc dec** *(see Note)* in next 2 sts; [sc in next st, sc dec in next 2 sts] 7 times; join in first sc. *(16 sc)*

Fasten off.

Rnd 18: Join C in first sc; ch 1, dc dec in corresponding 2 sts 3 rows below, sk next st on working rnd behind dc dec, sc in back lp of next st, [dc dec in front lps of next 2 sts 3 rows below, sk next st on working rnd behind dc dec, sc in back lp of next st] 7 times; join in first sc. *(16 sts)*

Rnd 19: Ch 1, sc dec in first 2 sc; [sc dec] 7 times; join in first sc. *(8 sc)*

Rnd 20: Sl st in next 7 sc; join in joining sl st.

Fasten off and weave in all ends.

HANGING LOOP
Cut 20-inch length of matching yarn. Thread through top of ornament. Tie ends in bow.

ring; join in **back lp** *(see Stitch Guide)* of first sc.

Rnd 2: Ch 1, 2 sc in same lp as joining; working in back lps only, 2 sc in each rem sc; join in back lp of first sc. *(16 sc)*

Rnd 3: Ch 1, 2 sc in same lp as joining; working in back lps only, sc in next sc, [2 sc in next sc, sc in next sc] 7 times; join in first sc. *(24 sc)*

Fasten off.

Rnd 4: Join B in back lp of any sc; ch 1, sc in same lp and in back lp of next sc, 2 dc in front lp of next sc 3 rows below; [sc in back lp of next 2 sc, 2 dc in **front lp** *(see Stitch Guide)* of corresponding sc 3 rows below,

Peppermint Candy Ornaments

DESIGNS BY SUE PENROD

SKILL LEVEL ⬛⬛◻◻
EASY

SIZE
2¼ inches in diameter

MATERIALS

Aunt Lydia's Classic
  Crochet size 10 crochet cotton
  (350 yds per ball):
    1 ball each #1 white *(A)*,
    #494 victory red *(B)*
Size B/1/ 2.25mm crochet hook or
  size needed to obtain gauge
Tapestry needle
White craft glue
20 inches ⅛-inch-wide silver
  ribbon (for 1 ornament)
Small container (for mixing stiff-
  ening solution)
Piece of cardboard
Plastic wrap
Straight pins

GAUGE
8 sc = 1 inch

Instructions

PEPPERMINT CANDY ORNAMENT
Row 1: With A, ch 15; sc in 2nd ch from hook and in next 2 chs, hdc in next ch, dc in next 6 chs, hdc in next ch, sc in next 3 chs, change to B by drawing lp through; cut A, turn. *(14 sts)*

Row 2: Ch 1, sc in each st, turn.

Row 3: Ch 1, sc in first 3 sc, hdc in next sc, dc in next 6 sc, hdc in next sc, sc in next 3 sc, change to A; cut B, turn.

Row 4: Ch 1, sc in each sc, turn.

Row 5: Ch 1, sc in first 3 sc, hdc in next sc, dc in next 6 sc, hdc in next sc, sc in next 3 sc; change to B; cut A, turn.

Rows 6–33: [Work rows 2–5] 7 times.

Rows 34 & 35: Rep rows 2 and 3.

Row 36: Ch 1, sl st in each st and in sk ch of beg ch-15.

Fasten off, leaving a 12-inch end. Weave in other end.

ASSEMBLY
Thread end in tapestry needle; weave needle in and out of row ends along 1 side. Draw thread to gather row ends tog in center. Secure ends. Rep on opposite side.

FINISHING
Step 1: Make stiffening mixture of 60 percent white glue and 40 percent water. Mix well in small container such as paper cup. Cover cardboard with plastic wrap.

Step 2: Place trim in mixture to saturate.

Step 3: Remove trim from mixture and place flat on plastic-covered cardboard, shaping as necessary. Let dry.

Step 4: Cover piece with clear plastic wrap. Cut ribbon in half and tie bows on either end to secure plastic wrap.

PEPPERMINT PINWHEEL ORNAMENT
Row 1: With A, ch 15; sc in 2nd ch from the hook and in next 2 chs, hdc in next ch, dc in next 6 chs, hdc in next ch, sc in next 3 chs; change to B by drawing lp through; drop A, turn. *(14 sts)*

Row 2: Ch 1, sc in next 3 sc, hdc in next hdc, dc in next 6 dc, hdc in next hc, sc in next 3 sc, turn.

Row 3: Rep Row 2.

Row 4: Ch 1, sc in next 3 sc, hdc in hdc, dc in next 6 dc, hdc in next hdc, sc in next 3 sc; change to A; drop B, turn.

Row 5: Ch 1, sc in next 3 sc, hdc in hdc, dc in next 6 dc, hdc in next hdc, sc in next 3 sc; change to B; drop A, turn.

Rows 6–17: [Work rows 2–5] 3 times.

Rows 18 & 19: Rep rows 2 and 3.

Row 20: Ch 1, sc in next 3 sc, hdc in hdc, dc in next 6 dc, hdc in next hdc, sc in next 3 sc, turn.

Row 21: Ch 1, sl st in each st and in unused sc of beg ch-15.

Fasten off, leaving a 12-inch end. Weave in other end.

ASSEMBLY
Thread end in tapestry needle; weave needle in and out of row ends. Draw thread to gather row ends tog. Secure ends.

Rep to gather other side closed.

FINISHING
Work same as Finishing for Peppermint Candy Ornament

PEPPERMINT SPIRAL ORNAMENT
Rnd 1 (RS): With B, ch 2; 7 sc in 2nd ch from the hook; change to A by drawing lp through; drop B. *(7 sc)*

Rnd 2: 2 sc in each sc; change to B; drop A. *(14 sc)*

Rnd 3: 2 sc in each sc; change to A; drop B. *(28 sc)*

Rnd 4: Sc in each sc; change to B; drop A.

Rnd 5: Sc in each sc; change to A; drop B.

Rnd 6: [Sc in next 3 sc, 2 sc in next sc] 7 times; change to B; drop A. *(35 sc)*

Rnd 7: [Sc in next 4 sc, 2 sc in next sc] 7 times; change to A; drop B. *(42 sc)*

Rnd 8: [Sc in next 6 sc, 2 sc in next sc] 6 times; change to B; drop A. *(48 sc)*

Rnd 9: Rep rnd 5.

Rnd 10: [Sc in next 7 sc, 2 sc in next sc] 6 times; change to B; drop A. *(54 sc)*

Rnd 11: Rep rnd 5.

Rnd 12: Rep rnd 4.

Rnd 13: [Sc in next 7 sc, sk next sc, sc in next sc] 6 times; change to A; drop B. *(48 sc)*

Rnd 14: [Sc in next 6 sc, sk next sc, sc in next sc] 6 times; change to B; drop A. *(42 sc)*

Rnd 15: [Sc in next 5 sc, sk next sc, sc in next sc] 6 times; change to A; drop B. *(36 sc)*

Rnd 16: [Sc in next 4 sc, sk next sc, sc in next sc] 6 times; change to B; drop A. *(30 sc)*

Rnd 17: [Sc in next 4 sc, sk next sc, sc in next sc] 6 times; change to A; drop B. *(24 sc)*

Rnd 18: Rep rnd 4.

Rnd 19: [Sc in next sc, sk next sc, sc in next sc] 8 times; change to B; drop A. *(16 sc)*

Rnd 20: Rep rnd 5.

Rnd 21: [Sc in next sc] in every other sc around, 4 sc.

Fasten off and weave in all ends.

FINISHING
Work same as Finishing for Peppermint Candy Ornament. 🌿

Santa Tree Skirt

DESIGN BY KATHLEEN STUART

SKILL LEVEL ■■□□
EASY

FINISHED SIZE
48 inches in diameter

MATERIALS

Lion Brand Chenille Thick
& Quick super bulky (super
chunky) yarn (100 yds per skein):
4 skeins #098 antique white (A)
3 skeins #131 forest green (B)
2 skeins #189 wine (C)
1 skein #124 khaki (D)
Size N/13/9mm crochet hook or
size needed to obtain gauge
12 black ½-inch buttons
6 red ½-inch buttons
Sewing needle and matching thread

GAUGE
2 dc = 1 inch

PATTERN NOTE
To change color, work last stitch
until 2 loops remain on hook; with
new color, yarn over and draw
through 2 loops on hook. Drop or
cut old color as specified. Do not
carry dropped color behind work;
use 2nd ball of yarn.

Instructions

PANEL
Make 6.
Row 1 (RS): With C, ch 4, 2 dc
in 4th ch from hook (beg 3 sk chs
count as a dc), turn. (3 dc)

Row 2: Ch 3 (counts as a dc on
this and following rows), dc in
first dc and in next dc; 2 dc in 3rd
ch of beg 3 sk chs, turn. (5 dc)

Row 3: Ch 3, dc in first dc and in
each rem dc to turning ch-3; 2 dc
in 3rd ch of turning ch-3, turn. (7 dc)

Rows 4–12: Rep row 3. (25 dc at
end of row 12)

Row 13: Ch 3, dc in first dc and in
each rem dc to turning ch-3; 2 dc
in 3rd ch of turning ch-3, changing
to A in last dc; cut C, turn. (27 dc)

Rows 14 & 15: Rep row 3. (31 dc
at end of row 15)

Row 16: Ch 3, dc in first dc and
in next 8 dc, changing to D in
last dc; drop A; dc in next 13 dc,
changing to A in last dc, drop D;
dc in next 8 dc, 2 dc in 3rd ch of
turning ch 3, turn. (33 dc)

Row 17: Ch 3, dc in first dc and
in next 11 dc, changing to D in
last dc; drop A; dc in next 9 dc,
changing to A in last dc, drop D;
dc in next 11 dc, 2 dc in 3rd ch of
turning ch 3, turn. (35 dc)

Rows 18 & 19: Rep row 3. (39 dc
at end of row 19)

Row 20: Rep row 3, changing to
B in last dc. (41 dc)

Row 21: Ch 3, dc in first dc and
in next dc, changing to A in last
dc; drop B; dc in next 37 dc,
changing to B in last dc; drop A;
dc in next dc, 2 dc in 3rd ch of
turning ch 3, turn. (43 dc)

Row 22: Ch 3, dc in first dc and
in next 5 dc, changing to A in
last dc; drop B; dc in next 31 dc,
changing to B in last dc; drop A;
dc in next 5 dc, 2 dc in 3rd ch of
turning ch 3, turn. (45 dc)

Row 23: Ch 3, dc in first dc and
in next 10 dc, changing to A in
last dc; drop B; dc in next 23 dc,
changing to B in last dc; drop A;
dc in next 10 dc, 2 dc in 3rd ch of
turning ch 3, turn. (47 dc)

Row 24: Ch 3, dc in first dc and
in next 15 dc, changing to A in
last dc; drop B; dc in next 15 dc,
changing to B in last dc; drop A;
dc in next 15 dc, 2 dc in 3rd ch of
turning ch 3, turn. (49 dc)

Row 25: Ch 3, dc in first dc and
in next 20 dc, changing to A in
last dc; drop B; dc in next 7 dc,
changing to B in last dc; drop A;
dc in next 20 dc, 2 dc in 3rd ch of
turning ch 3, turn. (51 dc)

Row 26: Ch 3, dc in first dc and in
next 24 dc, changing to A in last dc;
drop B; dc in next dc, changing to
B; drop A; dc in next 24 dc, 2 dc in
3rd ch of turning ch 3. (53 dc)

Fasten off and weave in all ends.

MUSTACHE
Make 6.
With A, ch 5, in 5th ch from hook
work (tr, ch 4, sl st); ch 5, in 5th ch
from hook work (tr, ch 4, sl st). Fasten
off, leaving an 8-inch end for sewing.

FINISHING
Step 1: With matching yarn, sew
panels tog along long sides,
leaving 2 panels unjoined for
opening.

Step 2: Referring to photo for placement and with sewing needle and
matching thread, sew 2 black
buttons to row 16 of each face for
eyes and sew 1 red button to each
face near center of row 17 for nose.

Step 3: Sew Mustache to each face
on row 18, underneath nose. ❦

Christmas Wreath

DESIGN BY MARY ANN FRITS

SKILL LEVEL
EASY

FINISHED SIZE
12 inches in diameter

MATERIALS
Mode Dea
  Caché bulky (chunky) weight
  yarn (1¾ oz/72 yds/50g per
  skein):
    4 skeins #2765 smartie (A)
Mode Dea Fur Sure super bulky
  (super chunky) weight yarn
  (1¾ oz/72 yds/50g per skein):
    1 skein #3722 totally pink (B)
Mode Dea Cheerio medium
  (worsted) weight yarn (1¾
  oz/104 yds/50g per skein):
    1 skein each #8625 peridot
    (C) and #8731 pink
    sapphire (D)
Mode Dea Prima bulky (chunky)
  weight yarn (1¾ oz/72 yds/50g
  per skein):
    1 skein #3781 raspberry (E)
Mode Dea Espree bulky (chunky)
  weight yarn (1¾ oz/90
  yds/50g) per skein):
    1 skein #2630 grassy (F)
Size I/9/5.5mm crochet hook or
  size needed to obtain gauge
Tapestry needle
12-inch diameter purchased
  plastic foam or straw wreath
Purchased decorative trims

Tacky craft glue

GAUGE
4 sc = 1 inch

Instructions

Row 1: With A, ch 26; sc in 2nd ch from hook and in next 11 chs, 3 sc in next ch; sc in next 12 chs, turn.

Note: *For **sc dec**, draw up lp in 2 sts indicated, yo and draw through all 3 lps on hook.*

Row 2: Ch 1, **sc dec** (see Note) in first 2 sc; sc in next 11 sc, 3 sc in next sc; sc in next 11 sc, sc dec in next 2 sc, turn.

Rows 3–6: Rep row 2. At end of row 6, change to B by drawing lp through; cut A, turn.

Rows 7–9: Rep row 2. At end of row 6, change to C by drawing lp through; cut B, turn.

Rows 10–13: Rep row 2. At end of row 6, change to E by drawing lp through; cut C, turn.

Rows 14–17: Rep row 2. At end of row 6, change to A by drawing

lp through; cut E, turn.

Rows 18–21: Rep row 2. At end of row 6, change to D by drawing lp through; cut A, turn.

Rows 22 & 23: Rep row 2. At end of row 6, change to F by drawing lp through; cut D, turn.

Rows 24 & 25: Rep row 2. At end of row 6, change to D by drawing lp through; cut F, turn.

Rows 26 & 27: Rep row 2. At end of row 27, change to A by drawing lp through; cut D, turn.

Rows 28–33: Rep row 2. At end of row 33, change to B by drawing lp through; cut A, turn.

Rows 34–87: [Work rows 7 through 33] twice. At end of row 87, do not change color.

Fasten off and weave in all ends.

FINISHING

Step 1: Place piece over Wreath. With tapestry needle, sew long sides tog. Sew beg ch to row 87.

Step 2: Glue purchased trims to Wreath. 🌿

Elf, Gingerbread Man & Snowman Shelf Sitters

DESIGN BY JENNINE KOREJKO

ELF

SKILL LEVEL ●●●□ INTERMEDIATE

FINISHED SIZE
9 inches tall seated, excluding legs

MATERIALS
Medium (worsted) weight yarn:
  2 oz/140 yds/56g green (A)
  small amount each of peach (B), white (C), rust (D), black (E)

Size G/6/4mm crochet hook or size needed to obtain gauge
Tapestry needle
12-inch square of plastic wrap: 2
1 cup uncooked rice
Polyester fiberfill
1 x 2-inch piece of cardboard

GAUGE
4 dc = 1 inch

PATTERN NOTE
Before starting project, make rice pouch as follows:

Place rice in center of 1 piece of plastic wrap, fold up corners and twist to secure; flatten pouch slightly. Wrap with 2nd piece of plastic wrap.

Instructions

BODY
Rnd 1 (RS): Starting at bottom with A, ch 3; 9 hdc in 3rd ch from hook *(beg 2 sk chs count as a hdc)*; join with a sl st in 2nd ch of beg 2 sk chs. *(10 hdc)*

Rnd 2: Ch 2 *(counts as a hdc on this and following rnds)*, hdc in same ch as joining; 2 hdc in each hdc; join in 2nd ch of beg ch-2. *(20 hdc)*

Rnd 3: Ch 2, hdc in same ch as joining and in next hdc; [2 hdc in next hdc, hdc in next hdc] 9 times; join in 2nd ch of beg ch-2. *(30 hdc)*

Rnd 4: Ch 2, hdc in same ch as joining and in next 2 hdc; [2 hdc in next hdc, hdc in next 2 hdc] 9 times; join in 2nd ch of beg ch-2. *(40 hdc)*

Rnd 5: Ch 2, hdc in same ch as joining and in next 3 hdc; [2 hdc in next hdc, hdc in next 3 hdc] 5 times; [2 hdc in next hdc, hdc in next hdc] 8 times; join in 2nd ch of beg ch-2. *(54 hdc)*

Rnd 6: Ch 2, hdc in each hdc; join in 2nd ch of beg ch-2.

Rnds 7–9: Rep rnd 6.

Note: For **hdc dec**, [yo, draw up lp in st indicated] twice; yo and draw through all 5 lps on hook.

Rnd 10: Ch 2, hdc in next 2 hdc, **hdc dec** *(see Note)* in next 2 hdc; [hdc in next 3 hdc, hdc dec in next 2 hdc] 9 times; hdc in next 4 hdc; join in 2nd ch of beg ch-2. *(44 hdc)*

Rnd 11: Rep rnd 6.

Rnd 12: Ch 2, hdc in next hdc, hdc dec; [hdc in next 2 hdc, hdc dec] 10 times; join in 2nd ch of beg ch-2. *(33 hdc)*

Rnds 13 & 14: Rep rnd 6.

Insert rice pouch *(see Pattern Note)* after rnd 14.

Rnd 15: Ch 2, hdc dec; [hdc in next hdc, hdc dec] 10 times; join

in 2nd ch of beg ch-2. *(22 hdc)*

Rnd 16: Rep rnd 6.

Rnd 17: Ch 2, hdc dec; [hdc in next hdc, hdc dec] 6 times; hdc in next hdc; join in 2nd ch of beg ch-2. *(15 hdc)*

Change to B by drawing lp through; cut A.

Note: *Stuff Body lightly with fiberfill.*

HEAD
Rnd 1 (RS): Ch 2, 2 hdc in each of next 2 hdc; [hdc in next hdc, 2 hdc in each of next 2 hdc] 4 times; join in 2nd ch of beg ch-2. *(25 hdc)*

Rnd 2: Ch 2, [2 hdc in next hdc, hdc in next 2 hdc] 8 times; join in 2nd ch of beg of ch-2. *(33 hdc)*

Rnd 3: Ch 2, hdc in each hdc; join in 2nd hc of beg of ch-2.

Rnds 4 & 5: Rep rnd 3.

Rnd 6: Ch 2, [hdc in next 2 hdc, hdc dec] 8 times. *(25 hdc)*

Rnd 7: Ch 2, hdc in next hdc, hdc dec; [hdc in next 2 hdc, hdc dec] 5 times; hdc in next hdc; join in 2nd ch of beg ch-2. *(19 hdc)*

Rnd 8: Ch 2, [hdc dec, hdc in next hdc] 6 times; join in 2nd ch of beg ch-2. *(13 hdc)*

Note: *Stuff Head firmly with fiberfill.*

Rnd 9: Ch 2, [hdc dec] 6 times; join in 2nd ch of beg ch-2. *(7 hdc)*

Fasten off, leaving a 6-inch end for sewing.

With tapestry needle, weave end through each st on last rnd. Pull tightly to close, and secure end.

Weave in all ends.

ARM
Make 2.
Rnd 1 (RS): Starting at hands with A, ch 3; 7 hdc in 3rd ch from hook *(beg 2 sk chs count as a hdc)*; join in 2nd ch of beg 2 sk chs. *(8 hdc)*

Rnd 2: Ch 2 *(counts as a hdc on this and following rnds)*, hdc in same ch as joining and in next hdc; [2 hdc in next hdc, hdc in next hdc] 3 times; join in 2nd ch of beg ch-2. *(12 hdc)*

Rnd 3: Ch 2, hdc in each hdc; join in 2nd ch of beg ch-2.

Rnd 4: Ch 2, hdc dec; [hdc in next hdc, hdc dec] 3 times; join in 2nd ch of beg ch-2. *(8 hdc)* Change to C by drawing lp through; cut A.

Rnd 5: Ch 2, hdc in each hdc; join in 2nd ch of beg ch-2. Change to D; cut C.

Rnd 6: Ch 2, hdc in each hdc; join in 2nd ch of beg ch-2. Change to C; cut D.

Rnds 7–12: [Work rnds 5 and 6] 3 times.

Rnd 13: Rep rnd 5.

Rnd 14: Ch 2, hdc in each hdc; join in 2nd ch of beg ch-2.

Fasten off, leaving a 6-inch end for sewing. Weave in other end.

LEG
Make 2.
Rnd 1 (RS): Starting at bottom of foot with A, ch 3; 7 hdc in 3rd ch from hook *(beg 2 sk chs count as an hdc)*; join in 2nd ch of beg ch-3. *(8 hdc)*

Rnd 2: Ch 2 *(counts as a hdc on this and following rnds)*, hdc in same ch as joining and in next hdc; [2 hdc in next hdc, hdc in next hdc] 3 times; join in 2nd ch of beg ch-2. *(12 hdc)*

Rnd 3: Ch 2, hdc in same ch as joining and in next 2 hdc; [2 hdc in next hdc, hdc in next 2 hdc] 3 times; join in 2nd ch of beg ch-2. *(16 hdc)*

Rnd 4: Ch 2, hdc in next hdc, hdc dec; [hdc in next 2 hdc, hdc dec] 3 times; join in 2nd ch of beg ch-2. *(12 hdc)*

Rnd 5: Ch 2, hdc dec; [hdc in next hdc, hdc dec] 3 times; join in 2nd ch of beg ch-2. *(8 hdc)* Change to C by drawing lp through; cut A.

Rnd 6: Ch 2, hdc in each hdc; join in 2nd ch of beg ch-2. Change to D; cut C.

Rnd 7: Ch 2, hdc in each hdc; join in 2nd ch of beg ch-2. Change to C; cut D.

Rnds 8–15: [Work rnds 6 and 7] 4 times.

Rnd 16: Rep rnd 6.

Rnd 17: Ch 2, hdc in each hdc; join in 2nd ch of beg ch-2.

Fasten off, leaving a 6-inch end for sewing. Weave in other end.

NOSE
Row 1 (RS): With B, ch 2; 2 sc in 2nd ch from hook, turn.

Row 2: Ch 1, sc in first sc, 2 sc in next sc.

Fasten off, leaving a 6-inch end for sewing. Weave in other end.

EARS
Left Ear
With B, ch 5; 2 hdc in 4th ch from hook *(beg 3 sk chs count as a dc);* in next ch work (hdc, sc, ch 1, sl st).

Fasten off, leaving a 6-inch end for sewing. Weave in other end.

Right Ear
With B, ch 3; in 2nd ch from hook work (sc, hdc); in next ch work (2 hdc, ch 3, sl st).

Fasten off, leaving a 6-inch end for sewing. Weave in other end.

HAT
Rnd 1 (RS): Starting at top of hat with D, ch 3; 3 hdc in 3rd ch from hook *(beg sk 2 chs count as a hdc);* join in first ch of beg ch-3. *(4 hdc)*

Rnd 2: Ch 2 *(counts as a hdc on this and following rnds);* hdc in same ch as joining and in next hdc; 2 hdc in next hdc; hdc in next hdc; join in 2nd ch of beg ch-2. *(6 hdc)*

Rnd 3: Ch 2, hdc in same ch as joining and in next hdc; [2 hdc in next hdc, hdc in next hdc] twice; join in 2nd ch of beg ch-2. *(9 hdc)*

Rnd 4: Ch 2, hdc in same ch as joining and in next 2 hdc; [2 hdc in next hdc, hdc in next 2 hdc] twice; join in 2nd ch of beg-2. *(12 hdc)*

Rnd 5: Ch 2, hdc in same ch as joining and in next 3 hdc; [2 hdc in next hdc, hdc in next 3 hdc] twice; join in 2nd ch of beg ch-2. *(15 hdc)*

Rnd 6: Ch 2, hdc in same ch as

joining and in next 4 hdc; [2 hdc in next hdc, hdc in next 4 hdc] twice; join in 2nd ch of beg ch-2. *(18 hdc)*

Rnd 7: Ch 2, hdc in same ch as joining and in next 5 hdc; [2 hdc in next hdc, hdc in next 5 hdc] twice; join in 2nd ch of beg ch-2. *(21 hdc)*

Rnd 8: Ch 2, hdc in same ch as joining and in next 6 hdc; [2 hdc in next hdc, hdc in next 6 hdc] twice; join in 2nd ch of beg ch-2. *(24 hdc)*

Rnd 9: Ch 2, hdc in same ch as joining; [hdc in next 4 hdc, 2 hdc in next hdc] 4 times; hdc in next 3 hdc; join in 2nd ch of beg ch-2. *(29 hdc)*

Rnd 10: Ch 2, hdc in same ch as joining; [hdc in next 8 hdc, 2 hdc in next hdc] 3 times; hdc in next hdc; join in 2nd ch of beg ch-2. *(33 hdc)*

Rnd 11: Ch 2, hdc in each hdc; join in **back lp** *(see Stitch Guide)* of 2nd ch of beg ch-2, turn.

Brim

Rnd 1: Ch 2, working in back lps only, hdc in same lp as joining and in next 2 hdc; [2 hdc in next hdc, hdc in next 2 hdc] 10 times; join in 2nd ch of beg ch-2, turn. *(44 hdc)*

Rnd 2: Ch 2, working through both lps, sk next hdc, [sl st in next hdc, ch 2, sk next hdc] 21 times; join in first ch of beg ch-2.

Fasten off and weave in ends.

COLLAR

Row 1 (WS): With C and leaving an 8-inch end, loosely ch 20; hdc in 3rd ch from hook *(beg 2 sk chs count as a hdc);* 2 hdc in next ch; [hdc in next ch, 2 hdc in next ch] 8 times, turn. *(28 hdc)*

Row 2 (RS): Ch 2, [sk next hdc, sl st in next hdc] 13 times; ch 2, sk next hdc; join in first ch of beg ch-2.

Fasten off, leaving an 8-inch end. Weave in other end.

FINISHING

Step 1: Stuff Arms and Legs lightly with fiberfill.

Step 2: Fold over top of 1 Arm. Referring to photo for placement and working through both thicknesses with long end, sew in place on Body. Rep with rem Arm. Sew Legs to Body in same manner.

Step 3: For tassel, wind C lengthwise around cardboard 5 times. Cut yarn at 1 end. Holding 5 strands tog, fold over a 6-inch strand of yarn; tie 6-inch strand into knot. With separate 3-inch strand of yarn, wrap around folded strands

½ inch from fold; tie into knot and cut close. With long ends left from 6-inch strand, tack to top of Hat. Trim tassel ends to desired length.

Step 4: Fold Nose in half and sew along end of rows, using long end. Shape Nose and sew to face.

Step 5: Referring to photo for placement, sew Ears to Head.

Step 6: Place Collar around neck and tie long ends in bow at front. Trim ends as desired.

Step 7: With E, make 2 French knots *(see Fig. 1)* for eyes. With D, sew mouth, using straight st *(see Fig. 2).* 🌺

Fig. 1

Fig. 2

GINGERBREAD MAN

SKILL LEVEL ◼◼◼◻
INTERMEDIATE

FINISHED SIZE
7 inches tall seated, excluding legs

MATERIALS
Medium (worsted) weight yarn:
   3 oz/210 yds/84g tan *(A)*
   small amount of rust *(B)*, green *(C)*, white *(D)*, black *(E)*
Size G/6/4mm crochet hook or size needed to obtain gauge
Tapestry needle

12-inch square of plastic wrap: 2
1 cup uncooked rice
Polyester fiberfill
8-inch piece of silver cord

GAUGE
4 dc = 1 inch

PATTERN NOTE
Before starting project, make rice pouch as follows:
Place rice in center of 1 piece of plastic wrap, fold up corners and twist to secure; flatten pouch slightly. Wrap with 2nd piece of plastic wrap.

Instructions

BODY

Rnd 1 (RS): Starting at bottom with A, ch 3; 9 hdc in 3rd ch from hook *(beg 2 sk chs count as a hdc);* join with a sl st in 2nd ch of beg 2 sk chs. *(10 hdc)*

Rnd 2: Ch 2 *(counts as a hdc on this and following rnds),* hdc in same ch as joining; 2 hdc in each hdc; join in 2nd ch of beg ch-2. *(20 hdc)*

Rnd 3: Ch 2, hdc in same ch as joining and in next hdc; [2 hdc in next hdc, hdc in next hdc] 9 times; join in 2nd ch of beg ch-2. *(30 hdc)*

Rnd 4: Ch 2, hdc in same ch as joining and in next 2 hdc; [2 hdc in next hdc, hdc in next 2 hdc] 9 times; join in 2nd ch of beg ch-2. *(40 hdc)*

Rnd 5: Ch 2, hdc in same ch as joining and in next 3 hdc; [2 hdc in next hdc, hdc in next 3 hdc] 5 times; [2 hdc in next hdc, hdc in next hdc] 8 times; join in 2nd ch of beg ch-2. *(54 hdc)*

Rnd 6: Ch 2, hdc in each hdc; join in 2nd ch of beg ch-2.

Rnds 7–9: Rep rnd 6.

*Note: For **hdc dec**, [yo, draw up lp in st indicated] twice; yo and draw through all 5 lps on hook.*

Rnd 10: Ch 2, hdc in next 2 hdc, **hdc dec** *(see Note)* in next 2 hdc; [hdc in next 3 hdc, hdc dec in next 2 hdc] 9 times; hdc in next 4 hdc; join in 2nd ch of beg ch-2. *(44 hdc)*

Rnd 11: Rep rnd 6.

Rnd 12: Ch 2, hdc in next hdc, hdc dec; [hdc in next 2 hdc, hdc dec] 10 times; join in 2nd ch of beg ch-2. *(33 hdc)*

Rnds 13 & 14: Rep rnd 6. Insert rice pouch *(see Pattern Note)* after rnd 14.

Rnd 15: Ch 2, hdc dec; [hdc in next hdc, hdc dec] 10 times; join in 2nd ch of beg ch-2. *(22 hdc)*

Rnd 16: Rep rnd 6.

Rnd 17: Ch 2, hdc dec; [hdc in next hdc, hdc dec] 6 times; hdc in next hdc; join in 2nd ch of beg ch-2. *(15 hdc)*

Note: Stuff Body lightly with fiberfill.

HEAD
Rnd 1 (RS): Ch 2, 2 hdc in each of next 2 hdc; [hdc in next hdc, 2 hdc in each of next 2 hdc] 4 times; join in 2nd ch of beg ch-2. *(25 hdc)*

Rnd 2: Ch 2, [2 hdc in next hdc, hdc in next 2 hdc] 8 times; join in 2nd ch of beg of ch-2. *(33 hdc)*

Rnd 3: Ch 2, hdc in each hdc; join in 2nd hc of beg of ch-2.

Rnds 4 & 5: Rep rnd 3.

Rnd 6: Ch 2, [hdc in next 2 hdc,

hdc dec] 8 times. *(25 hdc)*

Rnd 7: Ch 2, hdc in next hdc, hdc dec; [hdc in next 2 hdc, hdc dec] 5 times; hdc in next hdc; join in 2nd ch of beg ch-2. *(19 hdc)*

Rnd 8: Ch 2, [hdc dec, hdc in next hdc] 6 times; join in 2nd ch of beg ch-2. *(13 hdc)*

Note: Stuff Head firmly with fiberfill.

Rnd 9: Ch 2, [hdc dec] 6 times; join in 2nd ch of beg ch-2. *(7 hdc)*

Fasten off, leaving a 6-inch end for sewing.

With tapestry needle, weave end through each st on last rnd. Pull tight to close, and secure end. Weave in all ends.

ARM
Make 2.
Rnd 1 (RS): Starting at hands with A, ch 3; 7 hdc in 3rd ch from hook *(beg 2 sk chs count as a hdc)*; join in 2nd ch of beg 2 sk chs. *(8 hdc)*

Rnd 2: Ch 2 *(counts as a hdc on this and following rnds)*, hdc in same ch as joining and in next hdc; 2 hdc in each rem hdc; join in 2nd ch of beg ch-2. *(16 hdc)*

Rnd 3: Ch 2, 2 hdc in each of next 3 hdc; hdc in next 5 hdc, 2 hdc in each of next 3 hdc; hdc in next 4 hdc; join in 2nd ch of beg

ch-2. *(22 hdc)*

Rnd 4: Ch 2, hdc dec; hdc in next 2 hdc, hdc dec; hdc in next 5 hdc, hdc dec; hdc in next 2 hdc, hdc dec; hdc in next 4 hdc; join in 2nd ch of beg ch-2. *(18 hdc)*

Rnd 5: Ch 2, hdc in next hdc, [hdc dec] 8 times; join in 2nd ch of beg ch-2. *(10 hdc)*

Rnd 6: Ch 2, hdc in each hdc; join in 2nd ch of beg ch-2.

Rnds 7–13: Rep rnd 6.

Fasten off, leaving an 8-inch end for sewing. Weave in other end.

LEG
Make 2.
Rnds 1–5: Rep rnds 1–5 of Arm.

Rnd 6: Ch 2, hdc in each hdc; joining in 2nd ch of beg ch-2.

Rnds 7–17: Rep rnd 6.

Fasten off, leaving an 8-inch end for sewing. Weave in other end.

BUTTONS
Make 4 with B.
Make 2 with C.
Ch 2, 10 sc in 2nd ch from hook; join in first sc.

Fasten off and weave in all ends.

OUTLINES

ARM OUTLINE
Make 2.
With D and leaving a 12-inch end, ch 30 loosely.

Fasten off, leaving a 12-inch end for sewing. Weave in other end.

LEG OUTLINE
Make 2.
With D and leaving a 12-inch end, ch 37 loosely.

Fasten off, leaving a 12-inch end for sewing. Weave in other end.

HEAD & BODY OUTLINE
With D and leaving an 18-inch end, ch 57 loosely.

Fasten off, leaving an 18-inch end for sewing. Weave in other end.

FINISHING
Step 1: Stuff Arms and Legs lightly with fiberfill. Referring to photo for placement and with ends left for sewing, sew Arm and Leg Outlines in place, using back bumps only of ch sts.

Step 2: Fold over top of 1 Arm. Referring to photo for placement and working through both thicknesses with long end, sew in place on Body. Rep with rem Arm. Sew Legs to Body in same manner.

Step 3: Referring to photo for placement, sew Head and Body Outline in place, using back bumps only of ch sts.

Step 4: With E, sew each button in place making an "X" in center. Sew 1 B button to each hand and each foot; sew 2 C buttons to Body.

Step 5: With E, make 2 French knots (see Fig. 1) for eyes. With E, sew mouth, using straight sts (see Fig. 2).

Step 6: Tie cord in bow and tack to center front of neck. 🌿

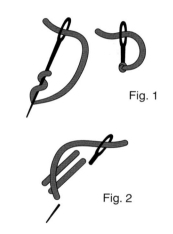

Fig. 1

Fig. 2

SNOWMAN

SKILL LEVEL⬛⬛⬛⬜
INTERMEDIATE

FINISHED SIZE
8 inches tall seated, excluding legs

MATERIALS
Medium (worsted) weight yarn:
   3 oz/210 yds/84g white (A)
   small amount each of gold (B), black (C), gray (D), rust (E), green (F)
Size G/6/4mm crochet hook or size needed to obtain gauge
Tapestry needle
12-inch square of plastic wrap: 2
1 cup uncooked rice
Polyester fiberfill
⅓-yd ¼-inch-wide white ribbon

GAUGE
4 dc = 1 inch

PATTERN NOTE
Before starting project, make rice pouch as follows:
Place rice in center of 1 piece of plastic wrap, fold up corners and twist to secure; flatten pouch slightly. Wrap with 2nd piece of plastic wrap.

Instructions

BODY
Rnd 1 (RS): Starting at bottom with A, ch 3; 9 hdc in 3rd ch from hook (beg 2 sk chs count as a hdc); join with a sl st in 2nd ch of beg 2 sk chs. (10 hdc)

Rnd 2: Ch 2 (counts as a hdc on this and following rnds), hdc in same ch as joining; 2 hdc in each hdc; join in 2nd ch of beg ch-2. (20 hdc)

Rnd 3: Ch 2, hdc in same ch as joining and in next hdc; [2 hdc in next hdc, hdc in next hdc] 9 times; join in 2nd ch of beg ch-2. (30 hdc)

Rnd 4: Ch 2, hdc in same ch as joining and in next 2 hdc; [2 hdc in next hdc, hdc in next 2 hdc] 9 times; join in 2nd ch of beg ch-2. (40 hdc)

Rnd 5: Ch 2, hdc in same ch as joining and in next 3 hdc; [2 hdc in next hdc, hdc in next 3 hdc] 5 times; [2 hdc in next hdc, hdc in next hdc] 8 times; join in 2nd ch of beg ch-2. (54 hdc)

Rnd 6: Ch 2, hdc in each hdc; join in 2nd ch of beg ch-2.

Rnds 7–9: Rep rnd 6.

Note: *For* **hdc dec**, *[yo, draw up lp in st indicated] twice; yo and draw through all 5 lps on hook.*

Rnd 10: Ch 2, hdc in next 2 hdc, **hdc dec** *(see Note)* in next 2 hdc; [hdc in next 3 hdc, hdc dec in next 2 hdc] 9 times; hdc in next 4 hdc; join in 2nd ch of beg ch-2. *(44 hdc)*

Rnd 11: Rep rnd 6.

Rnd 12: Ch 2, hdc in next hdc, hdc dec; [hdc in next 2 hdc, hdc dec] 10 times; join in 2nd ch of beg ch-2. *(33 hdc)*

Rnds 13 & 14: Rep rnd 6.

Insert rice pouch *(see Pattern Note)* after rnd 14.

Rnd 15: Ch 2, hdc dec; [hdc in next hdc, hdc dec] 10 times; join in 2nd ch of beg ch-2. *(22 hdc)*

Rnd 16: Rep rnd 6.

Rnd 17: Ch 2, hdc dec; [hdc in next hdc, hdc dec] 6 times; hdc in next hdc; join in 2nd ch of beg ch-2. *(15 hdc)*

Note: *Stuff Body lightly with fiberfill.*

HEAD
Rnd 1 (RS): Ch 2, 2 hdc in each of next 2 hdc; [hdc in next hdc, 2 hdc in each of next 2 hdc] 4 times; join in 2nd ch of beg ch-2. *(25 hdc)*

Rnd 2: Ch 2, [2 hdc in next hdc, hdc in next 2 hdc] 8 times; join in 2nd ch of beg of ch-2. *(33 hdc)*

Rnd 3: Ch 2, hdc in each hdc; join in 2nd hc of beg of ch-2.

Rnds 4 & 5: Rep rnd 3.

Rnd 6: Ch 2, [hdc in next 2 hdc, hdc dec] 8 times. *(25 hdc)*

Rnd 7: Ch 2, hdc in next hdc, hdc dec; [hdc in next 2 hdc, hdc dec] 5 times; hdc in next hdc; join in 2nd ch of beg ch-2. *(19 hdc)*

Rnd 8: Ch 2, [hdc dec, hdc in next hdc] 6 times; join in 2nd ch of beg ch-2. *(13 hdc)*

Note: *Stuff Head firmly with fiberfill.*

Rnd 9: Ch 2, [hdc dec] 6 times; join in 2nd ch of beg ch-2. *(7 hdc)*

Fasten off, leaving a 6-inch end for sewing.

With tapestry needle, weave end through each st on last rnd. Pull tight to close, and secure end. Weave in all ends.

ARM
Make 2.
Rnd 1 (RS): Starting at hands with A, ch 3; 7 hdc in 3rd ch from hook *(beg 2 sk chs count as a hdc)*; join in 2nd ch of beg 2 sk chs. *(8 hdc)*

Rnd 2: Ch 2 *(counts as a hdc on this and following rnds)*, hdc in same ch as joining and in next hdc; [2 hdc in next hdc, hdc in next hdc] 3 times; join in 2nd ch of beg ch-2. *(12 hdc)*

Rnd 3: Ch 2, hdc in same ch as joining and in next hdc; [2 hdc in next hdc, hdc in next hdc] 5 times; join in 2nd ch of beg ch-2. *(18 hdc)*

Rnd 4: Ch 2, hdc in next hdc, [hdc dec, hdc in next 2 hdc] 4 times; join in 2nd ch of beg ch-2. *(14 hdc)*

Rnd 5: Ch 2, hdc dec; [hdc in next hdc, hdc dec] 3 times; hdc in next 2 hdc; join in 2nd ch of beg ch-2. *(10 hdc)*

Rnd 6: Ch 2, hdc in each hdc; join in 2nd ch of beg ch-2.

Rnds 7–13: Rep rnd 6.

Fasten off, leaving a 6-inch end for sewing. Weave in other end.

LEG
Make 2.
Rnd 1 (RS): Starting at bottom of foot with A, ch 3; 7 hdc in 3rd ch from hook *(beg 2 sk chs count as an hdc)*; join in 2nd ch of beg ch-3. *(8 hdc)*

Rnd 2: Ch 2 *(counts as a hdc on this and following rnds)*, hdc in same ch as joining and in next hdc; [2 hdc in next hdc, hdc in next hdc] 3 times; join in 2nd ch of beg ch-2. *(12 hdc)*

Rnd 3: Ch 2, hdc in same ch as joining and in next hdc; [2 hdc in next hdc, hdc in next hdc] 5 times; join in 2nd ch of beg ch-2. *(18 hdc)*

Rnd 4: Ch 2, hdc in next hdc, [hdc dec, hdc in next 2 hdc] 4 times; join in 2nd ch of beg ch-2. *(14 hdc)*

Rnd 5: Ch 2, hdc dec; [hdc in next hdc, hdc dec] 3 times; hdc in next 2 hdc; join in 2nd ch of beg ch-2. *(10 hdc)*

Rnd 6: Ch 2, hdc in each hdc; join in 2nd ch of beg ch-2.

Rnds 7–17: Rep rnd 6.

Fasten off, leaving a 6-inch end for sewing. Weave in other end.

NOSE
Row 1 (RS): With B, ch 3; 2 hdc in 3rd ch from hook *(beg 2 sk chs count as a hdc)*, turn. *(3 hdc)*

Row 2: Ch 2, hdc in next hdc, 2 hdc in next hdc.

Fasten off, leaving turning ch-2 unworked and leaving a 6-inch end for sewing. Weave in other end.

HAT
Rnd 1 (RS): With C, ch 3; 11 hdc in 3rd ch from hook (beg 2 sk chs count as a hdc); join in 2nd ch of beg 2 sk chs. (12 hdc)

Rnd 2: Ch 2 (counts as a hdc on this and following rnds), hdc in same ch as joining; 2 hdc in each hdc; join in **back lp** (see Stitch Guide) of 2nd ch of beg ch-2. (24 hdc)

Rnd 3: Ch 2, working in back lps only, hdc in each hdc; join in 2nd ch of beg ch-2.

Rnd 4: Ch 2, working through both lps, hdc in each hdc; join in 2nd ch of beg ch-2.

Rnd 5: Rep rnd 4.

Rnd 6: Ch 2, hdc in each hdc; join in **front lp** (see Stitch Guide) of 2nd ch of beg ch-2.

Rnd 7: Ch 2, hdc in same lp as joining; working in front lps only, 2 hdc in each hdc; join in 2nd ch of beg ch-2. (48 hdc)

Fasten off and weave in ends.

SCARF
Row 1 (RS): With D, loosely ch 38; sc in 2nd ch from hook and in each rem ch; change to E by drawing lp through; cut D, turn. (37 sc)

Row 2: Ch 1, sc in first sc, [tr in next sc, sc in next sc] 18 times; change to D; cut E, turn.

Row 3: Ch 1, sc in first sc and in each rem st, turn.

Fasten off and weave in ends.

WREATH
With F, loosely ch 15, join to form a ring; ch 3, keeping last lp of each tr on hook, 2 tr in same ch as joining; yo and draw through all 3 lps—beg cl made; *keeping last lp on each tr on hook, 3 tr in next ch; yo and draw through all 4 lps on hook—cl made; rep from *13 times; join in 3rd ch of beg ch-3.

Fasten off and weave in ends.

FINISHING
Step 1: Stuff Arms and Legs lightly with fiberfill.

Step 2: Fold over top of 1 Arm. Referring to photo for placement and working through both thicknesses with long end, sew in place on Body. Rep with rem Arm. Sew Legs to Body in same manner.

Step 3: Fold Nose in half and using end left for sewing, sew along end of rows. Shape Nose and sew to face.

Step 4: For scarf fringe, cut 3-inch strands of D and E; use 3 strands for each knot. Tie 3 knots in each scarf end, matching yarn colors. Trim ends even.

Step 5: For Wreath, fold cls in half and sew top of sts to beg chain; pull slightly to form center of Wreath and secure. Push 1 cl forward and next cl back to shape Wreath.

Step 6: With E, make 11 French knots (see Fig. 1) on Wreath for berries. Wrap ribbon around 1 cl on Wreath and tie in bow. Tack Wreath to 1 Arm of Snowman.

Step 7: Referring to photo for placement, and with C, make 6 French knots for eyes and mouth. 🦃

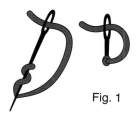

Fig. 1

Noel Stocking & Snowman Stocking

DESIGN BY KATHY WESLEY

NOEL STOCKING

SKILL LEVEL ◼◼◼◻
INTERMEDIATE

FINISHED SIZE
15 inches in circumference x 23 inches long

MATERIALS

Bernat Super Value medium (worsted) weight yarn (8 oz/445 yds/225g per skein):
1 skein each #07407 winter white *(A)*, #00610 royal blue *(B)*, #00607 berry *(C)*, #00609 kelly *(D)*
Size G/6/4mm crochet hook or size needed to obtain gauge
Tapestry needle
Sewing needle and matching thread
Stitch markers

GAUGE
8 hdc = 2 inches

SPECIAL STITCHES
Back post double crochet (bpdc): Yo, insert hook from back to front to back around **post** *(see Stitch Guide)* of st indicated, draw up lp, [yo, draw through 2 lps on hook] twice.

Front post double crochet (fpdc): Yo, insert hook from front to back to front around **post** *(see Stitch Guide)* of st indicated, draw up lp, [yo, draw through 2 lps on hook] twice.

Instructions

STOCKING

CUFF
Rnd 1 (RS): With A, ch 54; join with a sl st to form ring, being careful not to twist; ch 3 *(counts as a dc on this and following rnds)*, dc in each ch; join with a sl st in 3rd ch of beg ch-3. *(54 dc)*

Rnd 2: Ch 3, **bpdc** *(see Special Stitches)* around next dc; ***fpdc** *(see Special Stitches)* around next dc; bpdc around next dc; rep from * around; join in 3rd ch of beg ch-3; change to B by drawing lp through; cut A.

BODY
Rnd 1: Ch 1, 2 sc in same ch as joining; sk next dc; *2 sc in next dc; sk next dc; rep from * around; join in first sc.

Rnd 2: Ch 1, 2 sc in same sc as joining; sk next sc; *2 sc in next sc; sk next sc; rep from * around; join in first sc.

Rnds 3–10: Rep rnd 2. At end of rnd 10, change to A; cut B.

*Note: For **sc dec**, draw up lp in each of 2 sts indicated, yo and draw through all 3 lps on hook.*

Rnd 11: Ch 1, sc in same sc as joining; **sc dec** *(see Note)* in next 2 sc; sc in next 25 sc, sc dec in next 2 sc; sc in next 24 sc; join in first sc; change to C; drop A. *(52 sc)*

Note: Remainder of Body is worked in continuous rnds. Do not join; mark beg of rnds.

Rnd 12: Ch 2 *(counts as a hdc)*, hdc in each sc.

Rnd 13: Hdc in 2nd ch of beg ch-2 and in each hdc.

Rnd 14: Hdc in each hdc.

Rnds 15–34: Rep rnd 14. At end of rnd 34, change to D; drop C.

HEEL FLAP
Row 1: Sc in next 25 hdc, turn, leaving rem 27 sc unworked for instep.

Row 2: Ch 1, sc in each sc, turn.

Rows 3–12: Rep row 2.

TURNING HEEL
Row 1 (RS): Ch 1, sc in next 14 sc, turn, leaving rem 11 sts unworked.

Note: Dec are used on following rows to shape heel. They are worked in next sc on working row and in next unworked sc on Heel Flap.

Row 2: Ch 1, sc in next 3 sc, turn, leaving rem 11 sts unworked.

Row 3: Ch 1, sc in next 2 sc, sc dec in next sc and next unworked sc on row 12; sc in next sc on row 12, turn, leaving

rem 9 sc on row 12 unworked. *(4 sc)*

Row 4: Ch 1, sc in next 3 sc, sc dec in next sc and next unworked sc on row 1; sc in next sc on row 1, turn, leaving rem 9 sc on row 1 unworked. *(5 sc)*

Row 5: Ch 1, sc in next 4 sc, sc dec in next sc and next unworked sc on row 12; sc in next sc on row 12, turn, leaving rem 7 sc on row 12 unworked. *(6 sc)*

Row 6: Ch 1, sc in next 5 sc, sc dec in next sc and next unworked sc on row 1; sc in next sc on row 1, turn, leaving rem 7 sc on row 1 unworked. *(7 sc)*

Row 7: Ch 1, sc in next 6 sc, sc dec in next sc and next unworked sc on row 12; sc in next sc on row 12, turn, leaving rem 5 sc on row 12 unworked. *(8 sc)*

Row 8: Ch 1, sc in next 7 sc, sc dec in next sc and next unworked sc on row 1; sc in next sc on row 1, turn, leaving rem 5 sc on row 1 unworked. *(9 sc)*

Row 9: Ch 1, sc in next 8 sc, sc dec in next sc and next unworked sc on row 12; sc in next sc on row 12, turn, leaving rem 3 sc on row 12 unworked. *(10 sc)*

Row 10: Ch 1, sc in next 9 sc, sc dec in next sc and next unworked sc on row 1; sc in next sc on row 1, turn, leaving rem 3 sc on row 1 unworked. *(11 sc)*

Row 11: Ch 1, sc in next 10 sc, sc dec in next sc and next unworked sc on row 12; sc in next sc on row 12, turn, leaving rem sc on row 12 unworked. *(12 sc)*

Row 12: Ch 1, sc in next 11 sc, sc dec in next sc and next unworked sc on row 1; sc in next sc on row 1, turn, leaving rem sc

on row 1 unworked. *(13 sc)*

Row 13: Ch 1, sc in next 12 sc, sc dec in next sc and next unworked sc on row 12, turn.

Row 14: Ch 1, sc in next 12 sc, sc dec in next sc and next unworked sc on row 1. Fasten off.

GUSSET
Hold piece with RS facing you and last row worked at top; with A make slip knot on hook and join with a sc in 12th sc from right edge of row 14.

***Note:** Rnds 1 through 6 of Gusset are worked in continuous rnds. Do not join; mark beg of rnds.*

Rnd 1: Sc in next sc; working along side of Heel Flap in ends of rows, work 12 sc evenly spaced to last row of Flap; yo and draw up lp in next row, yo and draw up lp in first st of instep; yo and draw through all 3 lps on hook; *(mark st just made for Gusset)*; sc in next 25 sc, sc dec in next sc and first row of Heel Flap *(mark st just made for Gusset)*; working along side of Heel Flap in ends of rows, work 12 sc evenly spaced along other side of Heel Flap; sc in next 11 sc of row 14 of Heel. *(64 sc)*

Rnd 2: Sc in each sc to sc before first marked Gusset st; sc dec in next sc and marked st *(mark st just made)*; sc in next 25 sc, sc dec in next marked st and next sc *(mark st just made)*; sc in each sc to beg marker. *(62 sc)*

Rnds 3–6: Rep rnd 2. At end of rnd 6; join in first sc; change to C; drop A. *(54 sc at end of rnd 6)*

***Note:** Remove Gusset markers on following rnd.*

Rnd 7: Ch 3, dc in each sc; join in 3rd ch of beg ch-3; change to A; cut C.

Rnd 8: Ch 1, 2 sc in same ch as joining; sk next dc; *2 sc in next dc; sk next dc; rep from * around; join in first sc.

Rnd 9: Ch 1, 2 sc in same sc; sk next sc; *2 sc in next sc; sk next sc; rep from * around; join in first sc; change to D; cut A.

Rnd 10: Ch 3, dc in each sc; join in 3rd ch of beg ch-3.

Rnd 11: Ch 3, fpdc around next dc; *dc in next dc; fpdc around next dc; rep from * around; join in 3rd ch of beg ch-3; change to A; cut D.

Rnds 12 & 13: Rep rnds 8 and 9. At end of Rnd 13, change to C; cut A.

Rnd 14: Rep rnd 10, changing to A at end of rnd; cut C.

Rnd 15: Ch 1, sc in each sc; join in first sc.

Rnds 16–20: Rep rnd 15. Fasten off.

TOE SHAPING
Fold sock flat having Heel centered in bottom of foot. Mark sts on each side. You should have 26 sts between each marker. With D make slip knot on hook and join with a sc in 13th sc from right marker on bottom of foot *(mark st just made as beg of rnd)*.

***Note:** Toe is worked in continuous rnds. Do not join; mark beg of rnds.*

Rnd 1: *Sc in each sc to 2nd sc before marked side sc; sc dec; sc in next sc *(mark sc just made)*, sc dec; rep from * once; sc in each sc to beg marker. *(50 sc)*

Rnd 2: Sc in each sc.

Rnd 3: *Sc in each sc to 2nd sc

before marked sc; sc dec; sc in next sc *(mark sc just made)*, sc dec; rep from * once; sc in each sc to beg marker.

Rnd 4: Rep rnd 2.

Rnds 5–12: Rep rnd 3. *(14 sc at end of rnd 12)*

Fasten off and weave in ends.

ANGEL

With A, ch 4; 5 dc in 4th ch from hook *(beg 3 sk chs count as a dc)—head made*; ch 12; join in 3rd ch of beg 3 sk chs—*halo made*. Fasten off.

Hold piece with WS facing you and unused lp of beg ch at top; join A in unused lp.

Row 1 (WS): Ch 5 *(counts as a dc and a ch-3 sp on this and following rows)*, in unused lp work *(5 dc, ch 3, dc)*, turn.

Row 2 (RS): Ch 5, in next ch-3 sp work [dc, ch 3] twice; 2 dc in next dc; ch 1, 2 dc in each of next 3 dc; ch 1, 2 dc in next dc; ch 3, in next turning ch-3 sp work [dc, ch 3] twice; dc in same sp, turn.

Row 3: Ch 5, in each of next 3 ch-3 sps work (dc, ch 3, dc); dc in next 2 dc, in next dc work (dc, ch 1, dc)—*shell made*; sk next dc, in each of next 2 dc work (dc, ch 1, dc)—*shell made*; sk next dc, in next dc work (dc, ch 1, dc)—*shell made*; dc in next 2 dc, in each of next 2 ch-3 sps work (dc, ch 3, dc); in turning ch-5 sp work [dc, ch 3] twice; dc in same sp. Fasten off.

Hold piece with RS facing you; sk first 4 ch-3 sps and next dc; join A in next dc.

Row 4: Ch 3 *(counts as a dc)*, dc in next 2 dc, in next ch-1 sp work shell; in next ch-1 sp work [dc, ch 1] twice; dc in same sp; in next ch-1 sp work [dc, ch 1] twice; dc in same sp; shell in next ch-1 sp; dc in next 3 dc, turn.

Row 5: Ch 2, keeping last lp of each dc on hook, dc in next 2 dc, yo and draw through all 3 lps on hook—*beg cl made*; shell in each of next 2 ch-1 sps; in next ch-1 sp work [dc, ch 1] twice; dc in same sp; in next ch-1 sp work [dc, ch 1] twice; dc in same sp; shell in each of next 2 ch-1 sps; sk next dc, keeping last lp of each dc on hook, dc in next 2 dc and in 3rd ch of beg ch-3, yo and draw through all 4 lps on hook—*cl made*; turn.

Row 6: Ch 1, sk cl, sl st in next dc, in next ch-1 sp, in next 2 dc and in next ch-1 sp; ch 4 *(counts as a dc and a ch-1 sp)*; dc in same sp as last sl st made; shell in next ch-1 sp; in next ch-1 sp work [dc, ch 1] twice; dc in same sp; in next ch-1 sp work [dc, ch 1] twice; dc in same sp; shell in each of next 2 ch-1 sps, turn.

Row 7: Ch 3, shell in each of next 3 ch-1 sps; in next ch-1 sp work [dc, ch 1] twice; dc in same sp, in next ch-1 sp work [dc, ch 1] twice; dc in same sp, shell in each of next 2 ch-1 sps, in turning ch-4 work (dc, ch 1, 2 dc), turn.

Row 8: Ch 3, dc in next ch-1 sp, shell in each of next 8 ch-1 sps; dc in next ch-1 sp and in 3rd ch of turning ch-3, turn.

Row 9: Ch 3, dc in next dc, shell in each of next 8 ch-1 sps; sk next dc, dc in next dc and in 3rd ch of turning ch-3, turn.

Row 10: Ch 3, in first dc work (hdc, sc); in each of next 8 ch-1 sps work (sc, hdc, dc, hdc, sc); in 3rd ch of turning ch-3 work (sc, hdc, dc).

Fasten off and weave in all ends.

NOEL

With A, ch 95.

Fasten off and weave in ends.

HANGER

Hold 1 strand of B and 1 strand of A tog; ch 26; sc in 2nd ch from hook and in each rem ch.

Fasten off and weave in ends.

FINISHING

Step 1: Sew Toe.

Step 2: Fold Hanger in half. Referring to photo for placement, with desired-size lp above edge of Stocking, sew ends in place on WS of Stocking.

Step 3: Referring to photo for placement, sew Angel to Stocking, leaving skirt and arms unattached.

Step 4: Referring to photo for placement, pin chain to spell NOEL. Sew in place with sewing needle and matching thread. 🎄

SNOWMAN STOCKING

SKILL LEVEL

FINISHED SIZE
15 inches in circumference x 23 inches long

MATERIALS
Bernat Super Value
medium (worsted) weight yarn (8 oz/445 yds/225g per skein): 1 skein each #07407 winter white *(A)*, #00610 royal blue *(B)*, #00607 berry *(C)*, #00609 kelly *(D)*, #07421 black *(E)*
Aunt Lydia's Classic Crochet size 10 crochet cotton (350 yds per ball):
    1 ball #1 white *(F)*

Size G/6/4mm crochet hook or
size needed to obtain gauge
Size 7/1.65mm steel crochet hook
(for snowflakes)
Tapestry needle
Sewing needle and matching
thread
Stitch markers

GAUGE
8 hdc = 2 inches

SPECIAL STITCHES
**Back post double crochet
(bpdc):** Yo, insert hook from back
to front to back around **post** (see
Stitch Guide) of st indicated,
draw up lp, [yo, draw through 2
lps on hook] twice.

**Front post double crochet
(fpdc):** Yo, insert hook from front
to back to front around **post** (see
Stitch Guide) of st indicated,
draw up lp, [yo, draw through 2
lps on hook] twice.

Instructions

STOCKING

CUFF
Rnd 1 (RS): With A, ch 54; join
with a sl st to form ring, being
careful not to twist; ch 3 (counts
as a dc on this and following
rnds), dc in each ch; join with a sl
st in 3rd ch of beg ch-3. (54 dc)

Rnd 2: Ch 3, **bpdc** (see Special
Stitches) around next dc; *fpdc
(see Special Stitches) around
next dc; bpdc around next dc;
rep from * around; join with a sl st
in 3rd ch of beg ch-3; change to
B by drawing lp through; cut A.

BODY
Rnd 1: Ch 1, 2 sc in same ch as
joining; sk next dc; *2 sc in next
dc; sk next dc; rep from * around;
join in first sc.

Rnd 2: Ch 1, 2 sc in same sc as

joining; sk next sc; *2 sc in next
sc; sk next sc; rep from * around;
join in first sc.

Rnds 3–10: Rep rnd 2. At end of
rnd 10, change to A; cut B.

Note: For **sc dec**, draw up lp in
each of 2 sts indicated, yo and
draw through all 3 lps on hook.

Rnd 11: Ch 1, sc in same sc as
joining; **sc dec** (see Note) in next 2
sc; sc in next 25 sc, sc dec in next
2 sc; sc in next 24 sc; join in first
sc; change to C; drop A. (52 sc)

Note: Remainder of Body is
worked in continuous rnds. Do
not join; mark beg of rnds.

Rnd 12: Ch 2 (counts as a hdc),
hdc in each sc.

Rnd 13: Hdc in 2nd ch of beg
ch-2 and in each hdc.

Rnd 14: Hdc in each hdc.

Rnds 15–34: Rep rnd 14. At end
of rnd 34, change to D; drop C.

HEEL FLAP
Row 1: Sc in next 25 hdc, turn,
leaving rem 27 sc unworked for
instep.

Row 2: Ch 1, sc in each sc, turn.

Rows 3–12: Rep row 2.

TURNING HEEL
Row 1 (RS): Ch 1, sc in next
14 sc, turn, leaving rem 11 sts
unworked.

Note: Dec are used on following rows to shape heel. They are
worked in next sc on working
row and in next unworked sc on
Heel Flap.

Row 2: Ch 1, sc in next 3
sc, turn, leaving rem 11 sts
unworked.

Row 3: Ch 1, sc in next 2 sc, sc
dec in next sc and next unworked
sc on row 12; sc in next sc on
row 12, turn, leaving rem 9 sc on
row 12 unworked. (4 sc)

Row 4: Ch 1, sc in next 3 sc, sc
dec in next sc and next unworked
sc on row 1; sc in next sc on row
1, turn, leaving rem 9 sc on row 1
unworked. (5 sc)

Row 5: Ch 1, sc in next 4 sc, sc
dec in next sc and next unworked
sc on row 12; sc in next sc on
row 12, turn, leaving rem 7 sc on
row 12 unworked. (6 sc)

Row 6: Ch 1, sc in next 5 sc, sc
dec in next sc and next unworked
sc on row 1; sc in next sc on row
1, turn, leaving rem 7 sc on row 1
unworked. (7 sc)

Row 7: Ch 1, sc in next 6 sc, sc
dec in next sc and next unworked
sc on row 12; sc in next sc on
row 12, turn, leaving rem 5 sc on
row 12 unworked. (8 sc)

Row 8: Ch 1, sc in next 7 sc, sc
dec in next sc and next unworked
sc on row 1; sc in next sc on row
1, turn, leaving rem 5 sc on row 1
unworked. (9 sc)

Row 9: Ch 1, sc in next 8 sc, sc
dec in next sc and next unworked
sc on row 12; sc in next sc on
row 12, turn, leaving rem 3 sc on
row 12 unworked. (10 sc)

Row 10: Ch 1, sc in next 9 sc, sc
dec in next sc and next unworked
sc on row 1; sc in next sc on row
1, turn, leaving rem 3 sc on row 1
unworked. (11 sc)

Row 11: Ch 1, sc in next 10
sc, sc dec in next sc and next
unworked sc on row 12; sc in
next sc on row 12, turn, leaving
rem sc on row 12 unworked.
(12 sc)

Row 12: Ch 1, sc in next 11 sc, sc dec in next sc and next unworked sc on row 1; sc in next sc on row 1, turn, leaving rem sc on row 1 unworked. *(13 sc)*

Row 13: Ch 1, sc in next 12 sc, sc dec in next sc and next unworked sc on row 12, turn.

Row 14: Ch 1, sc in next 12 sc, sc dec in next sc and next unworked sc on row 1. Fasten off.

GUSSET

Hold piece with RS facing you and last row worked at top; with A make slip knot on hook and join with a sc in 12th sc from right edge of row 14.

Note: Rnds 1 through 6 of Gusset are worked in continuous rnds. Do not join; mark beg of rnds.

Rnd 1: Sc in next sc; working along side of Heel Flap in ends of rows, work 12 sc evenly spaced to last row of Flap; yo and draw up lp in next row, yo and draw up lp in first st of instep; yo and draw through all 3 lps on hook; *(mark st just made for Gusset);* sc in next 25 sc, sc dec in next sc and first row of Heel Flap *(mark st just made for Gusset);* working along side of Heel Flap in ends of rows, work 12 sc evenly spaced along other side of Heel Flap; sc in next 11 sc of row 14 of Heel. *(64 sc)*

Rnd 2: Sc in each sc to sc before first marked Gusset st; sc dec in next sc and marked st *(mark st just made);* sc in next 25 sc, sc dec over next marked st and next sc *(mark st just made);* sc in each sc to beg marker. *(62 sc)*

Rnds 3–6: Rep rnd 2. At end of rnd 6; join in first sc; change to C; drop A. *(54 sc)*

Note: Remove Gusset markers on following rnd.

Rnd 7: Ch 3, dc in each sc; join in 3rd ch of beg ch-3; change to A; cut C.

Rnd 8: Ch 1, 2 sc in same ch as joining; sk next dc; *2 sc in next dc; sk next dc; rep from * around; join in first sc.

Rnd 9: Ch 1, 2 sc in same sc; sk next sc; *2 sc in next sc; sk next sc; rep from * around; join in first sc; change to D; cut A.

Rnd 10: Ch 3, dc in each sc; join in 3rd ch of beg ch-3.

Rnd 11: Ch 3, fpdc around next dc; *dc in next dc; fpdc around next dc; rep from * around; join in 3rd ch of beg ch-3; change to A; cut D.

Rnds 12 & 13: Rep rnds 8 and 9. At end of Rnd 13, change to C; cut A.

Rnd 14: Rep rnd 10, changing to A at end of rnd; cut C.

Rnd 15: Ch 1, sc in each sc; join in first sc.

Rnds 16–20: Rep rnd 15. Fasten off.

TOE SHAPING

Fold sock flat having Heel centered in bottom of foot. Mark sts on each side. You should have 26 sts between each marker. With D make slip knot on hook and join with a sc in 13th sc from right marker on bottom of foot *(mark st just made as beg of rnd).*

Note: Toe is worked in continuous rnds. Do not join; mark beg of rnds.

Rnd 1: *Sc in each sc to 2nd sc before marked side sc; sc dec; sc in next sc *(mark sc just made)*, sc dec; rep from * once; sc in each sc to beg marker. *(50 sc)*

Rnd 2: Sc in each sc.

Rnd 3: *Sc in each sc to 2nd sc before marked sc; sc dec; sc in next sc *(mark sc just made)*, sc dec; rep from * once; sc in each sc to beg marker.

Rnd 4: Rep rnd 2.

Rnds 5–12: Rep rnd 3. *(14 sc at end of rnd 12)*

Fasten off and weave in ends.

SNOWFLAKE
Make 3.

Rnd 1: With steel hook and F, ch 4; join with a sl st to form ring; ch 4 *(counts as a dc and a ch-1 sp)*, dc in ring, ch 2; * in ring work (dc, ch 1, dc); ch 2; rep from * 4 times; join with a sl st in 3rd ch of beg ch-4.

Rnd 2: Sl st in next ch-1 sp, in same sp work (sc, ch 7, sl st in 4th ch from hook, ch 3, sc)—*point made;* sc in next ch-2 sp, ch 3, sl st in sc just made—*picot made;* * in next ch-1 sp work (sc, ch 7, sl st in 4th ch from hook, ch 3, sc)—*point made*; sc in next ch-2 sp, ch 3, sl st in sc just made—*picot made*; rep from * 4 times; join in first sc.

Fasten off, leaving 12-inch end for sewing.

SNOWMAN
Row 1 (RS): With G hook and A, ch 16; sc in 2nd ch from hook and in each rem ch, turn. *(15 sc)*

Row 2: Ch 1, 2 sc in first sc; sc in each sc to last sc; 2 sc in last sc, turn. *(17 sc)*

Row 3: Ch 1, 2 sc in first sc; sc in each sc to last sc; 2 sc in last sc, turn. *(19 sc)*

Row 4: Ch 1, sc in each sc, turn.

Row 5: Ch 1, 2 sc in first sc; sc in each sc to last sc; 2 sc in last sc, turn. *(21 sc)*

Rows 6 & 7: Rep row 4.

Note: For **sc dec**, *draw up lp in each of 2 sts indicated, yo and draw through all 3 lps on hook.*

Row 8: Ch 1, **sc dec** (see Note) over first 2 sc; sc in each sc to last 2 sc; sc dec in last 2 sc, turn. *(19 sc)*

Row 9: Ch 1, sc dec; sc in each sc to last 2 sc; sc dec, turn. *(17 sc)*

Rows 10–12: Rep row 9. *(11 sc at end of row 12)*

Row 13: Ch 1, sc dec; sc in next 6 sc, sc dec, turn, leaving rem sc unworked. *(8 sc)*

Row 14: Ch 7, sc in 2nd ch from hook and in next ch, hdc in next ch, 2 hdc in next ch; sc in next 2 chs, sc in next 8 sc, turn. *(15 sts)*

Row 15: Ch 7, sc in 2nd ch from hook and in next ch, hdc in next ch, 2 hdc in next ch; sc in next 2 chs and in next 12 sc, turn, leaving rem 3 sc unworked. *(19 sts)*

Row 16: Ch 1, sk first sc, sc dec; sc in next 13 sc, turn, leaving rem 3 sc unworked. *(14 sc)*

Row 17: Ch 1, sk first sc, sc dec; sc in next 11 sc, turn. *(12 sc)*

Row 18: Ch 1, sc in each sc, turn.

Row 19: Ch 1, sc dec; sc in next 8 sc, sc, turn. *(10 sc)*

Row 20: Ch 1, sc dec; sc in next 6 sc, dec, turn. *(8 sc)*

Row 21: Ch 1, [sc dec] 4 times, turn. *(4 sc)*

Row 22: Ch 1, sc in each sc, turn.

Row 23: Ch 1, 2 sc in first sc; sc in next 2 sc, 2 sc in next sc, turn. *(6 sc)*

Row 24: Ch 1, sc in each sc, turn.

Row 25: Ch 1, 2 sc in first sc; sc in next 4 sc, 2 sc in next sc, turn. *(8 sc)*

Row 26: Ch 1, sc in each sc, turn.

Row 27: Ch 1, sc dec; sc in next 4 sc, sc dec, turn. *(6 sc)*

Row 28: Ch 1, sc dec; sc in next 2 sc, sc dec. *(4 sc)*

Fasten off, leaving long end for sewing.

HAT
Row 1 (RS): With G hook and E, ch 11; sc in 2nd ch from hook and in each rem ch, turn.

Row 2: Ch 1, sc in each sc, turn.

Row 3: Ch 1, sl st in first 4 sc, ch 1, sc in same sc as last sl st made and in next 3 sc, turn, leaving rem 3 sc unworked.

Row 4: Ch 1, sc in each sc, turn.

Row 5: Ch 1, sc in each sc.

Fasten off, leaving long end for sewing.

SCARF
With G hook and D, ch 46; sc in 2nd ch from hook and in each rem ch. Fasten off.

FRINGE
For Fringe, cut 4 (3-inch) strands of green; use 1 strand for each knot. Fold strand in half. Draw folded end through 1 short end of scarf. Pull ends through fold and tighten knot. Tie 2 knots at each end of scarf. Trim ends even.

HANGER
Hold 1 strand of A and 1 strand of B tog; ch 26; sc in 2nd ch from hook and in each rem ch.

Fasten off and weave in ends.

FINISHING
Step 1: Sew Toe.

Step 2: Fold Hanger in half. Referring to photo for placement, with desired-size lp above edge of stocking, sew ends in place on WS of stocking.

Step 3: Starch Snowflakes. Referring to photo for placement, sew Snowflakes to Stocking.

Step 4: Tie Scarf around Snowman's neck. Referring to photo for placement, sew Snowman to Stocking. Tack ends of Scarf to Stocking as desired. Sew Hat on top of Snowman. 🍂

Whimsical Santa & Snowman Ornaments

DESIGN BY DEBBIE TABOR

SKILL LEVEL ⬤◼◻◻
EASY

FINISHED SIZES
Santa Ornament: 7 inches tall x 10 inches in circumference

Snowman Ornament: 7 inches tall x 12 inches in circumference

MATERIALS FOR SANTA ORNAMENT
Red Heart
Classic medium (worsted) weight yarn (3½ oz/190 yds/99g per skein):
1 skein each #912 cherry red (A), #246 sea coral (B), #12 black (C), #737 pink (D)
Moda Dea Zing light (light worsted) weight yarn (1¾ oz/87 yds/50g per skein):
1 ball #1316 pearl (E)
Red Heart Baby Clouds super bulky (super chunky) weight yarn (6 oz/140 yds/170g per skein):
1 skein #9311 cloud (F)
Size I/9/5.5mm crochet hook or size needed to obtain gauge
Tapestry needle
Polyester fiberfill
Cardboard
Stitch markers

MATERIALS FOR SNOWMAN ORNAMENT
Red Heart
Classic medium (worsted) weight yarn (3½ oz/190 yds/99g per skein):
1 skein each #912 cherry red (A), #676 emerald green (B), #245 orange (C), #12

black (D), #737 pink (E)
Moda Dea Zing light (light
worsted) weight yarn (1¾ oz/87
yds/50g) per skein:
1 ball #1316 pearl (F)
Size H/8/5mm crochet hook or
size needed to obtain gauge
Tapestry needle
Polyester fiberfill

GAUGE
12 sts = 3 inches; 12 rnds =
3 inches

Instructions

SANTA ORNAMENT

HAT & HEAD
Note: *Piece is worked in continuous rnds. Do not join; mark beg of rnds.*

Rnd 1 (RS): Starting at top of Hat and with A, ch 4; join with a sl st to form ring; ch 1, 10 sc in ring.

Rnd 2: Sc in each sc.

Rnd 3: Rep rnd 2.

Rnd 4: [Sc in next sc, 2 sc in next sc] 5 times. *(15 sc)*

Rnd 5: Sc in each sc.

Rnd 6: [Sc in next sc, 2 sc in next sc, sc in next sc] 5 times. *(20 sc)*

Rnds 7 & 8: Rep rnd 2. Fasten off.

Rnd 9: Join E in first sc; sc in each sc.

Rnd 10: [Sc in next 2 sc, 2 sc in next sc, sc in next sc] 5 times. *(25 sc)*

Rnd 11: Rep rnd 2. Fasten off.

Rnd 12: Join F in first sc; sc in each sc.

Rnd 13: Sc in next 2 sc, 2 sc in next sc; sc in next 2 sc; change to B by drawing lp through; cut F; [sc in next 2 sc, 2 sc in next sc, sc in next 2 sc] twice; change to F; cut B; [sc in next 2 sc, 2 sc in next sc, sc in next 2 sc] twice. *(30 sc)*

Rnd 14: Sc in next 6 sc; change to B; cut F; sc in next 12 sc; change to F; cut B; sc in next 12 sc. *(30 sc)*

Rnds 15 & 16: Rep rnd 14.

Rnd 17: Rep rnd 2.

Rnd 18: [Sc in next 2 sc, sk next sc, sc in next 2 sc] 6 times. *(24 sc)*

Rnd 19: [Sc in next 2 sc, sk next sc, sc in next sc] 6 times. *(18 sc)*

Rnd 20: [Sc in next sc, sk next sc, sc in next sc] 6 times. *(12 sc)*

Rnd 21: [Sc in next sc, sk next sc, sc in next sc] 4 times. *(8 sc)*

Fill with fiberfill.

Rnd 22: [Sc in next sc, sk next sc] 4 times. *(4 sc)*

Rnd 23: [Sl st in next sc, sk next sc] twice.

Fasten off and weave in all ends.

NOSE
Rnd 1: With B, ch 4; join with a sl st to form ring; 2 sc in each ch. Do not join. *(8 sc)*

Rnd 2: Sc in each sc; join in first sc.

Fasten off, leaving a 6-inch end for sewing.

POMPOM
Cut 2 (2½-inch-diameter) cardboard circles. Cut a hole in center of each, about ½ inch in diameter. Thread a tapestry needle with length of E doubled. Holding both circles tog, insert needle through center hole, over outside edge, through center again *(see Fig. 1)* until entire circle is covered and center hole is filled (thread more length of yarn as needed).

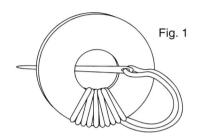

Fig. 1

With sharp scissors, cut yarn between circles all around the circumference *(see Fig. 2).*

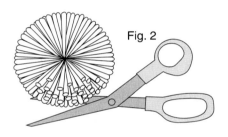

Fig. 2

Using 2 (12-inch) strands of E, slip yarn between circles and overlap yarn ends 2 or 3 times *(see Fig. 3)* to prevent knot from slipping, pull tightly and tie into a knot. Remove cardboard and fluff out pompom by rolling between hands. Trim even with scissors, leaving tying ends for attaching pompom.

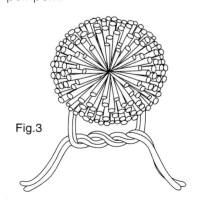

Fig.3

FINISHING

Step 1: Referring to photo for placement, sew Nose to face.

Step 2: Sew pompom to top of Hat.

Step 3: With C, make 1 French knot *(see Fig. 4)* for mouth and sew eyes, using straight st *(see Fig. 5)*. With D and using straight sts, sew cheeks.

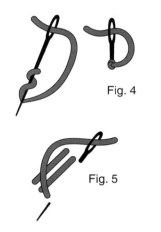

Fig. 4

Fig. 5

SNOWMAN ORNAMENT

HAT & HEAD
Note: *Piece is worked in continuous rnds. Do not join; mark beg of rnds.*

Rnd 1 (RS): Starting at top of hat and with A, ch 4; join with a sl st to form ring; ch 1, 10 sc in ring. Fasten off.

Rnd 2: Join B in first sc; sc in each sc. Fasten off.

Rnd 3: Join A in first sc; sc in each sc. Fasten off.

Rnd 4: Join B in first sc; sc in same sc, 2 sc in next sc; [sc in next sc, 2 sc in next sc] 4 times. *(15 sc)* Fasten off.

Rnd 5: Join A in first sc; sc in each sc. Fasten off.

Rnd 6: Join B in first sc; sc in

each sc. Fasten off.

Rnds 7 & 8: Rep rnds 5 and 6.

Rnd 9: Join A in first sc; sc in same sc, 2 sc in next sc; sc in next sc, [sc in next sc, 2 sc in next sc, sc in next sc] 4 times. *(20 sc)* Fasten off.

Rnd 10: Rep rnd 6.

Rnd 11: Rep rnd 5.

Rnd 12: Join B in first sc; sc in same sc and in next sc, 2 sc in next sc; sc in next 2 sc, [sc in next 2 sc, 2 sc in next sc, sc in next 2 sc] 3 times. *(24 sc)* Fasten off.

Rnd 13: Rep rnd 5.

Rnd 14: Join B in first sc; sc in same sc, 2 sc in next sc; sc in next sc, [sc in next sc, 2 sc in next sc, sc in next sc] 7 times. *(32 sc)* Fasten off.

Rnd 15: Join A in first sc; ch 1, hdc in each sc. Fasten off.

Rnd 16: Join F in first hdc; sc in each hdc.

Rnd 17: [Sc in next 2 sc, 2 sc in next sc, sc in next sc] 8 times. *(40 sc)*

Rnd 18: Sc in each sc.

Rnds 19–26: Rep rnd 18.

Rnd 27: [Sc in next 2 sc, sk next sc, sc in next 2 sc] 8 times. *(32 sc)*

Rnd 28: [Sc in next 2 sc, sk next sc, sc in next sc] 8 times. *(24 sc)*

Rnd 29: [Sc in next sc, sk next sc, sc in next sc] 8 times. *(16 sc)*

Rnd 30: [Sc in next 2 sc, sk next sc, sc in next sc] 4 times. *(12 sc)*

Rnd 31: [Sc in next sc, sk next sc, sc in next sc] 4 times. *(8 sc)*

Rnd 32: [Sc in next sc, sk next sc] 4 times. *(4 sc)*

Rnd 33: [Sl st in next sc, sk next sc] twice.

Fasten off and weave in all ends.

NOSE
Note: *Nose is worked in continuous rnds. Do not join rnds unless otherwise stated; mark beg of rnds.*

Rnd 1 (RS): With C, ch 3; join with a sl st to form ring; 2 sc in each ch. *(6 sc)*

Rnd 2: Sc in each sc.

Rnd 3: Rep rnd 2.

Rnd 4: Sc in each sc; join in first sc.

Fasten off, leaving a 6-inch end for sewing.

FINISHING
Step 1: Referring to photo for placement, sew Nose to face.

Step 2: With D, make 2 French knots *(see Fig. 4)* for eyes. With E and using straight sts *(see Fig. 5)*, sew cheeks on either side of Nose. With D, sew mouth using straight st over cheeks.

Step 3: Fold tip of Hat over and tack to secure. 🍃

Christmas Tree Table Topper

DESIGN BY KAREN HAY

SKILL LEVEL ◖■■▢▢
EASY

FINISHED SIZE
14 inches high x 20 inches in
diameter at base

MATERIALS
Medium (worsted) weight
   yarn (2½ oz/120 yds/71g per
   skein):
   4 skeins #2903 green *(A)*
   1 skein each #2904 lace *(B)*,
   #2902 red *(C)*, #2901 white
   (D), #2907 glitter ombré *(E)*
Size H/8/5mm crochet hook or
   size needed to obtain gauge
Tapestry needle
6 yds ¼-inch-wide gold ribbon
14 x 14-inch piece poster board

GAUGE
5 sc = 1 inch

Instructions

TREE
Note: *Tree is worked in continuous rnds. Do not join unless
specified; mark beg of rnds.*

Rnd 1 (RS): With A make slip
knot on hook; wrap end of yarn
counterclockwise around index
finger of hand holding hook; slide
ring off finger; 6 dc in ring. Pull
yarn end to tighten ring.

Rnd 2: 2 sc in each dc. *(12 sc)*

Rnd 3: [Sc in next sc, dc in next
sc] 6 times.

Rnd 4: [Sc in next sc, 2 dc in
next dc] 6 times. *(18 sts)*

Rnd 5: [Sc in next sc, 2 dc in next
dc, dc in next dc] 6 times. *(24 sts)*

Rnd 6: *2 sc in next sc; in each
of next 3 dc work (sl st, ch 5,
sl st)—*bough made*; rep from *
around.

Rnd 7: [2 sc in next sc, sc in
next sc, sk next bough] 6 times.
(18 sc)

Rnd 8: [Sc in next sc, dc in next
sc] 9 times.

Rnd 9: [Sc in next sc, 2 dc in
next dc] 9 times. *(27 sts)*

Rnd 10: [Sc in next sc, 2 dc in
next dc, dc in next dc] 9 times.
(36 sts)

Rnd 11: *2 sc in next sc; in each

of next 3 dc work (sl st, ch 5,
sl st)—*bough made*; rep from *
around.

Rnd 12: [2 sc in next sc, sc in
next sc, sk next bough] 9 times.
(27 sc)

Rnd 13: [Sc in next 2 sc, dc in
next sc] 9 times.

Rnd 14: [Sc in next 2 sc, 2 dc in
next dc] 9 times. *(36 sts)*

Rnd 15: [Sc in next 2 sc, 2 dc in
next dc, dc in next dc] 9 times.
(45 sts)

Rnd 16: *Sc in next sc, 2 sc in
next sc; in each of next 3 dc work

(sl st, ch 5, sl st)—*bough made*; rep from * around.

Rnd 17: [2 sc in next sc, sc in next 2 sc, sk next bough] 9 times. *(36 sc)*

Rnd 18: *Sc in next 2 sc, dc in next sc; rep from * around.

Rnd 19: *Sc in next 2 sc, 2 dc in next dc; rep from * around. *(48 sts)*

Rnd 20: *Sc in next 2 sc, 2 dc in next dc; dc in next dc; rep from * around. *(60 sts)*

Rnd 21: *Sc in next sc, 2 sc in next sc; in each of next 3 dc work (sl st, ch 5, sl st)—*bough made*; rep from * around.

Rnd 22: [2 sc in next sc, sc in next 2 sc, sk next bough] 9 times. *(48 sc)*

Rnd 23: *Sc in next 3 sc, dc in next sc; rep from * around.

Rnd 24: *Sc in next 3 sc, 2 dc in next dc; rep from * around. *(60 sts)*

Rnd 25: *Sc in next 3 sc, 2 dc in next dc, dc in next dc; rep from * around. *(72 sts)*

Rnd 26: *Sc in next 2 sc, 2 sc in next sc; in each of next 3 dc work (sl st, ch 5, sl st)—*bough made*; rep from * around.

Rnd 27: *2 sc in next sc; sc in next 3 sc, sk next bough; rep from * around. *(60 sc)*

Rnd 28: *Sc in next 3 sc, dc in next sc; rep from * around.

Rnd 29: *Sc in next 3 sc, 2 dc in next dc; rep from * around. *(75 sts)*

Rnd 30: *Sc in next 2 sc, 2 dc in next dc, dc in next dc; rep from * around. *(90 sts)*

Rnd 31: *Sc in next 2 sc, 2 sc in next sc; in each of next 3 dc work (sl st, ch 5, sl st)—*bough made*; rep from * around.

Rnd 32: *2 sc in next sc; sc in next 2 sc, sk next bough; rep from * around. *(75 sc)*

Rnd 33: *Sc in next 4 sc, dc in next sc; rep from * around.

Rnd 34: *Sc in next 4 sc, 2 dc in next dc; rep from * around. *(90 sts)*

Rnd 35: *Sc in next 4 sc, 2 dc in next dc, dc in next dc; rep from * around. *(105 sts)*

Rnd 36: *2 sc in next sc; sc in next 3 sc, in each of next 3 dc work (sl st, ch 5, sl st)—*bough made*; rep from * around.

Rnd 37: *Sc in next 4 sc, 2 sc in next sc; sk next bough; rep from * around. *(90 sc)*

Rnd 38: *Sc in next 4 sc, dc in next sc; rep from * around.

Rnd 39: *Sc in next 4 sc, 2 dc in next dc; rep from * around. *(108 sts)*

Rnd 40: *Sc in next 4 sc, 2 dc in next dc, dc in next dc; rep from * around. *(126 sts)*

Rnd 41: *2 sc in next sc; sc in next 3 sc, in each of next 3 dc work (sl st, ch 5, sl st)—*bough made*; rep from * around.

Rnd 42: *Sc in next 4 sc, 2 sc in next sc; sk next bough; rep from * around. *(108 sc)*

Rnd 43: *Sc in next 5 sc, dc in next sc; rep from * around.

Rnd 44: *Sc in next 5 sc, 2 dc in next dc; rep from * around. *(126 sts)*

Rnd 45: *Sc in next 5 sc, 2 dc in next dc, dc in next dc; rep from *

around. *(144 sts)*

Rnd 46: *Sc in next 4 sc, 2 sc in next sc; in each of next 3 dc work (sl st, ch 5, sl st)—*bough made*; rep from * around.

Rnd 47: *Sc in next 6 sc, sk next bough; rep from * around. *(108 sc)*

Rnd 48: Sc in each sc.

Rnd 49: Rep rnd 48.

Rnd 50: Sc in each sc; join in first sc.

Fasten off and weave in ends.

BASE
Make 2.
Note: *Each base forms about ¾ of a circle.*

Row 1: With A, ch 31; sc in 2nd ch from hook and in each rem ch, turn. *(30 sc)*

Row 2: Ch 1, 2 sc in first sc; sc in each sc to last sc; 2 sc in last sc, turn. *(32 sc)*

Row 3: Ch 1, sc in each sc, turn.

Row 4: Rep row 3.

Row 5: Rep row 2. *(34 sc at end of row)*

Rows 6–8: Rep row 3.

Row 9: Rep row 2. *(36 sc at end of row)*

Rows 10–15: Rep row 3.

Note: *For **sc dec,** draw up lp in each of 2 sts indicated, yo and draw through all 3 lps on hook.*

Row 16: Ch 1, **sc dec** (see Note) in first 2 sc; sc in each sc to last 2 sc; sc dec in last 2 sc, turn. *(34 sc)*

Rows 17–19: Rep row 3.

Row 20: Rep row 16. *(32 sc at end of row)*

Rows 21 & 22: Rep row 3.

Row 23: Rep row 16. *(30 sc at end of row)*

Row 24: Rep row 3.

Rows 25 & 26: Rep row 16. *(26 sc at end of row 26)*

Row 27: Ch 1, sc dec in first 2 sc; sc dec in next 2 sc; sc in each sc to last 4 sc; [sc dec in next 2 sc] twice, turn. *(22 sc)*

Rows 28–31: Rep row 27. *(6 sc at end of row 31)*

Fasten off and weave in ends.

STAR
Make 3.
Rnd 1 (RS): With B make sl knot on hook; wrap end of yarn counterclockwise around index finger of hand holding hook; slide ring off finger; 8 dc in ring; join with a sl st in first sc. Pull yarn end to tighten ring.

Rnd 2: Ch 1, sc in same sc as joining, 2 sc in next sc; [sc in next sc, 2 sc in next sc] 3 times; join with a sl st in first sc. *(12 sc)*

Rnd 3: Ch 1, sc in same sc as join in and in next 2 sc, 2 sc in next sc; [sc in next 3 sc, 2 sc in next sc] 3 times; join with a sl st in first sc. *(15 sc)*

Note: *Points of Star are worked in rows.*

First Point
Row 1: Ch 1, sc in next 3 sc, turn, leaving rem sc unworked.

Row 2: Ch 1, sc dec in first 2 sc; sc dec in same sc as last part of sc dec just worked and next sc, turn. *(2 sc)*

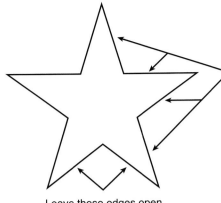

Sew these edges and corresponding edges on the other side.

Leave these edges open.

Row 3: Ch 1, sc dec, turn.

Row 4: Ch 1, sc in first sc, turn.

Row 5: Ch 1, sl st in first sc; working across next side in ends of rows, sl st evenly to row 1; sl st in same sc on rnd 3 as last sc of row 1 worked. Fasten off.

2nd Point
Row 1: Join B in first unused sc on rnd 3 from last point made; ch 1, sc in next 3 sc, turn, leaving rem sc unworked.

Rows 2–5: Rep rows 2–5 of First Point.

3rd–5th Points
Work same as 2nd Point.

Weave in all ends.

ORNAMENTS
Make 9 each of B, C, D & E.
Rnd 1 (RS): With yarn make slip knot on hook; wrap end of yarn counterclockwise around index finger of hand holding hook; slide ring off finger; 6 sc in ring; join with a sl st in first sc. Pull yarn end to tighten ring.

Rnd 2: Ch 1, 2 sc in same sc as joining and in each rem sc; join with a sl st in first sc. *(12 sc)*

Rnd 3: Ch 1, sc in same sc as joining and in each rem sc; join with a sl st in first sc. *(12 sc)*

Rnd 4: Ch 1, [sc dec] 6 times; join with a sl st in first sc. *(6 sc)*

Finish off and weave in ends.

ASSEMBLY
For each Ornament, cut 10-inch length of matching yarn. Draw through last rnd of Ornament and draw tight. Secure ends.

FINISHING
Step 1: Draw circle on poster board with radius equal to distance from rnd 1 of Tree to rnd 50. To draw a circle, cut a piece of yarn the same length as radius. Hold 1 end of yarn in center of poster board, and hold a pencil against the other end of the yarn. Hold yarn tight. Gently move pencil, drawing circle on poster board. Cut out circle and cut a large (approximately ¼ of the circle) pie-shaped wedge from circle. Form a cone from the poster board. The center of the circle forms the tip of the Tree, the cut edges of the pie-shaped wedge are overlapped to adjust size of cone. Slide cone in Tree.

Step 2: Overlap Bases and sew edges to rnd 50 of Tree to form flap. This allows Ornaments to be stored inside Tree.

Step 3: Cut 6-inch lengths of ribbon. Draw 1 length through last rnd of 1 Ornament and through ch-5 sp on any bough on Tree. Tie in bow. Rep with rem Ornaments.

Step 4: With B, sew tog edges of Stars indicated on diagram, leaving bottom edges open. Place on top of Tree. 🍂

Snowman Trio

DESIGN BY KATHLEEN STUART

SNOWMAN SODA BOTTLE COVER

SKILL LEVEL ▰▰▱▱ EASY

FINISHED SIZE
15 inches tall

MATERIALS
Bernat Soft Bouclé bulky (chunky) weight yarn (5 oz/255 yds/140g per skein) 1 skein #06713 white *(A)*
Lion Brand Homespun bulky (chunky) weight yarn (6 oz/185 yds/170g per skein):
    1 skein each #369 Florida Keys green *(B)* and #372 sunshine state *(C)*
Red Heart Classic medium (worsted) weight yarn (3½ oz/190 yds/99g per skein):
    3 yds #254 pumpkin *(D)*
Size J/10/6mm crochet hook or size needed to obtain gauge
Tapestry needle
Polyester fiberfill
2 black 12mm animal eyes
3 black ⅝-inch buttons
2 red 2-inch pompoms
Red chenille stem
2-liter soda bottle
Sewing needle and matching thread
Tacky craft glue

GAUGE
Rnds 1–3 = 2 inches

PATTERN NOTE
To change color, work last stitch until 2 loops remain on hook; with new color, yarn over and draw through 2 loops on hook. Cut old color.

Instructions

HEAD & BODY
Note: Head and Body are worked in continuous rnds. Do not join rnds unless otherwise stated; mark beg of rnds.

Rnd 1: Starting at top of Head with A, ch 2, 6 sc in 2nd ch from hook.

Rnd 2: 2 sc in each sc. *(12 sc)*

Rnd 3: [Sc in next sc, 2 sc in next sc] 6 times. *(18 sc)*

Rnd 4: [Sc in next 2 sc, 2 sc in next sc] 6 times. *(24 sc)*

Rnd 5: [Sc in next 3 sc, 2 sc in next sc] 6 times. *(30 sc)*

Rnd 6: [Sc in next 4 sc, 2 sc in next sc] 6 times. *(36 sc)*

Rnd 7: [Sc in next 5 sc, 2 sc in next sc] 6 times. *(42 sc)*

Rnd 8: Sc in each sc.

Rnds 9–16: Rep rnd 8.

Note: For **sc dec,** *draw up lp in 2 sts indicated, yo and draw through all 3 lps on hook.*

Rnd 17: Sc dec *(see Note)* in next 2 sc; *sc dec in next 2 sc; rep from * around. *(21 sc)*

Rnd 18: [Sc dec] 10 times; sc in next sc. *(11 sc)*

Rnd 19: 2 sc in each of next 10 sc; sc in next sc. *(21 sc)*

Rnd 20: 2 sc in each sc. *(42 sc)*

Place eyes between rnds 10 and 11, spacing eyes about 2 sts apart. Stuff Head with fiberfill.

Rnds 21–48: Rep rnd 8. At end of rnd 48, join with a sl st in first sc.

Fasten off and weave in ends.

NOSE

With D, ch 8, dc in 4th ch from hook and in each rem ch. Fasten off, leaving a 10-inch end for sewing.

SCARF

Rnd 1: With B, ch 62; sc in 2nd ch from hook; *ch 1, sk next ch, sc in next ch; rep from * across, changing to C in last sc; cut B, turn.

Rnd 2: Ch 1, sc in first sc, sc in next ch-1 sp; *ch 1, sk next sc, sc in next ch-1 sp; rep from * to last sc; sc in last sc, changing to B in last sc; cut C, turn.

Rnd 3: Ch 1, sc in first sc; *ch 1, sk next sc, sc in next ch-1 sp; rep from * to last sc; sc in last sc.

Fasten off and weave in ends.

FINISHING

Step 1: Roll Nose, starting at turning ch and roll toward last st and tack with long end to secure. Sew Nose to face below eyes.

Step 2: Sew buttons to front of Body.

Step 3: Glue 1 pompom to each end of chenille stem. Glue pompoms to side of head.

Step 4: Place Snowman over bottle. Tie Scarf around neck.

SNOWMAN TUBE COVER

SKILL LEVEL EASY

FINISHED SIZE
12 inches tall

MATERIALS
Red Heart Classic medium (worsted) weight yarn (3½ oz/190 yds/99g per skein):
1 skein each #1 white (A), #12 black (B), #912

cherry red (C)
3 yds #254 pumpkin (D)
Size G/6/4 mm crochet hook or size needed to obtain gauge
Tapestry needle
Polyester fiberfill
5 black ½-inch buttons
2 red 1-inch pompoms
1 paper towel cardboard tube
Small piece of cardboard
Small plastic bag filled with small amount of plastic pellets
Black fabric paint
Small paint-brush
Sewing needle and matching thread
Tacky craft glue
Stitch markers

GAUGE
5 sc = 1 inch

PATTERN NOTE
To change color, work last stitch until 2 loops remain on hook; with new color, yarn over and draw through 2 loops on hook. Cut old color.

Instructions

BODY, HEAD & HAT

Note: Body, Head and Hat are worked in continuous rnds. Do not join rnds unless otherwise stated; mark beg of rnds.

Rnd 1 (RS): Starting at bottom of Body with A, ch 24, join with a sl st to form a ring; sc in each ch. (24 sc)

Rnd 2: Sc in each sc.

Rnds 3–46: Rep rnd 2.

Rnds 47: Sc in each sc, changing to B in last sc. Cut A.

Rnd 48: Rep rnd 2.

Rnd 49: Working in **back lps** *(see Stitch Guide)* only, sc in each sc.

Rnds 50–57: Rep rnd 2.

*Note: For **sc dec**, draw up lp in 2 sts indicated, yo and draw through all 3 lps on hook.*

Rnd 58: Working in back lps only, [sc in next 4 sc, **sc dec** *(see Note)* in next 2 sc] 4 times. *(20 sc)*

Rnd 59: [Sc in next 3 sc, sc dec] 4 times. *(16 sc)*

Rnd 60: [Sc in next 2 sc, sc dec] 4 times. *(12 sc)*

Rnd 61: [Sc in next sc, sc dec] 4 times. *(8 sc)*

Rnd 62: [Sc dec] 4 times; join in first sc. *(4 sc)*

Fasten off and weave in ends.

HAT BRIM
Hold piece with RS facing you and bottom of Body at top; join B with a sl st in unused **front lp** *(see Stitch Guide)* of first sc on rnd 57; ch 3 *(counts as a dc)*, working in rem unused front lps, dc in next 2 sc, 2 dc in next sc; [dc in next 3 sc, 2 dc in next sc] 5 times; join with a sl st in 3rd ch of beg ch-3.

Fasten off and weave in ends.

FEET
Rnd 1 (RS): With B, ch 3; join with a sl st to form ring; ch 1, 11 sc in ring, join with a sl st in first sc.

Rnd 2: Ch 3, in same sc as joining work (dc, tr); 3 tr in next sc; dc in next sc, hdc in next sc, 2 sc in next sc; sc in next sc, 2 sc in next sc; hdc in next sc, dc in next sc, 3 tr in next sc; in last sc work (tr, dc, ch 3, sl st); join in joining sl st.

Rnd 3: Sc in next 3 chs of next

ch-3 sp, 2 hdc in each of next 4 sts; hdc in next 4 sts, in next st work (hdc, dc); dc in next st, in next st work (dc, hdc); hdc in next 4 sts, 2 hdc in each of next 4 sts, sc in next 3 chs of next ch-3 sp; join in first sc.

Fasten off, leaving an 8-inch end for sewing.

NOSE
Note: Nose is worked in continuous rnds. Do not join rnds unless otherwise stated; mark beg of rnds.

Rnd 1 (RS): With D, ch 2, 6 sc in 2nd ch from hook.

Rnd 2: Sc in each sc.

Rnd 3: Sc in each sc; join in first sc.

Fasten off, leaving a 6-inch end for sewing.

SCARF
With C, ch 50; hdc in 3rd ch from hook and in each rem ch.

Fasten off and weave in ends.

FINISHING
Step 1: Cut circle from cardboard to fit over end of cardboard tube. Place tube inside Body, Head and Hat, and glue circle to tube at bottom of Body.

Step 2: Place fiberfill inside tube to help keep tube from collapsing. For added weight, place small bag with plastic pellets inside tube near bottom as fiberfill is added.

Step 3: Sew Feet to bottom of Body.

Step 4: For ear muffs, glue 1 pompom to each side of Head, just below Hat.

Step 5: Referring to photo for placement, glue 2 buttons for eyes

to face. Sew Nose below eyes.

Step 6: Paint on mouth just below Nose using drops of fabric paint.

Step 7: Tie Scarf just below mouth. Tack in place, if desired.

Step 8: Glue rem buttons to front of Snowman, spacing about 2 to 3 rows apart. ✂

SNOWMAN WINE BOTTLE COVER

SKILL LEVEL ◼◻◻◻ EASY

FINISHED SIZE
13½ inches tall

MATERIALS
Bernat Soft Bouclé bulky (chunky) weight yarn (5 oz/255 yds/140g per skein): 1 skein #06713 white *(A)*
Lion Brand Jiffy bulky (chunky) weight yarn (3 oz/135 yds/85g per skein): 1 skein #109 royal blue *(B)*
Lion Brand Homespun bulky (chunky) weight yarn (6 oz/185 yds/170g per skein): 1 skein #307 antique red *(C)*
Red Heart Classic medium (worsted) weight yarn (3½ oz/190 yds/99g per skein): 1 skein #254 pumpkin *(D)*
Size J/10/6mm crochet hook or size needed to obtain gauge
Tapestry needle
Polyester fiberfill
9mm black animal eyes: 2
Sewing needle and matching thread

GAUGE
3 sc = 1 inch

PATTERN NOTE
To change color, work last stitch until 2 loops remain on hook; with new color, yarn over and draw through 2 loops on hook. Cut old color.

Instructions

HEAD & BODY

Note: *Head and Body are worked in continuous rnds. Do not join rnds unless otherwise stated; mark beg of rnds.*

Rnd 1 (RS): Starting at top of head with A, ch 2, 6 sc in 2nd ch from hook.

Rnd 2: 2 sc in each sc. *(12 sc)*

Rnd 3: [Sc in next sc, 2 sc in next sc] 6 times. *(18 sc)*

Rnd 4: [Sc in next 2 sc, 2 sc in next sc] 6 times. *(24 sc)*

Rnd 5: [Sc in next 3 sc, 2 sc in next sc] 6 times. *(30 sc)*

Rnd 6: Sc in each sc.

Rnds 7–12: Rep rnd 6.

Note: *For* **sc dec,** *draw up lp in 2 sts indicated, yo and draw through all 3 lps on hook.*

Rnd 13: *Sc in next 3 sc, **sc dec** (see Note) in next 2 sc; *sc in next 3 sc, sc dec in next 2 sc; rep from * 4 times. *(24 sc)*

Rnd 14: [Sc in next 2 sc, sc dec] 6 times. *(18 sc)*

Rnd 15: [Sc in next sc, sc dec] 6 times. *(12 sc)*

Rnd 16: [Sc in next sc, 2 sc in next sc] 6 times. *(18 sc)*

Rnd 17: [Sc in next 2 sc, 2 sc in next sc] 6 times. *(24 sc)*

Rnd 18: [Sc in next 3 sc, 2 sc in next sc] 6 times. *(30 sc)*

Place eyes between rnds 10 and 11, spacing eyes 2 sts apart. Stuff Head with fiberfill.

Rnds 19–45: Rep rnd 6. At end of rnd 45, join with a sl st in first sc.

Fasten off and weave in ends.

NOSE

With D, ch 6, hdc in 3rd ch from hook and in each rem ch. Fasten off, leaving a 10-inch end for sewing.

HAT

Row 1 (RS): With B, ch 15, sc in 2nd ch from hook and in each rem ch, turn.

Row 2: Ch 1, working in **back lps** *(see Stitch Guide)* only, sc in each sc, turn.

Rows 3–30: Rep row 2.

Row 31: Ch 1, hold row 1 and row 30 tog; working through both thicknesses at same time, sl st in each sc. Fasten off, leaving a 10-inch end. With yarn, weave through ends of each row and gather tog. Sew opening closed.

SCARF

With C, ch 61; sc in 2nd ch from hook, *dc in next ch, sc in next ch; rep from * to last ch; dc in last ch.

Fasten off and weave in ends.

FINISHING

Step 1: Roll Nose, starting at turning ch and roll toward last st and tack with long end to secure. Sew Nose to face below eyes.

Step 2: Sew Hat to top of head.

Step 3: Place Snowman over bottle. Tie Scarf around neck. 🌿

Glistening Tassel Cover

DESIGN BY DELSIE RHOADES

SKILL LEVEL ◼◼◻◻
EASY

FINISHED SIZE
6½ inches long, excluding hanger

MATERIALS
J.&P. Coats Royale Metallic Crochet size 10 crochet cotton (100 yds per ball):
1 ball #90G gold/gold
Lion Brand Lion Suede bulky (chunky) weight yarn (3 oz/122 yds/85g per skein):
1 ball each #140 rose, #132 olive, #146 fuchsia, #178 teal
Size 6/1.80mm steel crochet hook
Tapestry needle

GAUGE
7 sc = 1 inch

SPECIAL STITCH
Double triple crochet (dtr): Yo 3 times; insert hook in st indicated and draw lp through, [yo, draw through 2 lps on hook] 3 times.

Instructions

COVER
Make 4.
Row 1 (RS): With gold/gold, [ch 3, sl st in 3rd ch from hook] 23 times. Do not turn. Ch 1, sc in each sl st, turn. *(23 sc)*

Row 2: Ch 5 *(counts as a dtr)*, *dtr (see Special Stitch)* in next sc, ch 1, sk next sc, dtr in next sc, rep from * 6 times, dtr in last sc, turn.

Row 3: [Ch 5, sc in next ch-1 sp] 7 times, ch 5, sc in 5th ch of beg ch-5 of previous row, turn. *(8 ch-w5 sps)*

Row 4: Sl st in next ch-5 sp, ch 1, sc in same sp, [ch 5, sc in next ch-5 sp] 7 times, turn. *(7 ch-5 sps)*

Row 5: Ch 1, sc in next ch-5 sp, * ch 7, in 4th ch from hook work [sl st, ch 3] 3 times; sc in next ch-5 sp; rep from * across.

Fasten off and weave in ends.

TASSEL
Make 1 of each color.

Cut 32 (13-inch) strands of yarn.

Fold 30 strands in half and tie at fold with additional strand.

Wrap rem length around folded lengths, 1 inch from fold; tie in knot.

Trim ends even.

FINISHING
Step 1: Wrap Cover around top of Tassel. Sew ends tog.

Step 2: For hanging lps, cut 8-inch length of matching yarn for each Tassel. Thread end through top of Tassel. Knot ends tog to form lp. 🍂

Splendid Tabletops

Your buffet, party and dinner settings become special with these design ideas including table runners, wineglass tags, coasters and napkin rings.

Peppermint Wreath Coaster & Napkin Ring

DESIGNS BY SUE PENROD

SKILL LEVEL ■■□□ *EASY*

FINISHED SIZES
Coaster: 4 inches in diameter

Napkin Ring: 1¾ inches in diameter

MATERIALS
Aunt Lydia's Classic Crochet size 10 crochet cotton (350 yds per ball):
- 1 ball each #1 white *(A)*, #484 myrtle green *(B)*, #494 victory red *(C)*

Size B/1/2.25mm crochet hook or size needed to obtain gauge
Tapestry needle
White craft glue
Small container (for mixing stiffening solution)
Piece of cardboard
Plastic wrap
Straight pins

GAUGE
8 sc = 1 inch

Instructions

COASTER

CENTER
Note: *Center is worked in continuous rnds. Do not join unless specified; mark beg of rnds.*

Rnd 1: With A, ch 2, 16 hdc in 2nd ch from hook. *(16 hdc)*

Rnd 2: Hdc in each hdc.

Rnd 3: [Hdc in next hdc, 2 hdc in next hdc] 8 times. *(24 hdc)*

Rnd 4: [Hdc in next hdc, 2 hdc in next hdc] 12 times. *(36 hdc)*

Rnd 5: [Hdc in next hdc, 2 hdc in next hdc] 18 times. *(54 hdc)*

Rnd 6: [Hdc in next hdc, 2 hdc in next hdc] 27 times. *(81 hdc)*

Rnd 7: Rep rnd 2.

Rnd 8: Hdc in each hdc; join in first hdc.

Fasten off and weave in ends.

EDGING
Row 1: With A, ch 101, sc in 2nd ch from hook and in each rem ch, turn. *(100 sc)*

Row 2: Ch 1, sc in first sc and in each rem sc, turn.

Row 3: Ch 1, sc in first sc and in each rem sc, change to B by drawing lp through; cut A, turn.

Row 4: Rep row 2.

Row 5: Ch 1, sc in first sc and in each rem sc, change to C by drawing lp through; cut B, turn.

Row 6: Rep row 2.

Row 7: Ch 1, sc in first sc and in each rem sc.

Fasten off and weave in all ends.

NAPKIN RING
Row 1 (RS): With A, ch 51; sc in 2nd ch from the hook and each rem ch, turn. *(50 sc)*

Row 2: Ch 1, sc in each sc; change to B by drawing lp through; cut A, turn.

Row 3: Ch 1, sc in each sc, turn.

Row 4: Ch 1, sc in each sc; change to C by drawing lp through cut B, turn.

Row 5: Rep row 3.

Row 6: Ch 1, sc in each sc.

Fasten off and weave in ends.

FINISHING
Step 1: Make stiffening mixture of 60 percent white glue and 40 percent water. Mix well in small container such as paper cup. Cover cardboard with plastic wrap.

Step 2: Place Coaster Edging and Napkin Ring in mixture to saturate.

Step 3: Remove from mixture. Shape Edging in circle on top of Center, working ends tog. Pin if necessary to hold in place. Let dry. Shape Napkin Ring in circle, working ends tog. Pin if necessary to hold shape. Let dry.

Step 4: Glue Edging to Center. 🍃

Lustrous Table Runner & Centerpiece

BY LAURA POLLEY

LUSTROUS TABLE RUNNER

SKILL LEVEL ◼◼◼◻
INTERMEDIATE

FINISHED SIZE
18 x 42 inches

MATERIALS
Lion Brand Glitterspun medium (worsted) weight ribbon yarn (1¾ oz/115 yds/50g per skein):
    5 skeins #60573 silver *(A)*
    4 skeins #64707 gold *(B)*
Size K/10½/6.5mm crochet hook or size needed to obtain gauge
Tapestry needle

GAUGE
In pattern: 15 sts = 4 inches

SPECIAL STITCH
Long double crochet (long dc):
Yo, working over next ch-1 sp, insert hook in sk sc on 2nd row below, yo, draw lp through and up to height of working row, [yo, draw through 2 lps on hook] twice.

PATTERN NOTE
To change color, work last stitch until 2 loops remain on hook; with new color, yarn over and draw through 2 loops on hook. Carry old color along edge.

Instructions

CENTER
Row 1 (RS): With B, ch 158; sc in 2nd ch from hook and in each rem ch, turn. *(157 sc)*

Row 2: Ch 1, sc in first sc; *ch 1, sk next sc, sc in next sc; rep from * across, changing to A in last sc, turn.

Row 3: Ch 1, sc in first sc; ***long dc** (see Special Stitch) in next sk sc on 2nd row below; sc in next sc; rep from * across, turn.

Row 4: Rep row 2, changing to B at end of row.

Row 5: Rep row 3.

Rows 6–69: [Work rows 2–5] 16 times.

Row 70: Ch 1, sc in first sc and in each rem st.

Fasten off and weave in all ends.

EDGING

Rnd 1 (RS): Hold center with RS facing you and row 1 to right; join A with sl st in end of row 1 in upper right corner; ch 1, 3 sc in same sp as joining, working across side in ends of rows, work 65 sc evenly spaced to row 70; 3 sc in end of row 70; working across row 70, sc in each sc; working across next side in ends of rows, 3 sc in end of row 70; work 65 sc evenly spaced

down to row 1; 3 sc in end of row 1; working across next side in unused lps of beg ch, sc in each lp; join with sl st in first sc. *(456 sc)*

Rnd 2: Ch 1, sl st in next sc, dc in next sc, ch 3, 4 dc over **post** *(see Stitch Guide)* of last dc made; *sk next 3 sc, dc in next sc, ch 3, 4 dc over post of last dc made; rep from * to last sc; sc in last sc; join in first sl st. Fasten off.

Rnd 3: Join B with sl st in 3rd ch of first ch-3 on previous rnd; ch 1, sc in same ch as joining; *sl st in **back lp** *(see Stitch Guide)* only of next 4 dc, working over previous rnd, tr in first sk sc of next 3-sc group on 2nd rnd below, sc in 3rd ch of next ch-3; rep from * to last 4 dc; sl st in back lp only of last 4 dc, tr in first sk sc on 2nd rnd below; join in first sc.

Fasten off and weave in all ends.

LUSTROUS CENTERPIECE

SKILL LEVEL
INTERMEDIATE

FINISHED SIZE
Diameter at top opening: approximately 6¾ inches

Diameter at base: approximately 7½ inches

MATERIALS
Lion Brand Glitterspun bulky (chunky) weight ribbon yarn (1¾ oz/115 yds/50g per skein):
   3 skeins #60573 silver *(A)*
   1 skein #64707 gold *(B)*
Size G/6/4mm crochet hook or size needed to obtain gauge
Tapestry needle

GAUGE
Rnds 1–6 = 3 inches in diameter

SPECIAL STITCH
Long double crochet (long dc): Yo, working over next ch-1 sp, insert hook in sk sc on 2nd row below, yo, draw lp through and up to height of working row, [yo, draw through 2 lps on hook] twice.

PATTERN NOTE
To change color, work last stitch until 2 loops remain on hook; with new color, yarn over and draw through 2 loops on hook. Carry old color along edge.

Instructions

Rnd 1 (RS): With A, ch 4; join with sl st to form ring; ch 1, working over B, 8 sc in ring; join with sl st in first sc.

Note: *Continue to work following rnds over B.*

Rnd 2: Ch 1, 2 sc in same sc as joining and in each rem sc; join in first sc. *(16 sc)*

Rnd 3: Rep rnd 2. *(32 sc at end of row)*

Rnd 4: Ch 1, sc in same sc and in each rem sc; join in first sc.

Rnd 5: Ch 1; sc in first sc, 2 sc in next sc; *sc in next sc, 2 sc in next sc; rep from * around; join in first sc. *(48 sc)*

Rnd 6: Rep rnd 4.

Rnd 7: Ch 1, sc in same sc and in next sc, 2 sc in next sc; *sc in next 2 sc, 2 sc in next sc; rep from * around; join in first sc. *(64 sc)*

Rnd 8: Rep rnd 4.

Rnd 9: Ch 1; sc in same sc and in next 2 sc, 2 sc in next sc; *sc in next 3 sc, 2 sc in next sc; rep from * around; join in first sc. *(80 sc)*

Rnd 10: Rep rnd 4.

Rnd 11: Ch 1; sc in same sc and in next 3 sc; *sc in next 4 sc, 2 sc in next sc; rep from * around; join in first sc. *(96 sc)*

Rnd 12: Rep rnd 4.

Rnd 13: Ch 1; sc in same sc and in next 4 sc; *sc in next 5 sc, 2 sc in next sc; rep from * around; join first sc. *(112 sc)*

Rnd 14: Rep rnd 4.

Rnd 15: Ch 1; sc in same sc and in next 5 sc, 2 sc in next sc; *sc in next 6 sc, 2 sc in next sc,

rep from * around; join in first sc. *(128 sc)*

Rnd 16: Rep rnd 4.

Rnd 17: Ch 1; sc in same sc and in next 6 sc, 2 sc in next sc; *sc in next 7 sc, 2 sc in next sc; rep from * around; join in first sc. *(144 sc)*

Rnds 18–31: rep rnd 4.

Note: *For **sc dec,** draw up lp in each of 2 sts indicated, yo and draw through all 3 lps on hook.*

Rnd 32: Ch 1; sc in same sc and in next 6 sc, **sc dec** *(see Note)* in next 2 sc; *sc in next 7 sc, sc dec

in next 2 sc, rep from * around; join in first sc. *(128 sc)*

Rnds 33–35: Rep rnd 4.

Rnd 36: Ch 1, sc in same sc and in next 5 sc, sc dec; *sc in next 6 sc, sc dec; rep from * around; join in first sc. Change to B by drawing lp through; work over A on following rnd. *(112 sc)*

Rnd 37: Ch 1, sc in same sc and in each rem sc in each sc; join in **front lp** *(see Stitch Guide)* of first sc. Change to A by drawing lp through; work over B on following rnd. Turn.

Rnd 38 (WS): Ch 1, sc in same lp as joining and in back lp of each rem sc; join in first sc. Fasten off B.

EDGING
Rnd 39: Ch 3 *(counts as a dc)*, sk next 2 sc; *dc in next sc, ch 3, 4 dc over **post** *(see Stitch Guide)* of last dc made; sk next 3 sc; rep from * around; dc in same sc as beg ch-3 made; ch 3, 3 dc over post of last dc made; join in 3rd ch of beg ch-3. Fasten off.

Rnd 40: Hold piece with WS facing you; join A in first dc of 3-dc group made on rnd 39; loosely sl st in next 2 dc and in joining sl st of previous rnd, working over previous rnd, tr in first sk sc of next 3-sc group on 2nd row below, sc in 3rd ch of next ch-3; *loosely sl st in next 4 dc, working over previous rnd, tr in first sk sc of next 3-sc group on 2nd row below, sc in 3rd ch of next ch-3, rep from * around; join in joining sl st.

Fasten off and weave in all ends.

FINISHING
Fold Edging to RS along rnd 38. ❧

Candy Cane & Holly Beverage Tags

DESIGN BY SUE PENROD

CANDY CANE BEVERAGE TAG

SKILL LEVEL

FINISHED SIZE
1¾ inches long

MATERIALS
Aunt Lydia's Classic Crochet size 10 crochet cotton (350 yds per ball):
    1 ball each #1 white (A), #484 myrtle green (B), #421 goldenrod (C), #494 victory red (D), #493 French rose (E)
Size B/1/2.25mm crochet hook or size needed to obtain gauge
Tapestry needle
6mm jump rings: 4
25mm stemware hoops: 4
6mm glass beads:
    2 each of 4 different colors
White craft glue
Small container (for mixing stiffening solution)
Piece of cardboard
Plastic wrap
Straight pins

GAUGE
8 sc = 1 inch

Instructions

CANDY CANE
Make 4.

WHITE STRIPE
Make 4.
With A, ch 12, sc in 2nd ch from hook and in next 6 chs, 3 sc in next ch; working in unused lps on opposite side of beg ch, sc in next 4 chs. *(11 sc)*

Fasten off and weave in ends.

COLOR STRIPE
Make 1 each of B, C & D.
Ch 12, sc in 2nd ch from hook and in next 6 chs, 3 sc in next ch; working in unused lps on opposite side of beg ch, sc in next 4 chs. *(11 sc)*

Fasten off and weave in ends.

FINISHING
Step 1: Make stiffening mixture of 60 percent white glue and 40 percent water. Mix well in small container such as paper cup. Cover cardboard with plastic wrap.

Step 2: Place Stripes in mixture to saturate.

Step 3: Remove Stripes from mixture. For each Candy Cane, twist 1 White Stripe and 1 Color Stripe tog (not too tightly) and shape. Pin Candy Canes in place on cardboard. Let dry.

Step 4: Attach 1 jump ring in top of each Candy Cane. On 1 hoop, slide 1 glass bead, 1 jump ring and 1 additional matching bead. Rep with rem hoops.

BEADS & HOLLY BEVERAGE TAG

SKILL LEVEL

FINISHED SIZE
1¾ inches long

MATERIALS
Aunt Lydia's Classic Crochet size 10 crochet cotton (350 yds per ball):
    1 ball #484 myrtle green
Size B/1/2.25mm crochet hook or size needed to obtain gauge
Tapestry needle
25mm stemware hoops: 4
6mm glass beads:
    4 each of 4 different colors
White craft glue
Small container (for mixing stiffening solution)
Piece of cardboard
Plastic wrap
Straight pins

GAUGE
8 sc = 1 inch

Instructions

LEAF
Make 4.
Row 1: Ch 8, sc in 2nd ch from hook and in next 5 chs, 3 sc in next ch; working in unused lps on opposite side of beg ch, sc in next 4 chs, turn. *(13 sc)*

Row 2: Ch 1, sc in first 4 sc, 2 sc in each of next 3 sc; sc in next 4 sc, turn. *(14 sc)*

Row 3: Ch 1, sc in first 12 sc, turn, leaving rem sc unworked. *(12 sc)*

Row 4: Ch 1, sc in first 10 sc, turn, leaving rem sc unworked. *(10 sc)*

Row 5: Ch 1, sc in first 6 sc, ch 4, sl st in 2nd ch from hook, in next 2 chs, and in same sc as last sc made.

Fasten off and weave in ends.

FINISHING
Step 1: Make stiffening mixture of 60 percent white glue and 40 percent water. Mix well in small container such as paper cup. Cover cardboard with plastic wrap.

Step 2: Place leaves in mixture to saturate.

Step 3: Remove leaves from mixture and place flat on cardboard, shaping as necessary. Let dry.

Step 4: On 1 hoop, slide 2 glass beads, 1 Leaf and 2 additional matching beads. Rep with rem hoops. 🍃

Lacy Snowballs Table Set

DESIGNS BY MELODY MACDUFFEE

SKILL LEVEL
INTERMEDIATE

FINISHED SIZES
Place Mat: 12 x 18 inches

Circlet: 7½ inches in diameter

MATERIALS
Aunt Lydia's Classic Crochet
   size 10 crochet cotton (400 yds
   per ball):
      1 ball #1 white
Size 7/1.65mm steel hook or size
   needed to obtain gauge
Tapestry needle

GAUGE
Rnds 1 and 2 = 1 inch

Instructions

PLACE MAT
*Note: Place Mat is made in 8
rows of 14 motifs each as shown
in Diagram A on page 65.*

FIRST ROW
Motif A
Rnd 1: Ch 5, join with a sl st to
form ring; in ring work [sc, ch 3]
6 times; join with a sl st in first sc.
(6 sc)

Rnd 2: [5 sc in next ch-3 sp,
sl st in next sc] 5 times; 5 sc in
next ch-3 sp; join in joining sl st.
(30 sc)

Rnd 3: [Ch 3, sk next 2 sts, sl st
in next st] 11 times; ch 3; join in
first sc. *(12 ch-3 sps)*

Rnd 4: *In next ch-3 sp work

[2 sc, ch 3, sl st in **front lp** *(see
Stitch Guide)* of last sc made—
picot made, sc]; ch 2, sc in next
ch-3 sp, ch 2; rep from * 5 times
more; join in first sc.

Fasten off and weave in ends.

Motif B
Rnds 1–3: Work same as rnds
1–3 of Motif A.

Rnd 4: 2 sc in next ch-3 sp;
ch 1, sl st in tip of any picot
on completed motif, ch 1, sl st
in front lp of last sc made on
working motif; sc in same ch-3
sp; ch 2, sc in next ch-3 sp, ch
2, 2 sc in next ch-3 sp; ch 1, sl st
in tip of next picot on completed
motif, ch 1, sl st in front lp of last
sc made on working motif; sc in
same ch-3 sp; ch 2, sc in next
ch-3 sp, ch 2; *in next ch-3 sp
work (2 sc, picot, sc); ch 2, sc in
next ch-3 sp, ch 2; rep from * 3
times more; join in first sc.

Fasten off and weave in ends.

Work 12 additional Motifs
B, joining each motif to last
completed motif in 2 picots
opposite previously joined picots.

2ND ROW
Motif C
Rnds 1–3: Work same as rnds
1–3 of Motif A.

Rnd 4: 2 sc in next ch-3 sp; ch 1,
sl st in tip of picot to right of first
joined picot on first completed
Motif on last row made, ch 1, sl

st in front lp of last sc made on
working Motif; sc in same ch-3
sp; ch 2, sc in next ch-3 sp, ch 2;
*in next ch-3 sp work (2 sc, picot,
sc); ch 2, sc in next ch-3 sp, ch
2; rep from * 4 times more; join in
first sc.

Fasten off and weave in ends.

Motif D
Rnds 1–3: Work same as rnds
1–3 of Motif A.

Rnd 4: 2 sc in next ch-3 sp; ch
1, sl st in tip of 2nd picot to right
of joined picot on first completed
Motif on row, ch 1, sl st in front lp
of last sc made on working Motif;
sc in same ch-3 sp; ch 2, sc in
next ch-3 sp, ch 2, 2 sc in next
ch-3 sp; ch 1, sl st in tip of next
picot on completed Motif, ch 1,
sl st in front lp of last sc made on
working Motif; sc in same ch-3 sp;
ch 2, sc in next ch-3 sp, ch 2, 2 sc
in next ch-3 sp; ch 1, sl st in tip of
picot on next completed Motif on
previous row; ch 1, sl st in front lp
of last sc made on working Motif;
sc in same ch-3 sp; ch 2, sc in
next ch-3 sp, ch 2, *in next ch-3
sp work (2 sc, picot, sc); ch 2, sc
in next ch-3 sp, ch 2; rep from *
twice more; join in first sc.

Fasten off and weave in ends.

Work 12 additional Motifs D,
joining each motif to last
completed motif in 2 picots
opposite previously joined picots
and in 1 picot to completed
motif on previous row.

3RD—8TH ROWS

Work same as 2nd Row.

CENTER EDGING

Note: *Center Edging is worked in each center sp between joined motifs.*

Working in center sp between joined motifs, join crochet cotton in ch-2 sp to right of any joined picot; in same sp work (2 sc, picot, sc); in next ch-2 sp work (2 sc, picot, sc); ch 2; *in each of next 2 ch-2 sps on next motif work (2 sc, picot, sc); ch 2; rep from * twice more; join in first sc.

Fasten off and weave in ends.

CIRCLET

INNER MOTIF CIRCLE
Motif A

Rnds 1–4: Work same as rnds 1–4 of Motif A of Place Mat.

Motif B

Rnds 1–3: Work same as rnds 1–3 of Motif A of Place Mat.

Rnd 4: 2 sc in next ch-3 sp; ch 1, sl st in tip of any picot on first completed Motif on last row made, ch 1, sl st in front lp of last sc made on working Motif; sc in same ch-3 sp; ch 2, sc in next ch-3 sp, ch 2; *in next ch-3 sp work (2 sc, picot, sc); ch 2, sc in next ch-3 sp, ch 2; rep from * 4 times more; join in first sc.

Fasten off and weave in ends.

Motif C

Rnds 1–3: Work same as rnds 1–3 of Motif A of Place Mat.

Rnd 4: 2 sc in next ch-3 sp; ch 1, sl st in tip of picot opposite joined picot on last completed Motif, ch 1, sl st in front lp of last sc made on working Motif; sc in same ch-3 sp; ch 2, sc in next ch-3 sp, ch 2; *in next ch-3 sp work (2 sc, picot, sc); ch 2, sc in next ch-3 sp, ch 2; rep from * 4 times more; join in first sc join in first sc.

Fasten off and weave in ends.

Referring to Diagram B, work 6 additional Motifs C.

Motif D

Rnds 1–3: Work same as rnds 1–3 of Motif A of Place Mat.

Rnd 4: 2 sc in next ch-3 sp; ch 1, sl st in tip of picot opposite joined picot on last completed Motif, ch 1, sl st in front lp of last sc made on working Motif; sc in same ch-3 sp; ch 2, sc in next ch-3 sp, ch 2, in next ch-3 sp work (2 sc, picot, sc); ch 2, sc in next ch-3 sp, ch 2, 2 sc in next ch-3 sp; ch 1, sl st in tip of picot opposite joined picot on Motif A; ch 1, sl st in front lp of last sc made on working motif; sc in same ch-3 sp; ch 2, sc in next ch-3 sp, ch 2; *in next ch-3 sp work (2 sc, picot, sc); ch 2, sc in next ch-3 sp, ch 2; rep from * once more; join in first sc join in first sc.

Fasten off and weave in ends.

OUTER MOTIF CIRCLE
Motif E

Rnds 1–3: Work same as rnds 1–3 of Motif A of Place Mat.

Rnd 4: 2 sc in next ch-3 sp; ch 1, sl st in joined picot of Motif A and B; ch 1, sl st in front lp of last sc made on working Motif; sc in same ch-3 sp; ch 2, sc in next ch-3 sp, ch 2; 2 sc in next ch-3 sp; ch 1, sl st in next unused picot on Motif A; ch 1, sl st in front lp of last sc made on working motif; ch 1, sc in same ch-3 sp; ch 2, sc in next ch-3 sp, ch 2; *in next ch-3 sp work (2 sc, picot, sc); ch 2, sc in next ch-3 sp, ch 2; rep from * twice more; 2 sc in next ch-3 sp; ch 1, sl st in next unused picot on Motif B; ch 1, sl st in front lp of last sc made on working motif; ch 2, sc in next ch-3 sp, ch 2; join in first sc.

Fasten off and weave in ends.

Referring to Diagram B, work 9 additional Motifs E.

INNER EDGING
Join crochet cotton in tip of first unused inner picot of any motif on Inner Motif Circle; sc in same tip; *ch 3, sc in next sc, picot; ch 3, sc in tip of next picot, ch 1, sc in tip of next picot on next motif; rep from * 8 times more; ch 3, sc in next sc, picot; ch 3, sc in tip of next picot, ch 1; join in first sc.

Fasten off and weave in ends.

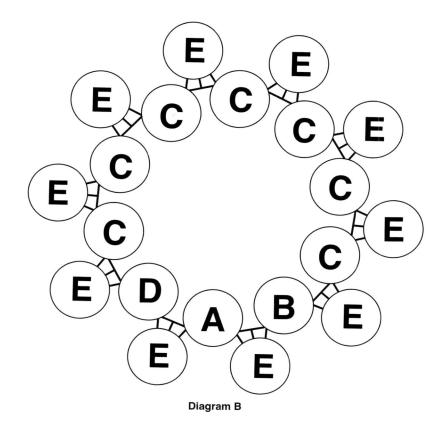

Diagram B

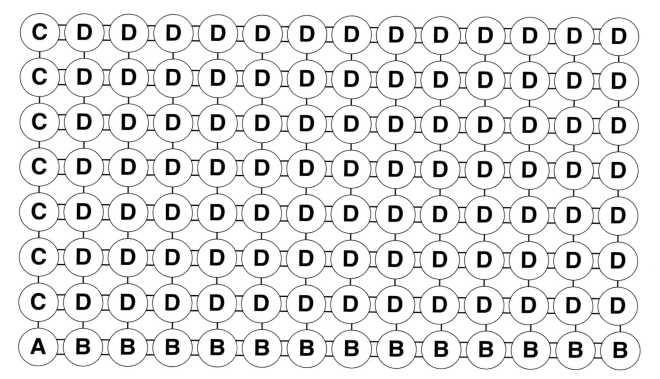

Diagram A

Elegant Edging

DESIGN BY DELSIE RHOADES

SKILL LEVEL EASY

FINISHED SIZE
2 inches x desired length

MATERIALS
J. & P. Coats Royale Classic
   Crochet size 10 crochet cotton
   (400 yds per ball):
     1 ball #201 white
Size 7/1.65mm steel crochet hook
   or size needed to obtain gauge
Tapestry needle

GAUGE
7 dc = 1 inch

Instructions

Note: Edging is worked lengthwise.

Row 1 (RS): Starting at narrow end, ch 12, dc in 4th ch from hook (*beg 3 sk chs count as a dc*) and in next 2 chs, ch 2, sk next 2 chs, dc in next 4 chs, turn.

Row 2: Ch 5 (*counts as a dc and a ch-2 sp on this and following rows*), sk next 2 dc, dc in next dc, 2 dc in next ch-2 sp; dc in next dc, ch 2, sk next 2 dc, dc in 3rd ch of beg 3 sk chs, turn.

Row 3: Ch 3 (*counts as a dc on this and following rows*), 2 dc in next ch-2 sp, dc in next dc, ch 2, sk next 2 dc, dc in next dc, 2 dc in sp formed by turning ch-5, dc in 3rd ch of turning ch-5, turn.

Row 4: Ch 5, sk next 2 dc, dc in next dc, ch 2, dc in next dc, ch 2, sk next 2 dc, dc in 3rd ch of turning ch-3, turn.

Row 5: Ch 3, 2 dc in next ch-2 sp; dc in next dc, ch 2, dc in next dc, 2 dc in sp formed by turning ch-5; dc in 3rd ch of turning ch-5, turn.

Row 6: Ch 5, sk next 2 dc, dc in next dc, 2 dc in next ch-2 sp; dc in next dc, ch 2, sk next 2 dc, dc in 3rd ch of turning ch-3, turn.

Rep rows 3–6 until edging is desired length.

Last row: Rep row 3. At end of row, do not turn.

BORDER
Rnd 1: Sc in last dc made; ch 3, working across next side in tops of edge sts, *dc in next edge st, ch 3; rep from * to row 1; dc in edge st of row 1, ch 3; working across next side in unused lps of beg ch, sc in first lp, ch 3, sk next 2 lps, sc in next lp, ch 3, sk next 2 unused chs, sc in next lp, ch 3, sk next 2 lps, sc in next lp, ch 3; working across next side in tops of edge sts, sc in edge st of row 1, ch 3; **dc in next edge st, ch 3; rep from ** to last row; sc in 3rd ch of turning ch-3 of last row, ch 3, sk next 2 dc, sc in next dc, ch 3, sc in next dc, ch 3, sk next 2 dc; join in first sc.

Rnd 2: Sl st in next ch-3 sp, sc in same sp, ch 3; *in next ch-3 sp work [dc, ch 3, sl st in 3rd ch from hook] 3 times; dc in same sp; ch 3, sk next ch-3 sp, sc in next ch-3 sp, ch 3; rep from * across bottom of edging to last ch-3 sp; sc in last ch-3 sp.

Fasten off and weave in ends. 🦅

Holiday Party Trims

DESIGNS BY DELSIE RHOADES

SKILL LEVEL ◼◻◻ EASY

FINISHED SIZES
Place Mat Trim: 2¾ x 13½ inches

Party Favor Trim: 2¾ x desired length

MATERIALS
- J. & P. Coats Royale Classic Crochet size 10 crochet cotton (350 yds per ball): 1 ball #420 cream
- 14 x 18 place mat
- Party favor
- Size 7/1.65mm steel hook
- Tapestry needle

GAUGE
8 dc = 1 inch

Instructions

PLACE MAT TRIM
Row 1 (RS): Starting at narrow end, ch 20, dc in 8th ch from hook (*beg 7 sk chs count as a ch-2 sp, a dc and a ch-2 sp*); [ch 2, sk next 2 chs, dc in next ch] 4 times, turn.

Row 2: Ch 5 (*counts as a dc and a ch-2 sp on this and following rows*), dc in next dc, ch 2, dc in next dc, 2 dc in next ch-2 sp; [dc in next dc, ch 2] twice; sk next 2 chs of beg 7 sk chs, dc in next ch, turn.

Row 3: Ch 5, dc in next dc, 2 dc in next ch-2 sp; dc in next dc, ch 5, sk next 2 dc, dc in next dc, 2 dc in next ch-2 sp; dc in next dc, ch 2, dc in 3rd ch of turning ch-5, turn.

Row 4: Ch 3 (*counts as a dc on this and following rows*), 2 dc in next ch-2 sp; dc in next dc, ch 5, sc in next ch-5 sp, ch 5, sk next 3 dc, dc in next dc, 2 dc in sp formed by turning ch-5; dc in 3rd ch of turning ch-5, turn.

Row 5: Ch 5, sk next 2 dc, dc in next dc, 3 dc in next ch-5 sp; ch 2, 3 dc in next ch-5 sp; dc in next dc, ch 2, dc in 3rd ch of turning ch-5.

Row 6: Ch 5, dc in next dc, ch 2, sk next 2 dc, dc in next dc, 2 dc in next ch-2 sp; dc in next dc, ch 2, sk next 2 dc, dc in next dc, ch 2, dc in 3rd ch of turning ch-5, turn.

Rows 7–38: [Work rows 3–6] 8 times.

Row 39: Ch 5, [dc in next dc, ch 2] twice; sk next 2 dc, [dc in next dc, ch 2] twice; dc in 3rd ch of turning ch-5. Do not turn.

BORDER
Rnd 1: Ch 4 (*counts as a sc and a ch-3 sp*); working across next side in top of edge dc, *sc in next dc, ch 3; rep from * to row 1; sc in edge dc of row 1, ch 3; working across next side in unused lps of beg ch, in next lp work [sc, ch 3] twice; sk next 2 chs, [sc in next lp, ch 3, sk next 2 chs] 4 times; in next ch work [sc, ch 3] twice; working across next side in top of edge dc, **sc in next edge dc, ch 3; rep from ** to last row; in 3rd ch of turning ch-5 of last row work [sc, ch 3] twice; [sc in next dc, ch 3] 5 times; join in first ch of beg ch-4.

Rnd 2: Sl st in next ch-3 sp, ch 1, sc in same sp; in next ch-3 sp work [dc, ch 1] 4 times; dc in same sp; *sc in next ch-3 sp, in next ch-3 sp work [dc, ch 1] 4 times; dc in same sp; rep from * around; join in first sc.

Fasten off and weave in ends.

PARTY FAVOR TRIM
Rows 1–6: Rep rows 1–6 of Place Mat Trim.

Rep rows 3–6 for desired length. At end of last row, do not turn.

BORDER
Work same as Border for Place Mat Trim. 🍂

Handsome Greetings

Send cards, wrap gifts and give bottled spirits that you have personalized with your hook, yarn, thread and warm holiday thoughts.

Greeting Cards

DESIGN BY NAZANIN FARD

SNOWMAN GREETING CARD

SKILL LEVEL INTERMEDIATE

FINISHED SIZE
2¼ x 3¾ inches

MATERIALS
DMC Cébélia size 10 crochet
  cotton (284 yds per ball):
    1 ball #0001 white *(A)*
Kreinik Ombré (17 yds per
  spool):
    1 spool #3200 solid pearl *(B)*
Kreinik 1/8 Ribbon (5½ yds per
  spool):
    1 spool #005HL black high
    luster *(C)*
Size 3/2.10 mm steel hook or size
  needed to obtain gauge
Tapestry needle
5 x 6½-inch Strathmore photo-
  frame card
CPE Felt Co. glimmer stiffened
  felt sheet (9 x 12 inches per
  sheet):
    4½ x 6 inch piece #0543 red
    small piece #3161 tangerine
    (for nose)
2 wiggly 2¼-inch eyes
2 green 8mm faceted heart-
  shaped stones
Tacky craft glue

GAUGE
7 dc = 1 inch

Instructions

SNOWMAN

HEAD
With 1 strand of A and 1 strand of
B held tog, ch 5; join with sl st to
form ring; ch 3 *(counts as a dc),*
13 dc in ring; join with sl st in 3rd
ch of beg ch-3. *(14 dc)*

Fasten off.

BODY
Rnd 1 (RS): Hold 1 strand of A
and 1 strand of B tog, ch 5; join

to form ring; ch 3 *(counts as a dc
on this and following rnd),* 15 dc
in ring; join in 3rd ch of beg ch-3.
(16 dc)

Rnd 2: Ch 3; *2 dc in each of
next 2 dc; dc in next dc; rep from
* around; join in 3rd ch of beg ch-
3. *(26 dc)*

Rnd 3: Hold head close to
body; sc in same ch as joining
on Head; working in rem dc
on Head, 2 sc in next dc; [sc
in next dc, 2 sc in next dc] 7
times; sc in same ch as joining
of rnd 2 of Body, working
around Body, 2 sc in next dc;
[sc in next dc, 2 sc in next dc]
12 times; join in first sc.

Fasten off and weave in all ends.

HAT
Row 1: With C, ch 10; sc in 2nd
ch from hook and in each rem sc,
turn. *(9 sc)*

Row 2: Ch 1, sc in each sc, turn.

Row 3: Sl st in first 3 sc, ch
3 *(counts as a dc on this and
following row),* dc in next 4 sc,
turn, leaving rem sts unworked.

Row 4: Ch 3, dc in each dc.

Fasten off and weave in ends.

FINISHING
Step 1: Insert red piece of felt in
card opening.

Step 2: Glue Snowman and Hat
in place on felt.

Step 3: For nose, cut small triangle piece from tangerine felt. Glue in place.

Step 4: Referring to photo for placement, glue eyes and hearts to Snowman.

CHRISTMAS TREE GREETING CARD

SKILL LEVEL ⬛⬛⬛◻ INTERMEDIATE

FINISHED SIZE
2 x 2½ inches

MATERIALS
Kreinik Fine (#8) Braid (11 yds per spool):
　　1 spool each #5982 forest green *(A)* and #022 brown *(B)*
Kreinik Tapestry (#12) Braid (11 yds per spool):
　　1 spool #007 pink *(C)*
Kreinik 1/16 Ribbon (5½ yds per spool):
　　1 spool #003 red *(D)*
Size 6/1.80mm steel hook or size needed to obtain gauge
Tapestry needle
1 gold star bead
5 x 6½-inch Strathmore photo-frame card
Over the Moon Press Family Traditions scrapbook paper (12 x 12 inches per sheet):
　　1 sheet #OTM285P diamond design
Tacky craft glue

GAUGE
7 dc = 1 inch

Instructions

TREE
Row 1 (RS): Starting at top of tree and with A, ch 4; in 4th ch from hook work (2 dc, ch 1, 2 dc), turn.

Row 2: Ch 1, sk first dc, sl st in

next dc and in next ch-1 sp, ch 3 *(counts as a dc on this and following rows)*, in same sp work (dc, ch 1, 2 dc); ch 1, sk next dc, in next dc work (2 dc, ch 1, 2 dc), turn.

Row 3: Ch 1, sk first dc, sl st in next dc and in next ch-1 sp, ch 3, in same sp work (dc, ch 1, 2 dc); in each of next 2 ch-1 sps work (2 dc, ch 1, 2 dc), turn.

Row 4: Ch 1, sk first dc, sl st in next dc and next ch-1 sp, ch 3, in same sp work (dc, ch 1, 2 dc); in next ch-1 sp work [2 dc, ch 1] twice; 2 dc in same sp; in next ch-1 sp work (2 dc, ch 1, 2 dc), turn.

Row 5: Ch 1, sk first dc, sl st in

next dc and next ch-1 sp, ch 3, in same sp work (dc, ch 1, 2 dc); (2 dc, ch 1, 2 dc) in next ch-sp, ch 1, in each of next 2 ch-1 sps work (2 dc, ch 1, 2 dc), turn.

Row 6: Ch 1, sk first dc, sl st in next dc and next ch-1 sp, ch 3, in same sp work (dc, ch 1, 2 dc); in each rem ch-1 sp work (2 dc, ch 1, 2 dc), turn.

Row 7: Ch 1, sl st in next dc and in next ch-1 sp, ch 3, 4 dc in same sp, 5 dc in each rem ch-1 sp. Fasten off.

TRUNK
Hold piece with RS facing you; sk first 10 dc on row 7; join B in next dc; ch 3, dc in next 4 dc.

Fasten off and weave in all ends.

STREAMER
Make 1 each of C & D.
Ch 50.

Fasten off and weave in ends.

FINISHING
Step 1: Referring to photo for placement, wrap Streamers around Tree, gluing ends on WS,

Step 2: Insert scrapbook paper in card opening.

Step 3: Glue Tree to paper. Glue star bead to top of tree.

POINSETTIA GREETING CARD

SKILL LEVEL
INTERMEDIATE

FINISHED SIZES
Poinsettia: 2¼ inches in diameter

Leaf: 2 x 1¼ inches

MATERIALS
DMC Traditions size 10 crochet cotton (350 yds per ball):
    1 ball each #5815 burgundy *(A)* and #5369 green *(B)*
Kreinik Blending Filament (40 yds per ball):
    1 spool #024HL burgundy *(C)*
    1 spool #009HL green *(D)*
Size 6/1.80mm steel hook or size needed to obtain gauge
Tapestry needle
5 x 6½-inch Strathmore photo-frame card
Over the Moon Press Family Traditions scrapbook paper (12 x 12 inches per sheet):
    1 sheet #OTM281P green crackle
    6 gold 3mm beads
Tacky craft glue

GAUGE
7 dc = 1 inch

Instructions

POINSETTIA
Row 1 (RS): With A and C held tog, ch 11; sc in 2nd ch from hook and in each rem ch, turn. *(10 sc)*

Row 2: Ch 1, sk first sc, sc in next sc, hdc in next sc, dc in next 5 sc, hdc in next sc, sc in next sc, turn.

Row 3: Ch 1, sc in first sc, hdc in next hdc, dc in next 5 dc, hdc in next hdc, sc in next sc and in sl knot at base of beg ch-11. Do not turn.

Row 4 (RS): Ch 11, sc in 2nd ch from hook and in each rem ch, turn.

Rows 5 & 6: Rep rows 2 and 3.

Rows 7–21: [Work rows 4–6] 5 times.

Fasten off and weave in ends.

Pull end of crochet cotton to tighten piece.

LEAF
Make 2.
Row 1 (RS): With B and D held tog, ch 15; sc in 2nd ch from hook and in next 12 chs, 2 sc in last ch; working in unused lps on opposite side of beg ch, sc in next 10 lps, turn.

Row 2: Ch 1, sc in first 10 sc, 2 sc in next sc; sc in next 10 sc, turn, leaving rem sc unworked.

Row 3: Ch 1, sc in first 10 sc, 2 sc in next sc; sc in next 9 sc, turn, leaving rem sc unworked.

Row 4: Ch 1, sc in first 9 sc, 2 sc in next sc; sc in next 8 sc, turn, leaving rem sc unworked.

Row 5: Ch 1, sc in first 8 sc. Fasten off, leaving rem sc unworked.

Weave in ends.

FINISHING
Step 1: Insert paper in card opening.

Step 2: Referring to photo for placement, glue Poinsettia and Leaves to paper.

Step 3: Glue beads to center of Poinsettia.

SNOWFLAKE GREETING CARD

SKILL LEVEL INTERMEDIATE

FINISHED SIZE
3½ inches in diameter

MATERIALS
DMC Cébélia size 10 crochet cotton (284 yds per ball):
 1 ball #0001 white *(A)*
Kreinik Japan Threads (44 yds per spool):
 1 spool #001J silver *(B)*
Size 6/1.80mm steel hook or size needed to obtain gauge
Tapestry needle
5 x 6½-inch Strathmore photo-frame card
CPE Felt Co. glimmer stiffened felt sheet (9 x 12 inches per sheet):
 4½ x 6 inch piece #GLM-0490 kelly
Tacky craft glue

GAUGE
7 dc = 1 inch

Instructions

Rnd 1 (RS): With A and B held tog, ch 6; join with sl st to form ring; ch 5 *(counts as a dc and a ch-2 sp),* in ring work [dc, ch 2] 7 times; join with sl st in 3rd ch of beg ch-5.

Rnd 2: Sl st in next ch-2 sp, ch 3 *(counts as a dc),* in same sp work (dc, ch 3, sl st in dc just made—*picot made;* 2 dc); ch 3; *in next ch-2 sp work (2 dc, picot, 2 dc); ch 3; rep from * around; join in 3rd ch of beg ch-3.

Rnd 3: [Ch 7, sl st in next ch-3 sp] 7 times; ch 7; join in joining sl st.

Rnd 4: Sl st in next 4 chs of next ch-7; *ch 5, sl st in last sl st made; ch 10, in 5th ch from hook work [sl st, ch 5] twice; sl st in same ch; ch 5, sl st in the next ch-7 sp; rep from * 6 times more; ch 5, sl st in last sl st made; ch 10, in 5th ch from hook work [sl st, ch 5] twice; sl st in same ch; ch 5; join in 4th sl st of beg 4 sl sts.

Fasten off and weave in ends.

FINISHING
Step 1: Insert felt in card opening.

Step 2: Glue snowflake to paper. 🌿

Be Merry Bottle Cover

DESIGNS BY ELLEN GORMLEY

SKILL LEVEL ■■□□
EASY

FINISHED SIZE
18 inches tall x 3 inches in diameter

MATERIALS

Moda Dea Cheerio medium (worsted) weight yarn (1¾ oz/104 yds/50g per skein):
  1 skein #8522 amethyst *or* #8731 pink sapphire (A)
  1 skein #8625 peridot (B)
Size I/9/5.5mm crochet hook or size needed to obtain gauge
Tapestry needle

GAUGE
Rnds 1–6 = 3 inches

SPECIAL STITCH
Double treble crochet (dtr): Yo 4 times, insert hook in st indicated, draw lp through, [yo, draw through 2 lps on hook] 4 times.

PATTERN NOTE
To change color, work last stitch until 3 loops remain on hook; with new color, yarn over and draw through all 3 loops on hook. Carry old color.

Instructions

COVER
Rnd 1: With A, ch 4; join with a sl st to form ring; ch 1, 6 sc in ring; join with a sl st in first sc.

Rnd 2: Ch 1, 2 sc in same sc and in each rem sc; join in first sc. *(12 sc)*

Rnd 3: Ch 1, sc in same sc; [2 sc in next sc, sc in next sc] 5 times; 2 sc in last sc; join in first sc. *(18 sc)*

Rnd 4: Ch 1, sc in same sc and in next sc; [2 sc in next sc, sc in next 2 sc] 5 times; 2 sc in last sc; join in first sc. *(24 sc)*

Rnd 5: Ch 1, sc in same sc and in next 2 sc; [2 sc in next sc, sc in next 3 sc] 5 times; 2 sc in last sc; join in first sc. *(30 sc)*

Rnd 6: Ch 1, sc in same sc and in next 3 sc; [2 sc in next sc, sc in next 4 sc] 5 times; 2 sc in last sc; join in first sc; join in **back lp** *(see Stitch Guide)* first sc. *(36 sc)*

Rnd 7: Ch 2 *(counts as a hdc on this and following rnds)*, working in back lps only, hdc in each rem sc; join in 2nd ch of beg ch-2.

Rnd 8: Ch 2, working through both lps, hdc in each rem hdc; join in 2nd ch of beg ch-2.

Rnd 9: Ch 2; change to B by drawing lp through; drop A; hdc in next hdc, changing to A; *hdc in next hdc, changing to B; hdc in next hdc, changing to A; rep from * to last 2 hdc; hdc in next hdc, changing to B; hdc in next hdc; join in 2nd ch of beg ch-2.

Rnd 10: Ch 2, change to A by drawing lp through; drop B; hdc in next hdc, changing to B; *hdc in next hdc, changing to A; hdc in next hdc, changing to B; rep from * to last 2 hdc; hdc in next hdc, changing to A; hdc in next hdc; join in 2nd ch of beg ch-2.

Rnds 11–24: Rep rnd 8.

Rnds 25 & 26: Rep rnds 9 and 10.

Rnds 27–30: Rep rnd 8.

Rnd 31: Ch 3 *(counts as a dc),*

CONTINUED ON PAGE 79

Last-Minute Gift Trim

DESIGN BY DELSIE RHOADES

SKILL LEVEL EASY

FINISHED SIZE
¾ inch x desired length

MATERIALS
J. & P. Coats Royale Classic
   Crochet size 10 crochet cotton
   (400 yds per ball):
      1 ball #201 white
Size 7/1.65mm steel hook or size
   needed to obtain gauge
Tapestry needle

GAUGE
4 dc = 1 inch

Instructions

Row 1 (RS): Ch 6, dc in 6th ch from hook, *ch 5, dc in last dc made; rep from * for every ¼-inch of desired length.

Row 2: Ch 1, working across long edge in ends of rows in sps formed by edge dc, 3 sc in each row, turn.

Row 3: Ch 4 (*counts as a dc and a ch-1 sp*); *sk next sc, dc in next 2 sc, ch 1; rep from * to last sc; dc in last sc, turn.

Row 4: Ch 1, sc in first dc, in each ch-1 sp and in each rem dc to turning ch-4; sc in sp formed by turning ch-4 and in 3rd ch of same turning ch.

Fasten off and weave in ends. ❧

Be Merry Bottle Cover CONTINUED FROM PAGE 77

dc in next 4 hdc, *ch 1, sk next hdc, dc in next 5 hdc; rep from * around; ch 1; join in 3rd ch of beg ch-3.

Rnd 32: Ch 2, hdc in each rem dc and in each ch; join in 2nd ch of beg ch-2.

Rnds 33–35: Rep rnd 8.

Rnd 36: Ch 2, working through both lps, hdc in each rem hdc; join in 2nd ch of beg ch-2. Change to B by drawing lp through; cut A.

Rnd 37: *Ch 11, sc in 2nd and 3rd chs from hook, hdc in next 2 chs, dc in next 2 chs, tr in next 2 chs, **dtr** (*see Special Stitch*) in next 2 chs; sk next 5 hdc, sl st in next hdc; rep from * 4 times more; ch 11, sc in 2nd and 3rd chs from hook, hdc in next 2 chs, dc in next 2 chs, tr in next 2 chs, dtr in next 2 chs; sk next 5 hdc; join in joining sl st.

Rnd 38: Ch 2, working behind sts made on rnd 37, sk next sk 2 hdc on rnd 36, sl st in next hdc; *ch 11, sc in 2nd and 3rd chs from hook, hdc in next 2 chs, dc in next 2 chs, tr in next 2 chs, dtr in next 2 chs; sk next 4 sk hdc on rnd 36, sl st in next hdc; rep from * 4 times more; ch 11, sc in 2nd and 3rd chs from hook, hdc in next 2 chs, dc in next 2 chs, tr in next 2 chs, dtr in next 2 chs; sk next 4 sk hdc; join in joining sl st.

Rnd 39: Ch 1, working behind sts made on rnds 37 and 38, sc in same st as joining and in each hdc of rnd 36; join in first sc.

Fasten off and weave in all ends.

TIE
With B, ch 81; sc in 2nd and 3rd chs from hook, hdc in next 2 chs, dc in next 2 chs, tr in next 2 chs, dtr in next 2 chs, tr in next 2 chs, dc in next 2 chs, hdc in next 2 chs, sc in next 50 chs, hdc in next 2 chs, dc in next 2 chs, tr in next 2 chs, dtr in next 2 chs, tr in next 2 chs, dc in next 2 chs, hdc in next 2 chs, sc in next 2 chs.

Fasten off and weave in ends.

FINISHING
Weave Tie in and out of ch-1 sps on rnd 31. Insert bottle. Tie knot in front. ❧

Throughout the House

Welcome your family and holiday guests with creations in every room, including afghans, throws, a tissue box cover, towel trims and hot pads.

Stained-Glass Flowers Afghan

DESIGN BY MELODY MACDUFFEE

SKILL LEVEL ■■■□
INTERMEDIATE

FINISHED SIZE
52 x 75 inches

MATERIALS
Red Heart Super Saver
  medium (worsted) weight yarn
  (7 oz/364 yds/198g per skein):
    2 skeins #365 coffee (A)
    1 skein each #320 cornmeal
      (B), #321 gold (C), #336
      warm brown (D), #330
      linen (E), #661 frosty green
      (F), #632 medium sage
      (G), #633 dark sage (H),
      #382 country blue (I), #380
      windsor blue (J), #387 soft
      navy (K)
Size K/10½/6.5mm crochet hook
  or size needed to obtain gauge
Tapestry needle

GAUGE
5 dc = 1 inch

SPECIAL STITCH
**Front post single crochet
(fpsc):** Insert hook from front to
back to front around **post** *(see
Stitch Guide)* of st indicated,
draw lp through, yo and draw
through 2 lps on hook.

Instructions

CORNER FLOWER
**Make 24 with F.
Make 24 with I.**
Rnd 1 (RS): With F or I, ch 4; join
with a sl st to form ring; ch 1, [sc
in ring, ch 3] 5 times; join with a
sl st in first sc.

Rnd 2: [In next ch-3 sp work
(sc, hdc, dc, tr, dc, hdc), ch 1] 5
times; join in first sc. Fasten off.

Note: *Work following rnd with
H if previous rnds were worked
with F, or K if previous rnds were
worked with I. Work in* **back lps**
(see Stitch Guide) only.

Rnd 3: Join in same sc as
joining; ch 1; *sc in next hdc, sc
in next dc, 3 sc in next tr; sc in
next dc, sc in next hdc, sk next
sc, working over next ch-1 sp,
sl st in beg ch-4 ring, sk next st;
rep from * 3 times; join in first sc.

FOUNDATION SQUARE
Make 12.
Note: *Work sts in back lps only
throughout unless otherwise
instructed.*

Rnd 1 (RS): With B, ch 4; join
with a sl st to form ring; [sc in
ring, ch 3] 4 times; join with a
sl st in first sc.

Rnd 2: [In next ch-3 sp work (sc,
hdc, dc, tr, dc, hdc, sc); sl st in
next sc] 3 times; in next ch-3 sp
work (sc, hdc, dc, tr, dc, hdc, sc);
join in joining sl st. Change to C
by drawing lp through; cut B.

Rnd 3: Ch 1; *sc in next 3 sts, 3
sc in tr; sc in next 3 sts, working
over next sl st, sl st in beg ch-4
ring; rep * 3 times; join in first sc.
Change to A; cut C.

Rnd 4: Ch 1, *sc in next st, hdc in
next st, dc in next st, 5 dc in next
st; dc in next st, hdc in next st,
sc in next st, sk next st, **fpsc** *(see
Special Stitch)* around vertical
threads of next sl st; sk next st;
rep from * 3 times; join in first sc.
Change to D; cut A.

Rnd 5: Ch 1; *sc in next 4 sts, 3
sc in next st—*corner made*; sc in
next 4 sts, sk next sc, sl st in next
sc, sk next sc; rep from * 3 times;
join in first sc. Fasten off.

Rnd 6: Join E in 2nd sc of any
corner; ch 1, corner in same sc;
sc in next 11 sts; [corner in next
st; sc in next 11 sts] 3 times; join
in first sc. Fasten off.

Rnd 7: Join F in 2nd sc of any
corner; ch 1, corner in same sc;

sc in next 13 sts, [corner in next
st, sc in next 13 sts] 3 times; join
in first sc. Fasten off.

Rnd 8: Join G in 2nd sc of any
corner; ch 1, corner in same sc;
sc in next 15 sts, [corner in next
st, sc in next 15 sts] 3 times; join
in first sc. Fasten off.

Rnd 9: Join H in 2nd sc of any
corner; ch 1, corner in same sc;
sc in next 17 sts, [corner in next
st, sc in next 17 sts] 3 times; join
in first sc. Fasten off.

Rnd 10: Join A in 2nd sc of any
corner; ch 1, corner in same sc;
sc in next 19 sts, [corner in next
st, sc in next 19 sts] 3 times; join
in first sc. Fasten off.

Rnd 11: Join D in 2nd sc of any
corner; ch 1, corner in same sc;
sc in next 21 sts, [corner in next
st, sc in next 21 sts] 3 times; join
in first sc. Fasten off.

CORNER SQUARE
Make 4.
Rnd 1: Join E in 2nd sc of any
corner Foundation Square; ch
1, corner in same sc; *sc in next
7 sts, hold 1 I-center Corner
Flower with WS of any flat side
facing WS of Foundation Square;
working through both thicknesses
at same time, sc in next st on
Foundation Square and 2nd sc of
nearest corner on Corner Flower;
sc in next 3 sts; sc in next st on
Foundation Square only, sk next
sl st on Corner Flower, sc in next
4 sts on both pieces; sc in next
7 sts on Foundation Square only;
corner in next st; rep from * once;
sc in next 7 sts, hold 1 I-center
Corner Flower with WS of any
flat side facing WS of Foundation
Square; working through both
thicknesses at same time, sc in
next st on Foundation Square
and 2nd sc of nearest corner
on Corner Flower; sc in next 3
sts; sc in next st on Founda-

tion Square only, sk next sl st on Corner Flower, sc in next 4 sts on both pieces; sc in next 7 sts on Foundation Square only; corner in next st; sc in next 7 sts, hold 1 F-center Corner Flower with WS of any flat side facing WS of Square; working through both thicknesses at same time, sc in next st on Foundation Square and 2nd sc of nearest corner on Corner Flower; sc in next 3 sts; sc in next st on Foundation Square only, sk next sl st on Corner Flower, sc in next 4 sts on both pieces; sc in next 7 sts on Foundaton Square only; join in first sc. Fasten off.

Rnd 13: Join B in 2nd sc of any corner; ch 1, corner in same sc; *sc in next 8 sts, working up around outer edge of next Corner Flower, [sc in next 3 unused sc, sk next sl st, sc in next 3 sts, 3 sc in next st] 3 times; sc in next 3 unused sc, sk next sl st, sc in next 3 sts; working across Foundation Square, sc in next 8 sts; corner in st; rep from * twice; sc in next 8 sts, working up around outer edge of next Corner Flower, [sc in next 3 unused sc, sk next sl st, sc in next 3 sts, 3 sc in next st] 3 times; sc in next 3 unused sc, sk next sl st, sc in next 3 sts; working across Foundation Square, sc in next 8 sts; join in first sc. Fasten off.

Rnd 14: Join C in 2nd sc of any corner; ch 1, corner in same sc; *sc in next 8 sts, sk next 2 sts, sc in next 2 sts, sk next st, sc in next 3 sts, 3 sc in next st; sc in next 3 sts, sk next st, sc in next 4 sts, 3 sc in next st; sc in next 4 sts, sk next st, sc in next 3 sts, 3 sc in next st; sc in next 3 sts, sk next st, sc in next 2 sts, sk next 2 sts, sc in next 8 sts, corner in next sc; rep from * twice; sc in next 8 sts, sk next 2 sts, sc in next 2 sts, sk next st, sc in next 3 sts, 3 sc in next st; sc in next 3 sts, sk next st, sc in next 4 sts, 3 sc in next

st; sc in next 4 sts, sk next st, sc in next 3 sts, 3 sc in next st; sc in next 3 sts, sk next st, sc in next 2 sts, sk next 2 sts, sc in next 8 sts; join in first sc. Fasten off.

Rnd 15: Join A in 2nd sc of any corner; ch 1, corner in same sc; *sc in next 9 sts, 2 sc in next st; sc in next 6 sts, ch 5, sc in **front lp** *(see Stitch Guide)* of 2nd sc of next corner on Rnd 10; ch 5, sk next 19 on rnd 14, sc in next 6 sts, 2 sc in next st; sc in next 9 sts, corner in next st; rep from * twice; sc in next 9 sts, 2 sc in next st; sc in next 6 sts, ch 5, sc

in front lp of 2nd sc of next corner on Rnd 10; ch 5, sk next 19 on rnd 14, sc in next 6 sts, 2 sc in next st; sc in next 9 sts; join in first sc.

Rnd 16: Join D in 2nd sc of any corner; ch 1, corner in same sc; *sc in next 11 sts, 2 sc in next st; sc in next 6 sts, sc in next 5 chs, sk next sc, sc in next 5 chs, sc in next 6 sts, 2 sc in next st; sc in next 11 sts, corner in next st; rep from * twice; sc in next 11 sts, 2 sc in next st; sc in next 6 sts, sc in next 5 chs, sk next sc, sc in next 5 chs, sc in next 6 sts, 2 sc

in next st; sc in next 11 sts; join in first sc.

Rnd 17: Join E in 2nd sc of any corner; ch 1, corner in same sc; *sc in next 12 sts, 2 sc in next st; sc in next 9 sts, sc in last 3 sts on rnd 14 before 2nd sc of corner, 3 sc in 2nd sc; sc in next 3 sts; sk next 6 sts on previous rnd, sc in next 9 sts, 2 sc in next st; sc in next 12 sts; rep from * twice; sc in next 12 sts, 2 sc in next st; sc in next 9 sts, sc in last 3 sts on rnd 14 before 2nd sc of corner, 3 sc in 2nd sc; sc in next 3 sts; sk next 6 sts on previous rnd, sc in next 9 sts, 2 sc in next st; join in first sc.

Note: *For* **hdc dec**, *yo, insert hook in st indicated, yo, draw lp through; insert hook in next st, yo, draw through lp, yo and draw through all 5 lps on hook. For* **dc dec**, *[yo, insert hook in st indicated, yo, draw lp through, yo, draw through 2 lps on hook] twice; yo and draw through all 3 lps on hook.*

Rnd 18: Join I in 2nd sc of any corner; ch 1, corner in same sc; *sc in next 17 sts, [**hdc dec** (see Note) in next 2 sts; **dc dec** (see Note) in next 2 sts] 3 times; hdc dec in next 2 sts; sc in next 3 sts; [hdc dec in next 2 sts; dc dec in next 2 sts] 3 times; hdc dec in next 2 sts; sc in next 17 sts, corner in next st; rep from * twice; sc in next 17 sts, [hdc dec in next 2 sts; dc dec in next 2 sts] 3 times; hdc dec in next 2 sts; sc in next 3 sts; [hdc dec in next 2 sts; dc dec in next 2 sts] 3 times; hdc dec in next 2 sts; sc in next 17 sts; join in first sc. Fasten off.

Note: *For* **sc dec**, *draw up lp in 2 sts indicated, yo and draw through all 3 lps on hook.*

Rnd 19: Join J in 2nd sc of any corner; ch 1, corner in same sc; *sc in next 3 sts, **sc dec** (see Note) in next 2 sts; sc in next 9 sts, sc dec in next 2 sts; hdc in next 2 sts, dc in next 4 sts, hdc in next 2 sts, sc in next st, hdc in next 2 sts, dc in next 4 sts, hdc in next 2 sts, sc dec in next 2 sts; sc in next 9 sts, sc dec in next 2 sts; sc in next 3 sts, corner in next st; rep from * twice; sc in next 3 sts, sc dec in next 2 sts; sc in next 9 sts, sc dec in next 2 sts; hdc in next 2 sts, dc in next 4 sts, hdc in next 2 sts, sc in next st, hdc in next 2 sts, dc in next 4 sts, hdc in next 2 sts, sc dec in next 2 sts; sc in next 9 sts, sc dec in next 2 sts; sc in next 3 sts; join in first sc. Fasten off.

Rnd 20: Join K in 2nd sc of any corner; ch 1, corner in same sc; *sc in next 47 sts, corner in next st; rep from * twice; sc in next 47 sts; join in first sc. Fasten off.

Rnd 21: Join A in 2nd sc of any corner; ch 1, corner in same sc; *sc in next 49 sts, corner in next st; rep from * twice; sc in next 49 sts; join in first sc.

Fasten off and weave in all ends.

SIDE SQUARE
Make 6.
Work same as Corner Square, joining 2 I-center Corner Flowers first and then 2 F-center Corner Flowers.

CENTER SQUARE
Make 2.
Work same as Corner Square, joining 4 F-center Corner Flowers.

ASSEMBLY
Join A in 2nd sc of any corner on 1 Corner Square; *ch 3, sl st in same st; *ch 1, sk next st, sl st in next st; rep from * to 2nd sc of next corner; in 2nd sc work (sl st, ch 3, sl st); work in same manner on rem 3 sides; join in joining sl st. Fasten off.

Note: *When joining rem Squares, refer to photo for placement of Squares.*

Join A in 2nd sc of any corner on 1 Side Square; ch 1, sl st in 2nd sc of corresponding corner on completed Square; ch 1, sl st in same st on working Square; *sl st in next ch-1 sp of Square to which you are attaching, sk next st on working Square, sl st in next st; rep from * to 2nd sc of next corner; sl st in 2nd sc, ch 1, sl st in 2nd sc of next corner on completed Square, ch 1, sl st in same sc on working Square; *ch 1, sk next st, sl st in next st; rep from * to 2nd sc of next corner; in 2nd sc work (sl st, ch 3, sl st); **ch 1, sk next st, sl st in next st; rep from ** to 2nd sc of next corner; in 2nd sc work (sl st, ch 3, sl st); ***ch 1, sk next st, sl st in next st; rep from *** to joining sl st; join in joining sl st.

Join rem Squares in same manner.

BORDER
Hold afghan with RS facing you; join A in any corner ch-3 sp; in same sp work (sc, ch 1, sc); *ch 1, sc in next ch-1 or ch-3 sp; rep from * to next corner ch-3 sp; in corner ch-3 sp work (sc, ch 1, sc); **ch 1, sc in next ch-1 or ch-3 sp; rep from ** to next corner ch-3 sp; in corner ch-3 sp work (sc, ch 1, sc); ***ch 1, sc in next ch-1 or ch-3 sp; rep from *** to next corner ch-3 sp; in corner ch-3 sp work (sc, ch 1, sc); ****ch 1, sc in next ch-1 or ch-3 sp; rep from **** to first sc; join in first sc.

Fasten off and weave in ends. 🍁

Blue Christmas Throw

DESIGN BY SVETLANA AVRAKH

SKILL LEVEL ◼◼◼◻
INTERMEDIATE

FINISHED SIZE
44 x 50 inches

MATERIALS
Bernat Denimstyle
 medium (worsted) weight yarn
 (3½ oz/196 yds/100g per ball):
 5 balls #03117 stonewash
  (A)
 2 balls each #03143 polo
  (B) and #03006 canvas (C)
 1 ball #03108 indigo (D)
Size I/9/5.5mm crochet hook or
 size needed to obtain gauge
Tapestry needle

GAUGE
12 dc = 4 inches

PATTERN NOTE
To change color, work last stitch
until 2 loops remain on hook; with
new color, yarn over and draw
through 2 loops on hook. Work
over color not in use.

Instructions

CENTER
Row 1 (RS): With A, ch 71; hdc
in 3rd ch from hook and in each
rem ch, turn. *(69 hdc)*

Row 2: Ch 2, hdc in first hdc and
in each rem hdc, turn.

Rep row 2 until piece measures
31 inches.

Fasten off and weave in ends.

BORDERS
Top Border
Row 1 (RS): Hold Center with RS
facing you and last row worked at
top; join D with a sl st in first hdc;
ch 1, 1 sc in each hdc, turn.

Row 2: Ch 1, sc in each sc.

Fasten off and weave in all ends.

Bottom Border
Row 1 (RS): Hold Center with RS
facing you and beg ch at top; join
D with a sl st in first unused lp of
beg ch; ch 1, 1 sc in same lp and
in each rem unused lp, turn.

Row 2: Ch 1, sc in each sc.

Fasten off and weave in ends.

Right Side Border
Row 1 (RS): Hold Center with RS
facing you and Bottom Border to
right; join D with a sl st in end of
last row of Bottom Border; ch 1,
work 96 sc evenly spaced across
side, turn.

Row 2: Ch 1, sc in each sc.

Fasten off and weave in all ends.

Left Side Border
Row 1 (RS): Hold Center with RS
facing you and Bottom Border to
left; join D with a sl st in end of
last row of Top Border; ch 1, work
96 sc evenly spaced across side,
turn.

Row 2: Ch 1, sc in each sc.

Fasten off and weave in all ends.

SECTIONS
Top Section
Row 1 (RS): Hold Center with
RS facing you and Top Border
at top; join C with sl st in end of
last row of Right Side Border;
ch 3 *(counts as a dc on this and
following rows)*, 2 dc in end of
next row, changing to B in last
dc; [dc in next 3 sc, changing
to C in last dc; dc in next 3 sc,
changing to B in last dc] 11
times; dc in next 3 sc, changing
to C in last dc; 2 dc in end of next
row of Left Side Border; dc in end
of next row, turn. *(75 dc)*

Row 2: Ch 3, dc in next 2 dc,
changing to B in last dc; [dc in
next 3 dc, changing to C in last

dc; dc in next 3 dc, changing to
B in last dc] 11 times; dc in next
3 dc, changing to C in last dc;
dc in next 2 dc and in 3rd ch of
beg ch-3, changing to B in last
dc, turn.

*Note: Change colors on following
rows in same manner.*

Row 3: Ch 3, dc in next 2 dc,
[with A, dc in next 3 dc; with B,
dc in next 3 dc] 11 times; with A,
dc in next 3 dc; with B, dc in next
2 dc and in 3rd ch of turning ch-
3, turn.

Row 4: Rep row 3, changing to C
in last dc.

Row 5: Ch 3, dc in next 2 dc,
[with B, dc in next 3 dc; with C,
dc in next 3 dc] 11 times; with B,
dc in next 3 dc; with C, dc in next
2 dc and in 3rd ch of turning ch-
3, turn.

Rows 6–17: [Work rows 2–5] 3
times.

Row 18: Rep row 2.

Fasten off and weave in all ends.

Bottom Section
Row 1 (RS): Hold Center with RS
facing you and Bottom Border at
top; join C with sl st in end of last
row of Left Side Border; ch 3, 2
dc in end of next row, [with B, dc
in next 3 sc; with C, dc in next 3
sc] 11 times; with B, dc in next
3 sc; with C, 2 dc in end of next
row of Right Side Border; dc in
end of next row, turn. *(75 dc)*

Rows 2–18: Rep rows 2–18 of
Top Section.

Right Side Section
Row 1: Hold Center with RS
facing you and Bottom Section
to right; join C in side of row 18
of Bottom Section; ch 3, dc in
base of edge dc of row 18 and

Row 4: Rep row 3, changing to C in last dc.

Row 5: Ch 3, dc in next 2 dc, [with B, dc in next 3 dc; with C, dc in next 3 dc] 24 times; with B, dc in next 3 dc; with C, dc in next 2 dc and in 3rd ch of turning ch-3, turn.

Rows 6–17: [Work rows 2–5] 3 times.

Row 18: Rep row 2.

Fasten off and weave in all ends.

Left Side Section
Row 1: Hold Center with RS facing you and Top Section to right; join C in side of row 18 of Top Section; ch 3, dc in base of edge dc of row 18 and in edge dc of next row; [with B, dc in top and base of next edge dc and in next edge; with C, dc in top and base of next edge dc and in next edge] 4 times; working across last row of Right Side Border, [with B, dc in next 3 sc; with C, dc in next 3 sc] 16 times; working across side of Bottom Section, [with B, dc in base and top of next edge dc and in next edge dc; with C, dc in base and top of next edge dc and in next edge] 5 times, turn.

Rows 2–18: Rep rows 2–18 of Right Side Section

EDGING
Rnd 1 (RS): Hold throw with RS facing you; join D in any corner; ch 1, 3 sc in same sp; *sc in each st to next corner; 3 sc in corner; rep from * twice; sc in each sc to first sc; join with a sl st in first sc.

Rnd 2: Ch 1, working from left to right, work **reverse sc** *(see Stitch Guide)* in each sc; join in first reverse sc.

Fasten off and weave in ends.

in edge dc of next row; [with B, dc in top and base of next edge dc and in next edge; with C, dc in top and base of next edge dc and in next edge] 4 times; working across last row of Left Side Border, [with B, dc in next 3 sc; with C, dc in next 3 sc] 16 times; working across side of Top Section, [with B, dc in base and top of next edge dc and in next edge dc; with C, dc in base and top of next edge dc and in next edge] 5 times, turn.

Row 2: Ch 3, dc in next 2 dc, [with B, dc in next 3 dc; with C, dc in next 3 dc] 24 times; with B, dc in next 3 dc; with C, dc in next 2 dc and in 3rd ch of beg ch-3, changing to B in last dc, turn.

Row 3: Ch 3, dc in next 2 dc, [with A, dc in next 3 dc; with B, dc in next 3 dc] 24 times; with A, dc in next 3 dc; with B, dc in next 2 dc and in 3rd ch of turning ch-3, turn.

Golden-Glow Throw

DESIGN BY CINDY ADAMS

SKILL LEVEL ■■□□
INTERMEDIATE

FINISHED SIZE
48 x 54 inches

MATERIALS
Caron Simply Soft medium
  (worsted) weight yarn (6
  oz/330 yds/168g per skein):
    3 skeins #9702 off-white *(A)*
    2 skeins #9703 bone *(B)*
Caron Simply Soft Brites medium
  (worsted) weight yarn (6
  oz/330 yds/168g per skein):
    2 skeins #9605 mango *(C)*
Size I/9/5.5mm crochet hook or
  size needed to obtain gauge
Tapestry needle
Stitch markers

GAUGE
Rnd 1 = 2 x 45 inches

SPECIAL STITCHES
Beginning popcorn (beg pc):
Ch 3, 4 dc in st indicated; drop lp
from hook, insert hook in first dc,
draw dropped lp through st and
lp on hook.

Popcorn (pc): 5 dc in st indicated; drop lp from hook, insert
hook in first dc, draw dropped lp
through st and lp on hook.

Instructions

FIRST STRIP
Foundation row: With B, [ch 4,
dc in 4th ch from hook] 41 times.
(41 ch-4 sps)

Rnd 1: Ch 1, working along dc
side of ch-4 sps, in first ch-4 sp
work (sc, 5 dc); sc in next ch-4
sp; *5 dc in next ch-4 sp; sc in
next ch-4 sp; rep from * to last
ch-4 sp; in last ch-4 sp work
(5 dc, sc, 5 dc); working over
opposite sides of same ch-4
sps, **sc in next ch-4 sp, 5 dc
in next ch-4 sp; rep from ** to
first sc; join with a sl st in first sc.
Fasten off.

Rnd 2: Join C with a sl st in sc
at opposite end of strip; in same
sc work [**beg pc** *(see Special
Stitches)*, ch 4, **pc** *(see Special
Stitches)*]; ch 3, sk next 2 dc, sc
in next dc, [ch 2, sk next 2 dc,
pc in next sc, ch 2, sk next 2 dc,
sc in next dc] 20 times; ch 3, sk
next 2 dc, in next sc work (pc,
ch 4, pc); ch 3, sk next 2 dc, sc
in next dc, [ch 2, sk next 2 dc,
pc in next sc, ch 2, sk next 2 dc,
sc in next dc] 20 times; ch 3, sk
next 2 dc; join with a sl st in beg
pc. Fasten off.

Rnd 3: Join B in first pc of 2-pc
group at either end; ch 1, sc in
same pc; 5 sc in next ch-4 sp; sc
in next st, 4 sc in next ch-3 sp;
sc in next st, [2 sc in next ch-2
sp, sc in next st] 40 times; 4 sc in
next ch-3 sp; sc in next st, 5 sc in
next ch-4 sp; sc in next st, 4 sc in
next ch-3 sp; sc in next st, [2 sc
in next ch-2 sp, sc in next st] 40
times; 4 sc in next ch-3 sp; join
with sl st in first sc.

Rnd 4: Ch 1, in same sc work
(sc, ch 2, dc); sk next sc, *in next
sc work (sc, ch 2, dc); sk next sc;
rep from * around; join with sl st
in first sc.

Rnd 5: Sl st in next ch-2 sp, ch 1,
sc in same sp; [ch 3, sc in next
ch-2 sp] 3 times; [ch 2, sc in next
ch-2 sp] 3 times; place marker
in last ch-2 sp made for joining
placement; [ch 2, sc in next ch-2
sp] 60 times; place marker in last
ch-2 sp made for joining placement; [ch 2, sc in next ch-2 sp]
twice; [ch 3, sc in next ch-2 sp] 3
times; ch 2; *sc in next ch-2 sp,
ch 2; rep from * to first sc; join
with sl st to first sc.

Fasten off and weave in all ends.

2ND–10TH STRIPS
Rnds 1–4: Work same as rnds
1–4 of First Strip.

Rnd 5: Sl st in first ch-2 sp, ch 1,
sc in same sp; [ch 3, sc in next
ch- 2 sp] 3 times; [ch 2, sc in next
ch-2 sp] 3 times; place marker
in last ch-2 sp made for joining
placement; [ch 2, sc in next ch-2
sp] 60 times; place marker in last
ch-2 sp made for joining placement; [ch 2, sc in next ch-2 sp]
twice; [ch 3, sc in next ch-2 sp]
3 times; [ch 2, sc in next ch-2
sp] twice; ch 1; hold WS of last
completed strip facing WS of
working strip; sl st in first marked
ch-2 sp on completed strip; ch 1;
on working strip, sc in next ch-2
sp; *ch 1, sl st in next ch-2 sp on
completed strip, ch 1; on working
motif, sc in next ch-2 sp; rep from
* 59 times; ch 2, sc in next ch-2
sp, ch 2; join in first sc.

Fasten off and weave in all ends.

11TH STRIP
Work same as 2nd Strip without
marking joining placements. 🍂

Sending Warm Wishes Afghan

DESIGN BY JOYCE NORDSTROM

SKILL LEVEL
EASY

FINISHED SIZE
54 x 64 inches

MATERIALS
Red Heart Super Saver
  medium (worsted) weight yarn
  (solids: 7 oz/364 yds/198g;
  multicolors: 5 oz/278 yds/141g
  per skein):
    3 skeins #967 holly & ivy *(A)*
    2 skeins #313 aran *(B)*
    1 skein each #631 light sage
      (C), #633 dark sage *(D)*,
      #374 country rose *(E)*,
      #378 claret *(F)*, #321
      gold *(G)*
Size J/10/6mm crochet hook or
  size needed to obtain gauge
Tapestry needle

GAUGE
14 sts = 4 inches

PATTERN NOTE
To change color, work last stitch
until 2 loops remain on hook; with
new color, yarn over and draw
through 2 loops on hook. Carry
unused yarns loosely up side until
needed again.

SPECIAL STITCHES
V-stitch (V-st): In st indicated
work (dc, ch 1, dc).

**Front post double crochet
(fpdc):** Yo, insert hook from
front to back to front around
post *(see Stitch Guide)* of st
indicated, draw lp through, [yo,
draw through 2 lps on hook]
twice.

Cross-stitch (X-st): Sk first st
indicated, dc in next st, fpdc
around sk st.

Instructions

CENTER
Row 1 (RS): With A, ch 174; dc
in 3rd ch from hook *(beg 2 sk chs
count as a hdc)* and in next ch;
*ch 3, sk next 3 chs, dc in next 2
chs; rep from * to last 5 chs; ch
3, sk next 3 chs, dc in next ch,
hdc in last ch; change to B by
drawing lp through; drop A, turn.

Row 2: Ch 3; *working over next
ch-3 of previous row, in 2nd sk ch
of next 3 sk chs on beg ch work
V-st *(see Special Stitches)*; ch 2,
sk next 2 dc; rep from * to last 2
dc; ch 2, sk last 2 dc, hdc in 2nd
ch of beg 2 sk chs; change to C;
drop B, turn.

Row 3: Ch 3; *working over next
ch-2 of previous row, **X-st** *(see
Special Stitches)* in 2 dc on 2nd
row below; ch 3, sk next V-st; rep
from * to turning ch; hdc in 2nd
ch of turning ch-3; change to A;
drop C, turn.

Rows 4–9: Rep rows 2 and 3,
working 1 row with A, 1 row B,
1 row D.

Rows 10–15: Rep rows 2 and 3,
working 1 row A, 1 row B, 1 row C.

Row 16: With A, rep row 2.

Row 17: With B, rep row 3.

Row 18: With B, rep row 2.

Row 19: With A, rep row 3.

Rows 20–25: Rep rows 2 and 3,
working 1 row B, 1 row G, 1 row A.

Rows 26–31: Rep rows 2 and 3,
working 1 row B, 1 row E, 1 row A.

Rows 32–39: Rep rows 2 and 3,
working 1 row B, 1 row F, 1 row A.

Rows 40–45: Rep rows 2 and 3,
working 1 row A, 1 row B, 1 row E.

Rows 46–51: Rep rows 2 and 3,
working 1 row A, 1 row B, 1 row G.

Rows 52–57: Rep rows 2 and 3,
working 1 row A, 1 row B, 1 row C.

Rows 58–65: Rep rows 2 and 3,
working 1 row A, 1 row B, 1 row D.

Rows 66–177: [Work rows 10-65]
twice.

Fasten off and weave in all ends.

BORDER
Rnd 1: Join B in any corner;
in same sp work (sc, ch 2,
sc)—*corner made;* *ch 1, sk next
sp or st, sc in next st or sp; rep
from * around and in each corner
working (sc, ch 2, sc)—*corner
made;* join with a sl st in first sc.

Rnd 2: Sl st in next ch-2 sp; ch 4
*(counts as a dc and a ch-1 sp on
this and following rnds)*; in same
sp work (dc, ch 1, V-st); *ch 1,

CONTINUED ON PAGE 97

Favorite Colors Gift Afghan

DESIGN BY JOYCE NORDSTROM

SKILL LEVEL ■■□□
EASY

FINISHED SIZE
50 x 70 inches

MATERIALS
Red Heart Super Saver
medium (worsted) weight yarn
(7 oz/364 yds/198g) per skein:
3 skeins each #313 aran
(A) and #330 linen (B)
18 oz of assorted scrap
colors
Size J/10/6mm crochet hook or
size needed to obtain gauge
Tapestry needle

GAUGE
14 sts = 4 inches

Instructions

AFGHAN

Row 1 (RS): With A, ch 171; 3 dc in 3rd ch from hook *(beg 3 sk chs count as a dc)*; *sk next 3 chs, sc in next 7 chs, sk next 3 chs, 7 dc in next ch; rep from * to last 14 chs; sk next 3 chs, sc in next 7 chs, sk next 3 chs, 4 dc in last ch; change to B by drawing lp through; cut A, turn.

Row 2: Ch 3, working in **back lps** *(see Stitch Guide)* only, hdc in first st; *ch 1, sk next st, hdc in next st; rep from * to last 2 sts; ch 1, sk next st, hdc in 3rd ch of beg 3 sk chs; change to scrap color; cut B, turn.

Row 3: Ch 1, working in **back lps** *(see Stitch Guide)* only, sc in first 4 sts, sk next hdc, next ch-1 sp, and next hdc; 7 dc in next ch-1 sp; *sk next hdc, next ch-1 sp and next hdc; sc in next 7 sts, sk next hdc, next ch-1 sp, and next hdc; 7 dc in next ch-1 sp; rep from * to last 8 sts; sk next hdc, next ch-1 sp, next hdc, and next ch-1 sp; sc in last 4 sts; change to A; cut scrap color, turn.

Row 4: Ch 4 *(counts as a hdc and a ch-1 sp)*; sk next st, working in back lps only, hdc in next st; *ch 1, sk next st, hdc in next st; rep from * across to last st; hdc in last st; change to B; cut A, turn.

Row 5: Ch 3, 3 dc in first st; *sk next hdc, next ch-1 sp, and next hdc; sc in back lp of next 7 sts, sk next hdc, next ch-1 sp, and next hdc; 7 dc in next ch-1 sp; rep from * to last 13 sts and turning ch; sk next hdc, next ch-1 sp, and next hdc; sc in back lp of next 7 sts, sk next hdc, next ch-1 sp, and next hdc; 3 dc in sp formed by turning ch-4; hdc in 3rd ch of turning ch-4; change to scrap color; cut B, turn.

Rep rows 2–5 until piece measures 62 inches from beg.

BORDER

Rnd 1: Hold Afghan with RS facing you; with A make slip knot on hook and join with a hdc in any corner; *ch 1, sk next st or sp, hdc in next sp or st; rep from * around, working (hdc, ch 3, hdc) in each corner; join in first hdc. Fasten off.

Rnd 2: With A, make slip knot on hook and join with a hdc in any corner ch-3 sp; ch 3, hdc in same sp; ch 1; *sk next st, hdc in next ch-1 sp, ch 1; rep from * around, working (hdc, ch 3, hdc) in ch-3 sp of each corner; join in first hdc. Fasten off.

Rnd 3: With scrap color, rep rnd 2.

Rnd 4: Sl st in next ch-3 sp; ch 3 *(counts as a dc)*, 8 dc in same sp; *sk next hdc, next ch-1 sp, and next hdc; sc in back lp of next 7 sts, sk next hdc, next ch-1 sp, and next hdc; 7 dc in next ch-1 sp; rep from * around, working 9 dc in each corner ch-3 sp and adjusting reps as necessary; join in 3rd ch of beg ch-3. Fasten off.

Rnd 5: Join A in any st; ch 1, working from left to right, work reverse sc *(see Stitch Guide)* in back lp of same st, ch 1, sk next st; *reverse sc in back lp of next st, ch 1, sk next st; rep from * around; join in first reverse sc.

Fasten off and weave in ends. 🦃

Festive Shell Bath Set

DESIGNS BY CINDY ADAMS

SKILL LEVEL
EASY

FINISHED SIZES
Tissue Box Cover: 5 x 5 x 6 inches

Towel Trim: 2½ x 16 inches

MATERIALS
Caron Simply Soft medium (worsted) weight yarn (6 oz/330 yds/168g per skein):
1 ball #9728 green (A)
Caron Simply Soft Brites medium (worsted) weight yarn (6 oz/330 yds/168g per skein):
1 skein each #9607 limelight (B) and #9608 blue mint (C)
Size I/9/5.5mm crochet hook or size needed to obtain gauge
Tapestry needle
Sewing needle and matching thread
2 hand towels

GAUGE
2 shells = 3½ inches

PATTERN NOTE
To change color, work last stitch until 2 loops remain on hook; with new color, yarn over and draw through 2 loops on hook. Cut old color.

Instructions

TISSUE BOX COVER
Foundation row: With A, ch 50; sc in 2nd ch from hook and in each rem ch, turn.

Row 1 (RS): Ch 3 *(counts as a dc on this and following rows)*, 2 dc in first sc; *sk next 2 sc, sc in next sc, sk next 2 sc, 5 dc in next ch—shell made; rep from * 6 times; sk next 2 sc, sc in next sc, sk next 2 sc, 3 dc in last sc, changing to B in last dc, turn.

Row 2: Ch 1 *(counts as a sc on this and following rows)*, [shell in next sc; sc in 3rd dc of next shell] 7 times; shell in next sc; sc in 3rd ch of beg ch-3, changing to C, turn.

Row 3: Ch 3, 2 dc in sp between same sc and next shell; [sc in 3rd dc of next shell, shell in next sc] 7 times; sc in 3rd dc on next shell, 3 dc in turning ch-1, changing to A in last dc, turn.

Row 4: Ch 1, [shell in next sc; sc in 3rd dc of next shell] 7 times; shell in next sc; sc in 3rd ch of beg ch-3, changing to B, turn.

Rows 5–12: [Work rows 3 and 4] 4 times, working in following color sequence: B, C, A, and changing to A in last dc of row 12.

Row 13: Ch 3, 2 dc in sp between same sc and next shell; [sc in 3rd dc of next shell, 3 dc in next sc] 7 times; sc in 3rd dc on next shell, 3 dc in turning ch-1.

Fasten off and weave in all ends.

FINISHING
With tapestry needle, sew ends of rows tog.

TOWEL TRIM
Make 2.
Foundation row: With A, ch 44; sc in 2nd ch from hook and in each rem ch, turn.

Row 1 (RS): Ch 3 *(counts as a dc on this and following rows)*, 2 dc in first sc; *sk next 2 sc, sc in next sc, sk next 2 sc, 5 dc in next ch—shell made; rep from * 5 times; sk next 2 sc, sc in next sc, sk next 2 sc, 3 dc in last sc, changing to B in last dc, turn.

Row 2: Ch 1 *(counts as a sc on this and following rows)*, [shell in next sc; sc in 3rd dc of next shell] 6 times; shell in next sc; sc in 3rd ch of beg ch-3, changing to C, turn.

Row 3: Ch 3, 2 dc in sp between same sc and next shell; [sc in 3rd dc of next shell, shell in next sc] 6 times; sc in 3rd dc on next shell, 3 dc in turning ch-1, changing to A in last dc, turn.

Row 4: Ch 1, sc in first dc, [shell in next sc, sc in 3rd dc of next shell] 6 times; shell in next sc; sc in 3rd ch of turning ch-3.

Fasten off and weave in all ends.

FINISHING
With sewing needle and matching thread, sew to towels. 🌿

Light Bulb Hot Pads

DESIGN BY KATHLEEN STUART

SKILL LEVEL ◼◻◻ EASY

FINISHED SIZE
9 inches long

MATERIALS
Caron Simply Soft
  Seasons medium (worsted)
  weight yarn (2½ oz/120
  yds/70g per skein):
    1 ball #2902 red/silver *or*
      #2903 green/silver *(A)*
Patons Canadiana medium
  (worsted) weight yarn (3½
  oz/201 yds/100g per skein):
    1 ball #00081 gold *(B)*
Size G/6/4mm crochet hook or
  size needed to obtain gauge
Tapestry needle

GAUGE
5 sc = 1 inch

Instructions

Note: Piece is worked in continuous rnds. Do not join unless specified; mark beg of rnds.

Rnd 1: With A, ch 2; 6 sc in 2nd ch from hook.

Rnd 2: [Sc in next sc, 2 sc in next sc] 3 times. *(9 sc)*

Rnd 3: [Sc in next 2 sc, 2 sc in next sc] 3 times *(12 sc)*

Rnd 4: [Sc in next 3 sc, 2 sc in next sc] 3 times. *(15 sc)*

Rnd 5: [Sc in next 4 sc, 2 sc in next sc] 3 times. *(18 sc)*

Rnd 6: [Sc in next 2 sc, 2 sc in next sc] 6 times. *(24 sc)*

Rnd 7: Sc in each sc.

Rnd 8: Rep rnd 7.

Rnd 9: [Sc in next 3 sc, 2 sc in next sc] 6 times. *(30 sc)*

Rnds 10 & 11: Rep rnd 7.

Rnd 12: [Sc in next 4 sc, 2 sc in next sc] 6 times. *(36 sc)*

Rnd 13: Rep rnd 7.

Rnd 14: [Sc in next 5 sc, 2 sc in next sc] 6 times. *(42 sc)*

Rnd 15: Rep rnd 7.

Rnd 16: [Sc in next 6 sc, 2 sc in next sc] 6 times. *(48 sc)*

Rnd 17: Rep rnd 7.

Rnd 18: [Sc in next 7 sc, 2 sc in next sc] 6 times. *(54 sc)*

Rnds 19–33: Rep rnd 7.

*Note: For **sc dec**, draw up lp*

in 2 sts indicated, yo and draw through all 3 lps on hook.

Rnd 34: [Sc in next 7 sc, **sc dec** *(see Note)* in next 2 sc] 6 times. *(48 sc)*

Rnd 35: [Sc in next 6 sc, sc dec] 6 times. *(42 sc)*

Rnd 36: [Sc in next 5 sc, sc dec] 6 times. *(36 sc)*

Rnd 37: [Sc in next 4 sc, sc dec] 6 times. *(30 sc)*

Rnd 38: [Sc in next 3 sc, sc dec] 6 times; change to B by drawing lp through; cut A. *(24 sc)*

Rnd 39: Rep rnd 7.

Rnd 40: Working in **back lps** *(see Stitch Guide)* only, sc in each sc.

Rnds 41–43: Rep rnd 40.

Joining row: Ch 1, fold row 43 in half, matching first sc and last sc of row; working through back lps of front sc and **front lps** *(see Stitch Guide)* of back sc only, sc in next 12 sc; ch 15, sl st in last sc made—*hanging lp made.*

Fasten off and weave in all ends. 🍃

Sending Warm Wishes Afghan CONTINUED FROM PAGE 91

sk next sc, V-st in next sc; rep from * around, working (V-st, ch 1, V-st) in each rem corner; join in 3rd ch of beg ch-4; change to C; cut B.

Rnd 3: Sl st in next ch-1 sp; ch 4, dc in same sp; ch 2, V-st in ch-1 sp of each V-st to center

ch-1 sp of next corner; *ch 2, V-st in center ch-1 sp and in ch-1 sp of each V-st to center ch-1 sp of next corner; rep from * twice; ch 2, V-st in center ch-1 sp and in ch-1 sp of each rem V-st; join in 3rd ch of beg ch-3. Sl st in 2nd ch of beg ch-4.

Rnd 4: Sl st in next ch-1 sp; ch 4, dc in same sp; in next ch-2 sp work (V-st, ch 1, V-st); *V-st in each V-st to next ch-2 sp; in ch-2 sp work (V-st, ch 1, V-st); rep from * twice; V-st in each V-st to beg ch-4; join in 3rd ch of beg ch-4.

Fasten off and weave in ends. 🍃

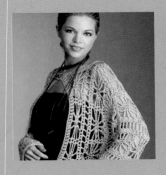   

Special Wearables & Quick Gifts

Please your loved ones with these unique designs, including sweaters, hat and scarf sets, a hostess apron, necklaces, stocking stuffers and even a dog coat.

Bright & Easy Bolero

DESIGN BY NAZANIN FARD

SKILL LEVEL ■□□□
EASY

FINISHED SIZES
Instructions given fit woman's size small; changes for medium and large are in [ ].

FINISHED GARMENT MEASUREMENTS
Chest: 40 [44, 48] inches

MATERIALS
Moda Dea Bow Ties bulky (chunky) weight yarn (1¾ oz/64 yds/50g per ball):
   10 [12, 14] balls #3738 pink lady
Size K/10½/6.5mm crochet hook or size needed to obtain gauge
Yarn needle

GAUGE
14 sc = 4 inches

Instructions

RIGHT SLEEVE
Row 1 (RS): Ch 53 [57, 61]; sc in 3rd ch from hook *(beg 2 sk chs count as a sc)*; *ch 1, sk next ch, sc in next ch; rep from * across, turn. *(52 [56, 60] sts)*

Row 2: Ch 2; *sc in next ch-1 sp, ch 1; rep from * to beg 2 sk chs; sc in 2nd ch of beg 2 sk chs, turn.

Row 3: Ch 2; *sc in next ch-1 sp, ch 1; rep from * to turning ch-2; sc in 2nd ch of turning ch-2, turn.

Row 4: Rep row 3.

Row 5: Ch 2, in next ch-1 sp work [sc, ch 1] twice; *sc in next ch-1 sp, ch 1; rep from * to last ch-1 sp; in last ch-1 sp work [sc, ch 1] twice; sc in 2nd ch of turning ch-2, turn. *(54 [58, 62] sts)*

Rows 6–9: Rep row 3.

Row 10: Rep row 5. *(56 [60, 64]*

sts at end of last row)

[Work rows 3–9] 3 times.

Rows 11–40: [Work rows 6–10] 6 times. *(68 [72, 76] sts at end of last row)*

BODY
Ch 41 for Back. Join another piece of yarn on other end of Right Sleeve for Front; ch 40. *(149 [153, 157] sts)*

Work as pattern on all sts for 6 [6, 7] inches. Divide for Front and Back.

BACK
Work in pattern as established in next 71 [74, 76] sts for 7 [8, 8] inches, ending at neck edge.

Fasten off.

RIGHT FRONT
Sk next 30 sts from neck edge; join in next st.

Row 1: Sk next 30 sts from neck edge; join in next st; ch 1, work in pattern across, turn.

Row 2: Ch 2, work in pattern to last 4 sts, turn, leaving rem sts unworked.

Row 3: Ch 2, work in pattern across, turn.

Row 4: Ch 1, work in pattern to last 4 sts, turn, leaving rem sts unworked.

Rep rows 3 and 4 twice. *(28 [30, 32] sts at end of last row)*

[Rep row 3] 3 times.

Fasten off.

LEFT FRONT
Row 1: Ch 29 [31, 33], sc in 3rd ch from hook *(beg 2 sk chs count as a sc)*; *ch 1, sk next ch, sc in

next ch; rep from * across, turn.

Row 2: Ch 2; *sc in next ch-1 sp, ch 1; rep from * to beg 2 sk chs; sc in 2nd ch of beg 2 sk chs, turn.

Row 3: Ch 2; *sc in next ch-1 sp, ch 1; rep from * to turning ch-2; sc in 2nd ch of turning ch-2, turn.

Row 4: Rep row 3.

Row 5: Ch 4, work in pattern in all sts, turn.

Rows 6–11: [Work rows 4 and 5] 3 times.

Row 12: Ch 2, work in pattern on all sts, ch 30; join to back and start working on left shoulder.

Work in pattern on all sts for 6 [6, 7] inches.

Fasten off.

LEFT SLEEVE
Row 1: Sk next 40 sts; join yarn; ch 2, work in pattern on next 69 [73, 77] sts, turn.

Row 2: Ch 2, work in pattern across, turn.

Row 3: Rep row 2.

Row 4: Ch 2, sk next ch-1 sp, sc in next ch-sp, work in pattern to last ch-1 sp; sk last ch-1 sp, sc in 2nd ch of turning ch-2.

Rows 5–7: Rep row 2.

Row 8: Rep row 4.

Rows 9–32: [Work rows 4–8] 6 times. *(53 [57, 61] sts at end of last row)*

Rows 33–36: Rep row 2.

Fasten off and weave ends.

FINISHING
Sew side seams and sleeve seams tog.

EDGING
Join yarn in center of back neck; ch 1; sc in same sp and in each st around back neck, front neckline, front edge and work 1 rnd of sc in every st around edge of Bolero; join in first sc.

Fasten off and weave in ends.

Golden Holiday Jacket

DESIGN BY TAMMY HILDEBRAND

SKILL LEVEL
INTERMEDIATE

FINISHED SIZES
Instructions given fit woman's small; changes for medium, large and X-large are in [ ].

FINISHED GARMENT MEASUREMENTS
Chest: 39¼ inches *(small)* [43¼ inches *(medium)*, 47¼ inches *(large)*, 51¼ inches *(X-large)*]

MATERIALS
Lion Brand Glitterspun medium (worsted) weight yarn (1¾ oz/115 yds/50g per skein): 6 [7, 8, 9] skeins #170 gold
Size K/10½/6.5mm crochet hook or size needed to obtain gauge
Tapestry needle
Decorative button
Sewing needle and matching thread

GAUGE
Pattern rows 1–7 = 5 inches

Instructions

BACK
Note: Back is worked lengthwise.

Row 1: Ch 56; dc in 4th ch from hook *(beg 3 sk chs count as a dc)* and in each rem ch, turn. *(54 dc)*

For Size Small Only
Continue with Back Body.

For Size Medium Only
Row 2: Ch 3 *(counts as a dc on this and following rows)*, dc in each rem dc and in 3rd ch of beg 3 sk chs, turn.

Continue with Back Body.

For Size Large Only
Row 2: Ch 3 *(counts as a dc on this and following rows)*, dc in each rem dc and in 3rd ch of beg 3 sk chs, turn.

Row 3: Ch 3, dc in each rem dc and in 3rd ch of turning ch-3, turn.

Continue with Back Body.

For Size X-Large Only
Row 2: Ch 3 *(counts as a dc on this and following rows)*, dc in each rem dc and in 3rd ch of beg 3 sk chs, turn.

Row 3: Ch 3, dc in each rem dc and in 3rd ch of turning ch-3, turn.

Row 4: Rep row 3.

Continue with Back Body.

BACK BODY
Row 1: Ch 3 *(counts as a dc on this and following rows)*, dc in next dc; *ch 5, [sk next 2 dc, tr in next dc] 3 times; ch 5, sk next 2 dc, dc in next 2 dc; rep from * twice; ch 5, [sk next 2 dc, tr in next dc] 3 times; ch 5, sk next 2 dc, dc in next dc and in 3rd ch of beg 2 sk chs or in 3rd ch of turning ch-3, turn. *(22 sts)*

Row 2: Ch 3, dc in next dc; *ch 4, sc in 5th ch of next ch-5 sp, in next 3 tr and in first ch of next ch-5 sp; ch 4, dc in next 2 dc; rep from * twice; ch 4, sc in 5th ch of next ch-5 sp, in next 3 tr and in first ch of next ch-5 sp; ch 4, dc in next dc and in 3rd ch of turning ch-3, turn. *(30 sts)*

Row 3: Ch 3, dc in next dc; *ch 5, sk next st, sc in next 3 sts, sk

next st, ch 5, dc in next 2 sts; rep from * twice; ch 5, sk next st, sc in next 3 sts, sk next st, ch 5, dc in next dc and in 3rd ch of turning ch-3, turn. *(22 sts)*

Row 4: Ch 3, dc in next dc; *[ch 2, tr in next st] 3 times; ch 2, dc in next 2 sts; rep from * twice; [ch 2, 2 tr in next st] 3 times; ch 2, dc in next dc and in 3rd ch of turning ch-3, turn.

Row 5: Ch 3; *dc in next st, [2 dc in next ch-2 sp; dc in next st] 4 times; rep from * 3 times; dc in 3rd ch of turning ch-3, turn. *(54 dc)*

Row 6: Ch 5 *(counts as a tr and a ch-1 sp)*, sk next st, tr in next st; *ch 1, sk next st, tr in next st; rep from * to last dc and turning ch-3; ch 1, sk last dc, tr in 3rd ch of turning ch-3, turn. *(26 tr)*

Row 7: Ch 3, 2 dc in next ch-1 sp; dc in each dc and in each ch-1 sp to turning ch-5; dc in sp formed by turning ch-5 and in 3rd ch of turning ch, turn. *(54 dc)*

For Size Small Only
Rows 8–21: [Work rows 1–7] twice.

Rows 22–26: Rep rows 1–5.

Fasten off and weave in ends.

Continue with Front Panel.

For Size Medium Only
Row 8: Ch 3, dc in each st, turn.

Rows 9–24: [Work rows 1–8] twice.

Rows 25–29: Rep rows 1–5.

Fasten off and weave in ends.

Continue with Front Panel.

For Size Large Only
Row 8: Ch 3, dc in each st, turn.

Row 9: Rep row 8.

Rows 10–18: Rep rows 1–9.

Rows 19–25: Rep rows 1–7.

Row 26: Ch 1, sc in each st, turn.

Row 27: Ch 1, sc in each sc, turn.

Rows 28–32: Rep rows 1–5.

Fasten off and weave in ends.

Continue with Front Panel.

For Size X-Large Only
Row 8: Ch 3, dc in each st, turn.

Rows 9 & 10: Rep row 8.

Rows 11–30: [Work rows 1–10] twice.

Rows 31–35: Rep rows 1–5.

Fasten off and weave in ends.

Continue with Front Panel.

FRONT PANEL
Make 2.

Note: *Front Panel is worked lengthwise.*

Row 1: Ch 56; dc in 4th ch from hook *(beg 3 sk chs count as a dc)* and in each rem ch, turn. *(54 dc)*

For Size Small Only
Continue with Front Body.

For Size Medium Only
Row 2: Ch 3 *(counts as a dc on this and following rows)*, dc in each rem dc and in 3rd ch of beg

3 sk chs, turn.

Continue with Front Body.

For Size Large Only
Row 2: Ch 3 *(counts as a dc on this and following rows)*, dc in each rem dc and in 3rd ch of beg 3 sk chs, turn.

Row 3: Ch 3, dc in each rem dc and in 3rd ch of turning ch-3, turn.

Continue with Front Body.

For Size X-Large Only
Row 2: Ch 3 *(counts as a dc on this and following rows)*, dc in each rem dc and in 3rd ch of beg 3 sk chs, turn.

Row 3: Ch 3, dc in each rem dc and in 3rd ch of turning ch-3, turn.

Row 4: Rep row 3.

Continue with Front Body.

FRONT BODY
For Size Small Only
Rows 1–7: Rep rows 1–7 of Back Body.

Rows 8–12: Rep rows 1–5.

Fasten off and weave in ends.

Continue with Sleeve.

For Size Medium Only
Row 1: Ch 3, dc in each rem st and in 3rd ch of turning ch-3, turn.

Rows 2–8: Rep rows 1–7 of Back Body.

Row 9: Ch 3, dc in each rem st and in 3rd ch of turning ch-3, turn.

Rows 10–14: Rep rows 1–5 of Back Body.

Fasten off and weave in ends.

Continue with Sleeve.

For Size Large Only
Row 1: Ch 3, dc in each rem st and in 3rd ch of turning ch-3, turn.

Row 2: Rep row 1.

Rows 3–9: Rep rows 1–7 of Back Body.

Rows 10 & 11: Rep row 1.

Rows 12–16: Rep rows 1–5 of Back Body.

Fasten off and weave in ends.

Continue with Sleeve.

For Size X-Large Only
Row 1: Ch 3, dc in each rem st and in 3rd ch of turning ch-3, turn.

Rows 2 & 3: Rep row 1.

Rows 4–10: Rep rows 1–7 of Back Body.

Rows 11–13: Rep row 1.

Rows 14–18: Rep rows 1–5 of Back Body.

Fasten off and weave in ends.

Continue with Sleeve.

ASSEMBLY
For side seam, hold 1 Front Panel and Back with WS tog. Beg with first st at lower edge on each piece, sew 28 sts tog for side seam and leaving rem sts unworked for armhole. Rep with rem Front Panel.

For shoulder seam, sew first 8 [10, 12, 14] rows of 1 Front Panel and Back tog beg at outside edge. Rep for 2nd shoulder seam.

EDGING
Hold piece with right front edge at top; make slip knot on hook and join with a sc in first unused lp of beg ch; working in

ch of next ch-5 sp, in next 3 tr, and in next ch of next ch-5 sp; ch 4; join in 3rd ch of beg ch-3. *(30 sts)*

Rnd 4: Ch 3, dc in next st; *ch 5, sk next st, sc in next 3 sts, sk next st, ch 5, dc in next 2 sts; rep from * twice; ch 5, sk next st, sc in next 3 sts, sk next st, ch 5; join in 3rd ch of beg ch-2. *(20 sts)*

Rnd 5: Ch 3, dc in next st; *[ch 2, tr in next st] 3 times; ch 2, dc in next 2 sts; rep from * twice; [ch 2, tr in next st] 3 times; ch 2; join in 3rd ch of beg ch-3.

Rnd 6: Ch 3, dc in next st; [2 dc in each ch-2 sp and dc in each st] around; join in 3rd ch of beg ch-3. *(52 dc)*

Rnd 7: Ch 5 *(counts as a tr and a ch-1 sp)*, sk first st; *tr in next st, ch 1, sk next st; rep from * around; join in 4th ch of beg ch-5. *(26 tr)*

Rnd 8: Ch 3, dc in next ch-1 sp; dc in each st and in each ch-1 sp; join in 3rd ch of beg ch-3. *(52 dc)*

Rnds 9–22: [Work rnds 2–8] twice.

Rnds 23–27: Rep rnds 2–6.

Fasten off and weave in ends.

LOWER BORDER
Row 1: Hold piece with lower edge at top; make slip knot on hook and join with a sc [sc, 2 sc, 2 sc] in end of first row of left Front Panel; working in ends of rem rows of right Front, Back, and left Front, work 2 sc in end of each dc row and 3 sc in end of each tr row to last row right Front Panel; sc [2 sc, 2 sc, 3 sc] in last row, turn. *(117 [132, 147, 162] sc)*

rem unused lps, sc in each lp; working around neck edge to left front edge, work 2 sc in end of each dc row and 3 sc in end of each tr row; working in corner of left front edge, ch 5—*button lp made*; working in unused lps of beg ch of left front edge, sc in each lp.

Fasten off.

SLEEVE
Make 2.
Rnd 1: Make slip knot on hook and join with a sc in center of 1 side seam, working around armhole opening, sc in each st and sp; join with a sl st in first sc. *(52 sc)*

Rnd 2: Ch 3 *(counts as a dc on this and following rnds)*, dc in next st; *ch 5, [sk next 2 sts, tr in next st] 3 times; ch 5, sk next 2 sts, dc in next 2 sts; rep from * twice; ch 5, [sk next 2 sts, tr in next st] 3 times; ch 5; join with a sl st in 3rd ch of beg ch-3. *(20 sts)*

Rnd 3: Ch 3, dc in next st; *ch 4, sc in 5th ch of next ch-5 sp, in next 3 tr, and in next ch of next ch-5 sp; ch 4, dc in next 2 dc; rep from * twice; ch 4, sc in 5th

Row 2: Ch 1, sc in first 2 sc, hdc in next 2 sc, dc in next sc, 2 dc in each of next 2 sc; dc in next sc, hdc in next 2 sc, sc in next 2 sc, *ch 3, sk next 3 sc, sc in next 2 sc, hdc in next 2 sc, dc in next sc, 2 dc in each of next 2 sc, dc in next sc, hdc in next 2 sc, sc in next 2 sc; rep from * across, turn.

For Size Small Only
Note: *For* **sc dec**, *draw up lp in 2 sts indicated, yo and draw through all 3 lps on hook.*

Row 3: Ch 1, **sc dec** *(see Note)* in first 2 sts; hdc in next 2 sts, dc in next 2 sts, 2 dc in each of next 2 sts; dc in next 2 sts, hdc in next 2 sts, sc dec in next 2 sts; *ch 3, sk next ch-3 sp, sc dec in next 2 sts; hdc in next 2 sts, dc in next 2 sts, 2 dc in each of next 2 sts; dc in next 2 sts, hdc in next 2 sts, sc dec in next 2 sts; rep from * across, turn.

Row 4: Ch 1, sc dec in first 2 sc; in each of next 9 sts work (dc, ch 1); sk next 2 sts; *working over next ch-3 sp, sc in ch-3 on 2nd row below, ch 2, sk next 2 sts, in each of next 9 sts work (dc, ch 1); dc in next st, ch 2, sk next 2 sts; rep from * 5 times; working over next ch-3 sp, sc in ch-3 on 2nd row below; ch 2, sk next 2 sts, in each of next 9 sts work (dc, ch 1); dc in next st, sc dec in last 2 sts, turn.

Row 5: Ch 1, sc in first st, [dc in next dc and in next ch-1 sp] 4 times; dc in next dc; *in next ch-1 sp work (2 dc, ch 3, sc in 3rd ch from hook, 2 dc); [dc in next dc and in next ch-1 sp] 4 times; dc in next dc, sl st in next sc, [dc in next dc and in next ch-1 sp] 4 times; dc in next dc; rep from * 6 times; in next ch-1 sp work (2 dc, ch 3, sc in 3rd ch from hook, 2 dc); [dc in next dc and in next ch-1 sp] 4 times; dc in next dc; sc in last st.

Fasten off and weave in ends.

For Size Medium Only
Row 3: Ch 1, sc in first st, sc dec in next 2 sts; hdc in next 2 sts, dc in next 2 sts, 2 dc in each of next 2 sts; dc in next 2 sts, hdc in next 2 sts, sc dec in next 2 sts; sc in next st; *ch 3, sk next ch-3 sp, sc in next st, sc dec in next 2 sts; hdc in next 2 sts, dc in next 2 sts, 2 dc in each of next 2 sts; dc in next 2 sts, hdc in next 2 sts, sc dec in next 2 sts, sc in next st; rep from * across, turn.

Row 4: Ch 1, sc in first st, sc dec; in each of next 9 sts work (dc, ch 1); sc in next st, sk next 2 sts; *working over next ch-3 sp, sc in ch-3 on 2nd row below, ch 2, sk next 2 sts, sc in next st, in each of next 9 sts work (dc, ch 1); dc in next st, sc in next st, ch 2, sk next 2 st; rep from * 5 times; working over next ch-3 sp, sc in ch-3 sp on 2nd row below, ch 2, sk next 2 sts, sc in next st, in each of next 9 sts work (dc, ch 1); dc in next st, sc in next st, sc dec, turn.

Row 5: Ch 1, sc in first 2 sts, [dc in next st, ch 1] 4 times; dc in next st; *in next ch-1 sp work (2 dc, ch 3, sc in 3rd ch from hook, 2 dc); [dc in next st, ch 1] 4 times; dc in next st, sc in next 2 sts, sl st in next st, [dc in next st, ch 1] 4 times; dc in next st; rep from * 6 times; in next ch-1 sp work (2 dc, ch 3, sc in 3rd ch from hook, 2 dc); [dc in next st, ch 1] 4 times; dc in next st, sc in last 2 sts.

Fasten off and weave in ends.

For Size Large Only
Row 3: Ch 1, sc dec in first 2 sts; sc dec in next 2 sts; hdc in next 2 sts, dc in next 2 sts, 2 dc in each of next 2 sts; dc in next 2 sts, hdc in next 2 sts, [sc dec in next 2 sts] twice; *ch 3, sk next ch-3 sp, sc in next st, [sc dec in next 2 sts] twice, hdc in next 2 sts, dc in next 2 sts, 2 dc in each of next 2 sts; dc in next 2 sts, hdc in next 2 sts, [sc dec in next 2 sts] twice, turn.

Row 4: Ch 1, sc dec in first 2 sts; sc dec; in each of next 9 sts work (dc, ch 1); sc dec; sk next 2 sts, *working over next ch-3, sc in ch-3 on 2nd row below, ch 2, sk next 2 sts, sc dec; in each of next 9 sts work (dc, ch 1); dc in next st, sc dec; sc in next st, ch 2, sk next 2 sts; rep from * 5 times; working over next ch-3 sp, sc in ch-3 on 2nd row below, ch 2, sk next 2 sts, sc dec; in each of next 9 sts work (dc, ch 1); dc in next st, [sc dec] twice, turn.

Row 5: Ch 1, sc in first 3 sts, [dc in next st, ch 1] 4 times; dc in next st; *in next ch-1 sp work (2 dc, ch 3, sc in 3rd ch from hook, 2 dc); [dc in next st, ch 1] 4 times; dc in next st, sc in next 3 sts, sl st in next st, [dc in next st, ch 1] 4 times; dc in next st, in next ch-1 sp work (2 dc, ch 3, sc in 3rd ch from hook, 2 dc); [dc in next st, ch 1] 4 times; dc in next st, sc in last 3 sts.

Fasten off and weave in ends.

For Size X-Large Only
Row 3: Ch 1, sc in first st, sc dec in first 2 sts; sc dec in next 2 sts; hdc in next 2 sts, dc in next 2 sts, 2 dc in each of next 2 sts, dc in next 2 sts, hdc in next 2 sts, [sc dec] twice; sc in next st; *ch 3, sk next ch-3 sp, sc in next st, [sc dec] twice; hdc in next 2 sts, dc in next 2 sts, 2 dc in each of next 2 sts; dc in next 2 sts, hdc in next 2 sts, [sc dec] twice; sc in next st; rep from * across, turn.

Row 4: Ch 1, sc in first st, [sc dec] twice; in each of next 9 sts work (dc, ch 1); [sc dec] twice; sc in next st, sk next 2

CONTINUED ON PAGE 156

Holiday Stripe Jacket

DESIGN BY LAURA POLLEY

SKILL LEVEL
INTERMEDIATE

FINISHED SIZES
Instructions given fit woman's X-small; changes for small, medium, large and X-large are in [ ].

FINISHED GARMENT MEASUREMENTS
Chest: 37 inches *(X-small)* [41 inches *(small),* 44 inches *(medium),* 48 inches *(large),* 51 inches *(X-large)*]

MATERIALS

Plymouth Encore D.K. light (DK) weight yarn (1¾ oz/150 yds/50g) per skein:
  7 [7, 8, 9, 10] skeins #9601 red *(A)*
  6 [6, 7, 8, 9] balls each #256 cream *(B)* and #204 hunter green *(C)*
Sizes E/4/3.5mm and F/5/4mm crochet hooks or sizes needed to obtain gauge
Tapestry needle
¾-inch red button
Sewing needle and matching thread

GAUGE
With F hook in pattern: 20 sts and 20 rows = 4 inches

PATTERN NOTE
To change color, work last stitch until 2 loops remain on hook; with new color, yarn over and draw through 2 loops on hook. Carry unused yarns loosely up side until needed again.

SPECIAL STITCH
Long double crochet (long dc): Yo, working over ch-1 sp indicated, insert hook in indicated sk sc on 2nd row below, draw up lp even with working row, [yo, draw through 2 lps on hook] twice.

Instructions

BACK
Row 1 (RS): With F hook and A, ch 94 [104, 112, 122, 130]; sc in 2nd ch from hook and in each rem ch, changing to B in last sc, turn. *(93 [103, 111, 121, 129] sc)*

Row 2: Ch 1, sc in first sc; *ch 1, sk next sc, sc in next sc; rep from * across, changing to C in last sc, turn.

Row 3: Ch 1, sc in first sc; *working over next ch-1 sp, **long dc** *(see Special Stitch)* in next sk sc on 2nd row below; sc in next sc; rep from * across changing to A in last sc, turn.

Rep rows 2 and 3, working 1 row of each color, until piece measures approximately 15 [16, 16½, 17½, 18] inches from beg, ending with a row 3.

ARMHOLE SHAPING
***Note:** On following rows, work in color sequence as established.*

Next row (WS): Sl st in first 9 [11, 15, 15, 19] sc; ch 1, sc in same sc as last sl st made; work in pattern as established to last 8 [10, 14, 14, 18] sc, turn, leaving rem sts unworked.

Work even in pattern as established until piece measures approximately 23½ [24½, 25½, 26½, 27½] inches from beg, ending with a RS row.

NECK SHAPING
Next row (WS): Ch 1, work in pattern across first 21 [23, 23, 29, 29] sts, turn, leaving rem sts unworked. *(21 [23, 23, 29, 29] sc)*

Work even in pattern as established until piece measures approximately 24 [25, 26, 27, 28] inches from beg, ending with a RS row.

Last row: Ch 1, sc in each st. Fasten off.

Hold piece with WS facing you; working color sequence as established, sk center 35 [37, 37, 35, 35] sts; rejoin yarn with a sl st in next st; ch 1, work in pattern across, turn. *(21 [23, 23, 29, 29] sts)*

Work even in pattern as established until piece measures approximately 24 [25, 26, 27, 28] inches from beg, ending with a RS row.

Last row: Ch 1, sc in each st.

Fasten off and weave in all ends.

RIGHT FRONT
Row 1 (RS): With F hook and A, ch 48 [52, 56, 62, 66]; sc in 2nd ch from hook and in each rem ch, changing to B in last sc, turn. *(47 [51, 55, 61, 65] sc)*

Row 2: Ch 1, sc in first sc; *ch 1, sk next sc, sc in next sc; rep from * across, changing to C in last sc, turn.

Row 3: Ch 1, sc in first sc; *long dc *(see Special Stitch)*, sc in next sc; rep from * across changing to A in last sc, turn.

Rep rows 2 and 3, working 1 row of each color, until piece measures same as Back to armhole, ending with a row 2.

ARMHOLE SHAPING
***Note:** On following rows, work in color sequence as established.*

Next row (RS): Ch 1, work in pattern as established to last 8 [10, 14, 14, 18] sts rem, turn, leaving rem sts unworked. *(39 [41, 41, 47, 47] sts)*

Work even in pattern as established until piece measures

approximately 16 [17, 17, 18, 19] inches from beg, ending with a RS row.

V-NECK SHAPING

Note: *For **sc dec**, draw up lp in 2 sts indicated, yo and draw through all 3 lps on hook.*

Row 1 (WS): Ch 1, work in pattern as established to last 2 sts, **sc dec** *(see Note)* in last 2 sts, turn. *(38 [40, 40, 46, 46] sts)*

Row 2 (RS): Ch 1, sc in first 2 sts; *long dc, sc in next sc; rep from * across, turn.

Row 3: Ch 1, work in pattern as established to last 3 sts; ch 1, sk next dc, sc dec, turn.

Row 4: Ch 1, sc in first sc; *long dc, sc in next sc, rep from * across, turn.

Rows 5–36: [Work rows 1–4] 8 times. *(21 [23, 23, 29, 29] sts at end of last row)*

Work even in pattern as established until piece measures same as Back to shoulders, ending with a RS row.

Last row: Ch 1, sc in each st.

Fasten off and weave in all ends.

LEFT FRONT

Work same as Right Front to Armhole Shaping. Fasten off at end of last row.

ARMHOLE SHAPING

Note: *On following rows, work in color sequence as established.*

Next row (RS): Hold piece with RS facing you; sk first 8 [10, 14, 14, 18] sts on last row worked; join next color in next st; work in pattern as established across, turn.

Work even in pattern as established until piece measures approximately 16 [17, 17, 18, 19] inches from beg, ending with a RS row.

V-NECK SHAPING
Row 1 (WS): Ch 1, sc dec in first 2 sts; sc in next st; *ch 1, sk next st, sc in next st; rep from * across, turn.

Row 2 (RS): Ch 1, work in pattern as established to last st; sc in last st, turn.

Row 3: Ch 1, sc dec in first 2 sts; *ch 1, sk next st, sc in next st; rep from * across, turn.

Row 4: Ch 1, sc in first st; *long dc, sc in next st, rep from * across, turn.

Rows 5–36: [Work rows 1–4] 8 times. (21, [23, 23, 29, 29] sts at end of last row)

Work even in pattern as established until piece measures same as Back to shoulders, ending with a RS row.

Last row: Ch 1, sc in each st.

Fasten off and weave in all ends.

SLEEVE
Make 2.
First row (RS): With F hook and A, ch 60 [60, 64, 64, 62]; sc in 2nd ch from hook and in each rem ch, changing to B in last sc, turn. (59 [59, 63, 63, 61] sc)

Row 2: Ch 1, sc dec sc in first 2 sts; sc in next sc; *ch 1, sk next sc, sc in next sc; rep from * to last 2 sc; sc dec in last 2 sc, changing to C, turn.

Row 3: Ch 1, sc in first 2 sts; *long dc, sc in next sc; rep from * to last st; sc in last st, changing to A, turn.

Row 4: Ch 1, sc dec sc in first 2 sts; *ch 1, sk next st, sc in next st; rep from * to last 3 sts; ch 1, sk next st, sc dec sc in last 2 sts, changing to B, turn.

Row 5: Ch 1, sc in first sc; *long dc, sc in next st; rep from * across, changing to C in last sc, turn.

Note: *On following rows, work in color sequence as established.*

Rows 6–17: [Work rows 2–5] 3 times. (43, [43, 47, 47, 47] sts at end of last row)

UPPER SLEEVE SHAPING
Row 18: Ch 1, 2 sc in first st; *ch 1, sk next st, sc in next st; rep from * to last 2 sts; ch 1, sk next st, 2 sc in last st, turn.

Row 19: Ch 1, sc in first 2 sts; *long dc, sc in next sc; rep from * to last st; sc in last st, turn.

Row 20: Ch 1, sc in first st, ch 1, sc in next st; *ch 1, sk next st, sc in next st; rep from * to last st; ch 1, sc in last st, turn.

Row 21: Ch 1, sc in first st, long dc in first sc on 2nd row below, sc in next sc; *long dc, sc in next st; rep from * to last ch-1 sp; long dc in last sc on 2nd row below, sc in last st, turn.

[Work rows 18–21] 11 [11, 11, 11, 13] times. (91 [91, 95, 95, 101] sts at end of last row)

Work in pattern as established until piece measures approximately 20 inches from beg, ending with a RS row.

Last row: Ch 1, sc in each st.

Fasten off and weave in all ends.

FINISHING
Sew shoulder seams. Sew Sleeves into armhole openings, matching center of Sleeves to shoulder seam and setting sides of Sleeves into armhole insets. Sew side and Sleeve seams.

EDGINGS
Lower Edging
Row 1 (RS): Hold Jacket with RS facing you and beg ch at top; with E hook, join A with a sl st in first unused lp of beg ch; ch 1, sc in same lp; working in rem unused lps of beg ch, sc in each rem lp, turn. (187 [205, 221, 243, 259] sc)

Row 2: Ch 1, sc in first sc and in each rem sc.

Fasten off and weave in ends.

Sleeve Edging
Row 1: Hold Sleeve with RS facing you and beg ch at top; with E hook, join A in first unused lp of beg ch; ch 1, sc in same lp; working in rem unused lps, sc in each lp; join with a sl st in first sc, turn. (59 [59, 63, 63, 61] sc)

Row 2: Ch 1, sc in first sc and each sc to first sc; join with a sl st in first sc.

Fasten off and weave in ends.

Rep on 2nd sleeve.

Neck Edging
Row 1: Hold Jacket with RS facing you and right front edge at top; with E hook, join A with a sl st in end of first row of Lower Edging; ch 1, sc in same sp as joining; sc evenly spaced up right front neck edge to beg V-Neck Shaping; 3 sc in corner of V-Neck Shaping; sc evenly spaced up right front neck edge to shoulder, down back neck shaping to st before corner; sc dec in st before corner and st after corner; sc in each st across center back neck edge to last st before corner; sc dec in last st before corner and

first st after corner; sc evenly spaced up side of back neck shaping to shoulder and down left front neck edge to corner of V-Neck Shaping; 3 sc in corner of V-Neck Shaping; sc evenly spaced down left front edge to last row of Lower Edging, turn.

Note: *Mark right front neck edging for 1 button at corner at* *beg of V-Neck Shaping.*

Row 2: Ch 1, sc in first sc and in each sc to corner of V-neck, ch 3, sk 3 sc in corner of V-neck— *buttonhole made;* sc in each rem sc, turn.

Row 3: Ch 1, sc in first sc and in each rem sc and working 5 sc in ch-3 sp at beg of right V-Neck Shaping, 3 sc in corner at beg of left front V-Neck Shaping, and sc dec at each inner corner of back neck as before.

Fasten off and weave in ends.

FINISHING
With sewing needle and matching thread, sew button opposite buttonhole. ❧

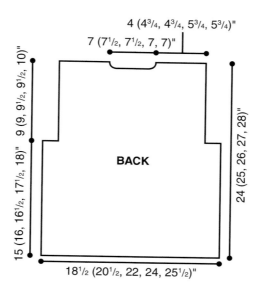

4 (4³/₄, 4³/₄, 5³/₄, 5³/₄)"

7 (7¹/₂, 7¹/₂, 7, 7)"

9 (9, 9¹/₂, 9¹/₂, 10)"

BACK

24 (25, 26, 27, 28)"

15 (16, 16¹/₂, 17¹/₂, 18)"

18¹/₂ (20¹/₂, 22, 24, 25¹/₂)"

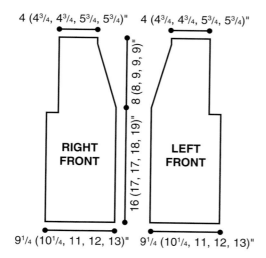

4 (4³/₄, 4³/₄, 5³/₄, 5³/₄)"   4 (4³/₄, 4³/₄, 5³/₄, 5³/₄)"

8 (8, 9, 9, 9)"

RIGHT FRONT

LEFT FRONT

16 (17, 17, 18, 19)"

9¹/₄ (10¹/₄, 11, 12, 13)"   9¹/₄ (10¹/₄, 11, 12, 13)"

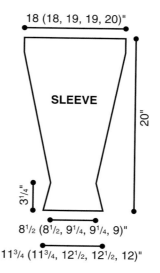

18 (18, 19, 19, 20)"

SLEEVE

20"

3¹/₄"

8¹/₂ (8¹/₂, 9¹/₄, 9¹/₄, 9)"

11³/₄ (11³/₄, 12¹/₂, 12¹/₂, 12)"

Holiday Walk Dog Coat

DESIGN BY LAURA POLLEY

SKILL LEVEL ■■■□ INTERMEDIATE

FINISHED SIZES
Instructions given fit small dog; changes for medium and large dogs are in [ ].

FINISHED GARMENT MEASUREMENTS
Chest: 14 [17, 20] inches

Back Length: 11 [13, 17¾] inches

MATERIALS

Plymouth Encore D.K. light (DK) weight yarn (1¾ oz/150 yds/50g per skein):
  1 [2, 3] skein(s) each #9601 red (A), #208 white (B) and #54 green (C)
Sizes E/4/3.5mm and F/5/3.75mm crochet hooks or sizes needed to obtain gauge
Tapestry needle
4 (5, 6) ½-inch red buttons
Sewing needle and matching thread

GAUGE
With F hook in pattern: 20 sts and 20 rows = 4 inches

PATTERN NOTE
To change color, work last stitch until 2 loops remain on hook; with new color, yarn over and draw through 2 loops on hook. Carry unused yarns loosely up side until needed again.

SPECIAL STITCH
Long double crochet (long dc): Yo, working over ch-1 sp indicated, insert hook in indicated sk sc on 2nd row below, draw up lp even with working row, [yo, draw through 2 lps on hook] twice.

Instructions

BODY
Row 1 (RS): With F hook and A, ch 44 [44, 48]; sc in 2nd ch from hook and in each rem ch, changing to B in last sc, turn. (43, [43, 47] sc)

Row 2: Ch 1, 2 sc in first sc; *ch 1, sk next sc, sc in next sc; rep from * to last 2 sc; ch 1, sk next sc, 2 sc in last sc, changing to C in last sc, turn.

Row 3: Ch 1, sc in first 2 sts; *working over next ch-1 sp, **long dc** (see Special Stitch) in next sk sc on 2nd row below; sc in next sc; rep from * to last st, sc in last st, changing to A, turn.

Row 4: Ch 1, sc in first st, ch 1, sc in next st; *ch 1, sk next st, sc in next st; rep from * to last st; ch 1, sc in last st, changing to B, turn.

Row 5: Ch 1, sc in first st, long dc in first sc on 2nd row below, sc in next sc; *long dc, sc in next sc; rep from * to last ch-1 sp; long dc in last sc on 2nd row below, sc in last st, changing to C, turn.

Note: On following rows, work in color sequence as established.

[Work rows 2–5] 3 [4, 5] times. (59, [63, 75] sts at end of last row)

Next row (WS): Ch 7 [13, 13], sc in 2nd ch from hook and in next 5 [11, 11] chs, work in pattern as established over next 59 [63, 75] sts, turn. (66 [76, 87] sts)

Next row (RS): Ch 7 [13, 13], sc in 2nd ch from hook and in next 5 [11, 11] chs; work in pattern as established over next 59 [63, 75] sts; sc in next 6 [12, 12] sc, turn. (71 [85, 101] sts)

Work even in pattern as established until piece measures approximately 6½ [8¼, 10¾] inches from beg, ending with a WS row.

RIGHT FRONT
Row 1 (RS): Ch 1, work in pattern as established across first 5 [7, 9] sts, turn, leaving rem of sts unworked.

Work even in pattern until Right Front measures approximately 2 [2, 3] inches from row 1, ending with a RS row.

Last row: Ch 1, sc in first st and in each rem st. Fasten off.

LEFT FRONT
Hold piece with RS facing you; sk next 61 [71, 83] unworked sts from Right Front, with F hook, join next color in sequence with a sl st in next st, ch 1, sc in same st; work in pattern over next 4 [6, 8] sts, turn.

Work even in pattern until Left Front measures approximately 2 [2, 3] inches from row 1, ending with a RS row.

Last row: Ch 1, sc in first st and in each rem st. Fasten off.

BACK
Hold piece with RS facing you; sk first 11 [13, 15] st from Right Front—leg opening made; with F hook, rejoin appropriate color

with a sl st in next st, ch 1, sc in same sc; work in pattern over next 38 [44, 52] sts, turn, leaving rem 11 [13, 15] sts unworked—leg opening made. (39 [45, 53] sts)

Work even in pattern as established until piece measures approximately 1½ [1½, 2½] inches from beg, ending with a WS row.

RIGHT NECK SHAPING
Row 1 (RS): Ch 1, work in pattern across first 11 [13, 15] sts, turn, leaving rest of row unworked.

Note: For **sc dec**, draw up lp in 2 sts indicated, yo and draw through all 3 lps on hook.

Row 2: Ch 1, **sc dec** (see Note) in first 2 sts; sc in next st; *ch 1, sk next dc, sc in next sc; rep from * across, turn. (10 [12, 14] sts)

Row 3: Ch 1, work in pattern as established to last st; sc in last st, turn.

Row 4: Ch 1, dec sc in first 2 sts; *ch 1, sk next dc, sc in next sc, rep from * across, turn. (9 [11, 13] sts)

Row 5: Ch 1, sc in first st; *long dc, sc in next st; rep from * across, turn.

Rows 6–9: Rep rows 2–5. (7, [9, 11] sts at end of last row)

Work even in pattern as established until piece measures approximately 3 [3½, 4½] inches from row 1, ending with a RS row.

Last row: Ch 1, sc in first st and in each rem st. Fasten off.

RIGHT NECK SHAPING
Row 1 (RS): Hold piece with RS facing you; sk 17 [19, 23] sts from Left Neck Shaping; with F hook, rejoin appropriate color in next st; ch 1, sc in same st; work in pattern as established over next 10 [12, 14] sts.

Row 2: Ch 1, work in pattern as established to last 2 sts; sc dec in last 2 sts, turn.

Row 3: Ch 1, sc in first 2 sts; *long dc, sc in next sc; rep from * across, turn.

Row 4: Ch 1, work in pattern as established to last 3 sts, ch 1, sk next dc, sc dec sc in last 2 sts, turn.

Row 5: Ch 1, sc in first sc; *long dc, sc in next sc; rep from * across, turn.

Rows 6–9: Rep rows 2–5. (7, [9, 11] sts at end of last row)

Work even in pattern as established until piece measures approximately 3 [3½, 4½] inches from row 1, ending with a RS row.

Last row: Ch 1, sc in first st and in each rem st.

Fasten off and weave in all ends.

FINISHING
Lay Body flat with RS facing you. Measure 1 [1½, 2] inches down from last row worked on each side of Back and mark row ends at these points with lp of waste yarn.

Turn last row of Right Front sideways, counterclockwise, and sew to 1 [1½, 2]-inch section of Back above marker (see schematic).

Turn last row of Left Front sideways, clockwise, and sew to opposite 1 [1½, 2]-inch section of Back above marker (see schematic).

EDGINGS
Neck Edging
Hold coat with RS facing you; with E hook, join A with a sl st in edge of last row of right neck edge; ch 1, sc in same sp as joining; work 47 [53, 67] sc evenly spaced around neck opening to last row of left neck edge. Fasten off.

Leg Opening Edgings
Hold coat with RS facing you; with E hook, join A with a sl st to right leg opening at lower inner corner of Right Front; ch 1, sc in same sp as joining; work 21 [23, 27] sc evenly spaced around entire leg opening; join with a sl st to first sc. Fasten off.

Rep for left leg opening, beg at lower inner corner of Left Front.

Lower Edging
Row 1 (RS): Hold coat with RS facing you; with E hook, join A with a sl st in sc at lower left corner of widest point of Body; ch 1, sc in same sp as [21, 29] sc evenly spaced down shaped body edge, 3 sc in lower corner; working in unused lps of beg ch,

sc in next 43 [43, 47] lps; 3 sc in next lower corner; work 17 [21, 29] sc evenly spaced up shaped body edge; sc in next 6 [12, 12] sc, turn. *(95 [115, 135] sc)*

Row 2: Ch 1, sc in first sc and in each rem sc.

Fasten off and weave in ends.

COLLAR
Note: Collar is worked sideways.

Row 1 (RS): With E hook and A, ch 9; sc in 2nd ch from hook and in each rem ch, turn. *(8 sc)*

Row 2: Ch 1, working in **back lps** *(see Stitch Guide)* only, sc in each sc, turn.

Rep row 2 until piece, when slightly stretched, fits around neck opening.

Fasten off and weave in ends.

Sew Collar to neck edging, easing to fit around neckline.

LEG TRIM
Make 2.
Row 1 (RS): With E hook and A, ch 9; sc in 2nd ch from hook and in each rem ch, turn. *(8 sc)*

Row 2: Ch 1, working in back lps only, sc in each sc, turn.

Rep row 2 until piece, when slightly stretched, fits around leg opening.

Fasten off and weave in ends.

BUTTONBAND
Hold coat with RS facing you and Left Front edge at top; with E hook, join A with a sl st in upper right-hand corner of Collar; ch 1.

Row 1 (RS): Hold coat with RS facing you and left opening at top; with E hook, join A with a sl st in

upper right-hand corner of Collar; ch 1; sc in same sp as joining; work 8 sc evenly spaced across Collar edge, 7 [9, 11] sc across last row of left back neck, 25 [30, 30] sc across Left Front to last row of lower edging, turn. *(40 [47, 57] sc)*

Row 2: Ch 1, sc in each sc, turn.

Rows 3 & 4: Rep row 2.

Fasten off and weave in ends.

Mark button band for 4 [5, 6] buttons, having first button ½ inch from upper edge of Collar and last button 1 inch from lower edge of Body and spacing rem buttons evenly between.

BUTTONHOLE BAND
Row 1 (RS): Hold coat with RS facing you and Right Front opening at top; with E hook, join A with a sl st in end of last row of lower edge of Body; ch 1, sc in same sp as joining; work 25 [30, 38] sc evenly spaced up Right Front, 7 [9, 11] sc across last row of Right Front, and 8 sc along

Collar edge to end of Collar, turn. *(40 [47, 57] sc)*

Row 2: Ch 1, sc in first sc and in each sc to first marker; ch 2, sk next 2 sc—*buttonhole made;* [sc in each sc to next marker, ch 2, sk next 2 sc—*buttonhole made*] twice [3, 4] times; sc in each rem sc, turn.

Row 3: Ch 1, sc in first sc and in each sc to next ch-2 sp, 2 sc in next ch-2 sp; [sc in each sc to next ch-2 sp, 2 sc in next ch-2 sp] 3 [4, 5] times; sc in each rem sc, turn.

Row 4: Ch 1, sc in each sc.

Fasten off and weave in ends.

FINISHING
Step 1: With sewing needle and matching thread, sew on buttons opposite buttonholes.

Step 2: Sew first and last row of each Leg Trim tog, forming tube. Sew 1 Leg Trim to each leg opening edging, easing to fit. 🌿

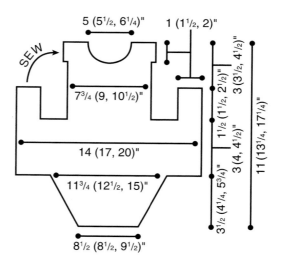

Plush Warmers for Mother & Child

DESIGNS BY DARLA SIMS

SKILL LEVEL EASY

SIZES FOR CAPELET
Instructions given fit woman's small; changes for medium, large, X-large and 2X-large are in [ ].

FINISHED GARMENT MEASUREMENTS
Lower edge: 51 [54, 57½, 60¾, 64] inches

SIZES FOR CARDIGAN & HAT
Instructions given fit child's size 6 months; changes for 12 months and 24 months are in [ ].

FINISHED GARMENT MEASUREMENT
Chest: 22 [24, 26] inches

MATERIALS FOR CAPELET
Patons Be Mine super bulky (super chunky) weight yarn (1¾ oz/89 yds/50g per skein):
    4 [5, 6, 7, 8] skeins #63320 lovely lilac (A)
Patons Pooch super bulky (super chunky) weight yarn (2⅖ oz/36 yds/70g per skein):
    3 [3, 4, 4, 5] skeins #65310 purple sunset (B)
Bernat Eye Lash super bulky (super chunky) weight yarn (1¾ oz/77 yds/50g per skein):
    1 skein #35315 flash (C)
Sizes H/8/5mm and I/9/5.5mm crochet hooks or sizes needed to obtain gauge
Stitch markers

MATERIALS FOR CARDIGAN & HAT
Patons Be Mine super bulky (super chunky) weight yarn (1¾ oz/89 yds/50g per skein):
    3 [3, 4] skeins #63320 lovely lilac (A)
Patons Pooch super bulky (super chunky) weight yarn (2⅖ oz/36 yds/70g per skein):
    1 skein #65310 purple sunset (B)
Bernat Eye Lash super bulky (super chunky) weight yarn (1¾ oz/77 yds/50g per skein):
    1 skein #35315 flash (C)
Sizes H/8/5mm and I/9/5.5mm crochet hooks or sizes needed to obtain gauge
Stitch markers

GAUGE
With I hook: 5 dc = 1 inches

Instructions

CAPELET
Note: *Capelet is worked from neck down.*

Row 1: Ch 66; dc in 4th dc from hook *(beg 3 sk chs count as a dc)*, dc in next 7 chs; *sk next 2 chs, in next ch work (2 dc, ch 1, 2 dc)—shell made;* sk next 2 chs, dc in next 4 chs, sk next 2 chs, in next ch work (2 dc, ch 1, 2 dc)—*shell made;* sk next 2 chs, dc in next 18 chs, sk next 2 chs, in next ch work (2 dc, ch 1, 2 dc)—*shell made;* sk next 2 chs, dc in next 4 chs, sk next 2 chs, in next ch work (2 dc, ch 1, 2 dc)—*shell made;* sk next 2 chs, dc in next 9 chs, turn.

Row 2: Ch 3 *(counts as a dc on this and following rows),* dc in next 7 dc; *2 dc in next dc; in ch-1 sp of next shell work shell; sk next 2 dc of same shell, 2 dc in next dc; dc in next 2 dc, 2 dc in next dc; in ch-1 sp of next shell work shell; sk next 2 dc of same shell, 2 dc in next dc, dc in next 16 dc, 2 dc in next dc, in ch-1 sp of next shell work shell; sk next 2 dc of same shell, 2 dc in next dc; dc in next 2 dc, 2 dc in next dc; in ch-1 sp of next shell work shell; sk next 2 dc of same shell, 2 dc in next dc; dc in next 7 dc and in 3rd ch of beg 3 sk chs, turn.

Row 3: Ch 3, dc in each dc to last dc before next shell; 2 dc in last dc; *shell in next shell; 2 dc in first dc after shell; dc in each dc to last dc before next shell; 2 dc in last dc; rep from * twice; shell in next shell; 2 dc in first dc after shell; dc in each rem dc and in 3rd ch of turning ch, turn.

Rows 4–8 [4–9, 4–10, 4–11, 4–12]: Rep row 3.

Row 9 [10, 11, 12, 13]: Ch 3;* dc in each dc to next shell; shell in next shell; rep from * 3 times; dc in each rem dc and in 3rd ch of turning ch-3, turn.

Rows 10 & 11 [11 & 12, 12 & 13, 13 & 14, 14 & 15]: Rep row 9 [10, 11, 12, 13].

Row 12 [13, 14, 15, 16]: Rep row 3.

Rows 13–16 [14–17, 15–18, 16–19, 17–20]: Rep row 9 [10, 11, 12, 13].

Note: *For **dc dec,** [yo, draw up lp in st indicated, yo, draw through 2 lps on hook] twice; yo and draw through all 3 lps on hook.*

Last row: Ch 3, dc in next 61 dc, **dc dec** *(see Note)* in next 2 dc; dc in each rem dc and in 3rd ch of turning ch-3, turn.

EDGING

Ch 1, sc in first dc; *ch 4, sk next dc, sc in next dc; rep from * to last dc and turning ch-3; ch 4, sk last dc, sc in 3rd ch of turning ch-3.

Fasten off and weave in ends.

COLLAR

Row 1: Hold piece with RS facing you and beg ch at top; join B in first unused lp of beg ch; ch 1, sc in same lp; working in rem unused lps, sc in each lp, turn.

Note: *Place marker above 2 dc on each side of each shell on last shell row worked.*

Row 2: Ch 3, dc in each dc, working 2 dc at each marker, turn.

Rep row 2 until piece measures 4½ inches from beg.

Fasten off and weave in ends.

TIE
Make 2.
With E hook, join C in edge of row 1 of Capelet; ch 46; hdc in 3rd ch from hook and in each rem ch; sl st in same sp as joining.

Fasten off and weave in ends.

CARDIGAN
Note: *Cardigan is worked from neck down.*

YOKE
Row 1 (RS): Ch 36, hdc in 3rd ch from hook *(beg 2 sk chs count as a hdc)* and in each rem ch, turn. *(35 hdc)*

Row 2: Ch 2 *(counts as a hdc on this and following rows)*; *hdc in next hdc, 2 hdc in next hdc; rep from * to last hdc and beg 2 sk chs; hdc in last hdc, 2 hdc in 2nd ch of beg 2 sk chs, turn. *(51 hdc)*

Row 3: Ch 2, hdc in next hdc and in 2nd ch of turning ch-2, turn.

Row 4: Ch 2, hdc in next hdc; * hdc in next 2 hdc, 2 hdc in next hdc; rep from * to last 2 hdc and turning ch-3; hdc in last 2 hdc and in 2nd ch of turning ch-3, turn. *(67 hdc)*

Row 5: Ch 2, hdc in next hdc, in each rem hdc and in 2nd ch of turning ch-2, turn.

Row 6: Ch 2, hdc in next 2 hdc; *2 hdc in next hdc; hdc in next 3 hdc; rep from * across, turn. *(83 hdc)*

For Size 6 Months Only
Row 7: Ch 2, hdc in next hdc, in each rem hdc and in 2nd ch of turning ch-2, turn.

Row 8: Rep row 7.

Continue with Body.

Size 12 Months Only
Row 7: Ch 2, hdc in next hdc, in each rem hdc and in 2nd ch of turning ch-2, turn.

Row 8: Ch 2, hdc in next 3 hdc; *2 hdc in next hdc; hdc in next 4 hdc; rep from * to last 4 hdc and turning ch-2; 2 hdc in next hdc;

hdc in last 3 hdc and in 2nd ch of turning ch-2, turn. *(99 hdc)*

Row 9: Rep row 7.

Continue with Body.

Size 24 Months Only
Row 7: Ch 2, hdc in next hdc and in each st to end. *(99 hdc)*

Row 8: Ch 2, hdc in next 4 hdc; *2 hdc in next hdc; hdc in next 5 hdc; rep from * to last 5 hdc; 2 hdc in next hdc; hdc in last 4 hdc and in 2nd ch of turning ch-2, turn. *(115 hdc)*

Rows 9 & 10: Rep row 7.

Continue with Body.

BODY
Row 1: Ch 2, hdc in next 11 [13, 15] hdc, ch 2—*underarm made*; sk next 22 [24, 26] hdc, hdc in next 23 [27, 31] hdc, ch 2—*underarm made*; sk next 22 [24, 26], hdc in next 12 [14, 16] hdc, turn. *(51 [59, 67] hdc)*

Row 2: Ch 2; *2 hdc in next hdc; hdc in next 7 hdc; rep from * to last 2 hdc and turning ch-2; 2 hdc in next hdc; hdc in last hdc and in 2nd ch of turning ch-2. *(59 [67, 75] hdc)*

Row 3: Ch 2, hdc in next hdc, in each rem hdc and in 2nd ch of turning ch-2, turn.

Row 4: Rep row 3.

Row 5: Ch 2, hdc in next hdc; *2 hdc in next hdc; hdc in next 7 hdc; rep from * to last 2 hdc and turning ch-2; 2 hdc in next hdc; hdc in last hdc and in 2nd ch of turning ch-2, turn. *(67 [75, 83] hdc)*

Row 6: Rep row 3.

Rep row 6 until Body measures 5½ [6, 8½] inches.

EDGING
Ch 1, sc in first hdc; *ch 4, sk next hdc, sc in next hdc; rep from * to last hdc and turning ch-2; ch 4, sk last hdc, sc in 2nd ch of turning ch-2.

Fasten off and weave in ends.

SLEEVE
Rnd 1: Join A in center of 1 underarm; ch 2 *(counts as a hdc on this and following rnds)*, work 25 [27, 29] hdc around Sleeve opening; join with a sl st in 2nd ch of beg ch-2, turn. *(26, [28, 30] hdc)*

Note: *For* **hdc dec**, *[yo, draw up lp in st indicated] twice; yo and draw through all 5 lps on hook.*

Rnd 2: Ch 2, **hdc dec** *(see Note)* in next 2 hdc; hdc to last hdc and turning ch-2; hdc dec in next hdc and 2nd ch of turning ch; join in 2nd ch of turning ch-2, turn. *(24 [26, 28] hdc)*

Rnd 3: Ch 2, hdc dec in next 2 hdc; hdc to last hdc and turning ch-2; hdc dec in next hdc and 2nd ch of turning ch; join in 2nd ch of turning ch-2, turn. *(22 [24, 26] hdc)*

Rnd 4: Ch 2, hdc dec in next 2 hdc; hdc to last hdc and turning ch-2; hdc dec in next hdc and 2nd ch of turning ch; join in 2nd ch of turning ch-2, turn. *(20 [22, 24] hdc)*

Rnd 5: Ch 2, hdc dec in next 2 hdc; hdc to last hdc and turning ch-2; hdc dec in next hdc and 2nd ch of turning ch; join in 2nd ch of turning ch-2, turn. *(18 [20, 22] hdc)*

Rnd 6: Ch 2, hdc in each rem hdc and in 2nd ch of turning ch; join in 2nd ch of turning ch-2, turn.

Rep rnd 6 until Sleeve measures 5½ [6, 8] inches from beg.

Fasten off and weave in ends.

EDGINGS
Sleeve Edging
Hold 1 Sleeve with RS facing you and last rnd work at top; join B in 2nd ch of turning ch-2; ch 1, sc in same ch as joining and in each rem hdc; join in first sc.

Fasten off and weave in ends.

Rep on other Sleeve.

Collar Edging
Row 1: Hold Cardigan with RS facing you and neck opening at top; join A in first st of neck edge; ch 1, sc in same st; work 35 sc evenly spaced along neck edge. Change to B by drawing lp through; cut A, turn. *(36 sc)*

Row 2: Ch 2, hdc in next 7 sc, [2 hdc in next sc; hdc in next 8 sc] 3 times; 2 hdc in next sc, turn. *(40 hdc)*

Row 3: Ch 2, hdc in next 8 hdc, [2 hdc in next hdc; hdc in next 9 hdc] 3 times; 2 hdc in 2nd ch of turning ch-2, turn. *(44 hdc)*

Row 4: Ch 2, hdc in each rem hdc and in 2nd ch of turning ch-2.

Fasten off and weave in all ends.

TIE
Make 2.
With E hook, join C in end of row 1 of Cardigan; ch 26; sc in 2nd ch from hook and in each rem ch; sl st in same sp as joining.

Fasten off and weave in ends.

HAT
Note: *Hat is worked in continuous rnds. Do not join; mark beg of rnds.*

Rnd 1: With H hook and A, ch 40 [42, 44]; join to form a ring; ch 1, sc in same ch as joining and in each rem ch.

Rnd 2: Sc in each sc.

Rnds 3–8 [3–8, 3–10]: Rep rnd 2.

Note: *For **sc dec**, draw up lp in 2 sts indicated, yo and draw through all 3 lps on hook.*

Rnd 9 [9, 11]: *Sc in next 3 sc, **sc dec** (see Note) in next 2 sc; rep from * around.

Rnds 10 & 11 [10 & 11, 12 & 13]: Rep rnd 9 [9, 11].

Rnds 12 &13 [12 & 13, 14 & 15]: Rep rnd 2.

Sc dec until 5 sc rem. Fasten off, leaving long end for sewing. Pull end to WS. With tapestry needle and end, sew top tog.

EDGING
Hold Hat with WS facing you and beg ch at top; with E hook, join B in first unused lp of beg ch; ch 1, sc in same lp; working in rem unused lps, sc in each lp; join in first sc.

Fasten off.

POMPOM
With H hook and C, ch 4; 9 dc in 4th ch from hook. Fasten off, leaving long end. Thread end in tapestry needle, pull yarn through top lps of sts and pull tog to form Pompom. Fasten off. Weave ends through top of Hat and sew to WS. ❧

Santa's Girl Floral Cardigan

DESIGN BY DONNA MAY

SKILL LEVEL
INTERMEDIATE

FINISHED SIZES
Instructions given fit child's size 2; changes for 4, 6 and 8 are in [ ].

FINISHED GARMENT MEASUREMENTS
Chest: 24 [26, 28, 30] inches

MATERIALS
Red Heart Baby Clouds super bulky (super chunky) weight yarn (6 oz/140 yds/170g per skein):
   2 [2, 2, 2] skeins #9074 pale pink *(A)*
TLC Amore medium (worsted) weight yarn (6 oz/278 yds/170g per skein):
   1 skein each #3625 celery *(B)* and #3752 hot pink *(C)*
Sizes H/8/5mm and K/10½/6.5mm crochet hooks or sizes needed to obtain gauge
Tapestry needle
4 [4, 5, 6] sets of large covered hook-and-eye fasteners
Stitch markers
Sewing needle and matching thread

GAUGE
With K hook and A: 8 sts and 8 rows = 4 inches

PATTERN NOTE
To change color, work last stitch until 2 loops remain on hook; with new color, yarn over and draw through 2 loops on hook. Cut old color.

Instructions

BODY
Note: *Body is worked in 1 piece to armholes.*

Row 1 (RS): With K hook and A, ch 46 [51, 56, 60]; sc in 2nd ch from hook and in each rem ch, turn. *(45 [50, 55, 59] sc)*

Row 2: Ch 1, 2 sc in first sc; sc in each sc to last sc; 2 sc in last sc, turn. *(47 [52, 57, 61] sc)*

Row 3: Ch 1, 2 sc in first sc; sc in each sc to last sc; 2 sc in last sc; turn. *(49 [54, 59, 63] sc)*

Row 4: Ch 1, sc in each sc, changing to H hook and B in last sc, turn.

Row 5: Ch 1, sc in first 4 sc; *in next sc work [sl st, ch 8] 3 times; sl st in same st; sc in next 9 [8, 9, 8] sc; rep from * 3 [4, 4, 5] times; in next sc work [sl st, ch 8] 3 times; sl st in same st; sc in next 4 sc, changing to K hook and A in last st, turn. *(44 [48, 53, 56] sc)*

Row 6: Ch 1, sc in first 4 sts; working in front of ch-8 lps made on previous rnd, *ch 1, sk next 3 ch-8 lps, sc in next 9 [8, 9, 8] sts; rep from * 3 [4, 4, 5] times; ch 1, sk next 3 ch-8 lps, sc in next 4 sc, turn. *(49 [54, 59, 63] sts)*

Row 7: Ch 1, sc in first sc; *insert hook through next ch-8 lp made on row 4 and sc in next sc on row 6; sc in next 5 sc, sk center ch-8 lp, insert hook in

next ch-8 lp and sc in next sc on row 6; sc in next 3 [2, 3, 2] sc; rep from * 3 [4, 4, 5] times; insert hook in next ch-8 lp and sc in next sc on row 6; sc in next 5 sc, sk center ch-8 lp, insert hook in next ch-8 lp and sc in next sc on row 6; sc in last sc, turn.

Row 8: Ch 1, sc in each sc, turn. *(49 [54, 59, 63] sc)*

Note: *On following row, when picking up center lp, twist lp over once to left to close lp forming stem.*

Row 9: Ch 1, sc in first 4 sc, changing to H hook and C in last sc; working over A, *work 6 dc all through center lp and in next sc on row 8, changing to K hook and A in last dc; working over C, sc in next 9 [8, 9, 8] sts, changing to H hook and in last sc; rep from * 3 [4, 4, 5] times; work 6 dc all through center lp and in next sc on row 8, changing to K hook and A in last dc; working over C, sc in last 4 sc, turn. Cut C.

Row 10: Ch 1, sc in first 4 sc; *ch 1, sk next 6 dc, sc in next 9 [8, 9, 8] sc; rep from * 3 [4, 4, 5] times; ch 1, sk next 6 dc, sc in last 4 sc, turn.

Row 11: Ch 1, sc in first sc and in each rem sc and in each ch-1 sp, turn. *(49 [54, 59, 63] sc)*

Rows 12–13 [12–17, 12–17, 12–17]: Ch 1, sc in each sc, turn.

Row 14 [18, 18, 18]: Ch 1, sc in first 13 [14, 15, 16] sc, sl st in next sc, ch 1, sc in next 21 [24, 27, 29] sc, sl st in next sc, ch 1, sc in next 13 [14, 15, 16] sc; ch 1, turn. *(47 [52, 57, 61] sc)*

RIGHT FRONT
Row 1 (RS): Ch 1, sc in first 13 [14, 15, 16] sc, turn. *(13 [14, 15, 16] sc)*

Rows 2–7 [2–7, 2–9, 2–11]: Ch 1, sc in each sc, turn.

RIGHT NECK SHAPING
Row 1 (WS): Ch 1, sc in first 9 [10, 11, 12] sc, turn, leaving rem 4 sc unworked. *(9 [10, 11, 12] sc)*

Row 2 (RS): Sl st in first sc, ch 1, sc in next 8 [9, 10, 11] sc, turn. *(8 [9, 10, 11] sc)*

Row 3: Ch 1, sc in first 7 [8, 9, 10] sc, turn, leaving last sc unworked. *(7 [8, 9, 10] sc)*

Row 4: Ch 1, sc in each sc, turn.

Row 5: Ch 1, sc in each sc.

Fasten off and weave in ends.

CENTER BACK
Row 1 (RS): Hold piece with RS facing you; join A with sl st in first sc from Right Front; ch 1, sc in same sc; sc in next 20 [23, 26, 28] sc, turn. *(21 [24, 27, 29] sc)*

Row 2: Ch 1, sc in each sc, turn.

Rows 3–12 [3–12, 3–14, 3–16]: Rep row 2.

Fasten off and weave in ends.

Note: *Mark center 10 sc.*

LEFT FRONT
Row 1 (RS): Hold piece with RS facing you; join A with sl st in first sc from Center Back; ch 1, sc in same sc and in each rem sc, turn. *(13 [14, 15, 16] sc)*

Row 2: Ch 1, sc in each sc, turn.

Rows 3–7 [3–7, 3–9, 3–11]: Rep row 2.

LEFT NECK SHAPING
Row 1 (WS): Sl st in first 4 sc; ch 1, sc in next 9 [10, 11, 12] sc, turn. *(9 [10, 11, 12] sc)*

Row 2 (RS): Ch 1, sc in first 8 [9, 10, 11] sc, turn, leaving rem sc unworked. *(8 [9, 10, 11] sc)*

Row 3: Sl st in first sc, ch 1, sc in next 7 [8, 9, 10] sc, turn. *(7 [8, 9, 10] sc)*

Row 4: Ch 1, sc in each sc, turn.

Row 5: Ch 1, sc in each sc.

Fasten off and weave in ends.

SLEEVE
Make 2.
Row 1 (RS): With K hook and A, ch 16 [17, 18, 18]; sc in 2nd ch from hook and in each rem ch, turn. *(15 [16, 17, 17] sc)*

Row 2: Ch 1, sc in each sc, turn.

Row 3: Ch 1, 2 sc in first st; sc in next 13 [14, 15] sc, 2 sc in last sc, turn. *(17 [18, 19, 19] sc)*

Row 4: Ch 1, sc in each sc, turn.

Rows 5 & 6: Rep row 4.

Row 7: Ch 1, 2 sc in first sc; sc in next 15 [16, 17] sc, 2 sc in last sc, turn. *(19 [20, 21, 21] sc)*

Rows 8–10: Rep row 4.

Row 11: Ch 1, 2 sc in first st; sc in next 17 [18, 19, 19] sts, 2 sc in last sc, turn. *(21 [22, 23, 23] sc)*

Rows 12–14: Rep row 4.

Row 15: Ch 1, 2 sc in first st; sc in next 19 [20, 21, 21] sc, 2 sc in last sc, turn. *(23 [24, 25, 25] sc)*

Rows 16–18: Rep row 4.

For Size 2 Only
Fasten off and weave in ends.

Sizes 4, 6 & 8 Only
Row 19: Ch 1, 2 sc in first sc; sc in next 24 [25, 25] sc, 2 sc in last

sc, turn. *(26 [27, 27] sc)*

Rows 20–22: Rep row 4.

For Size 4 Only
Fasten off and weave in ends.

For Size 6 Only
Rows 23 & 24: Rep row 4.

Fasten off and weave in ends.

For Size 8 Only
Row 23: Ch 1, 2 sc in first sc; sc in next 25 sc, 2 sc in last sc, turn. *(29 sc)*

Rows 24–26: Rep row 4.

Fasten off and weave in ends.

ASSEMBLY
Hold Front and Back tog, carefully matching sts; with tapestry needle and A, using overcast st, sew pieces tog at left shoulder seam over 7 [8, 9, 10] sts, leaving 10 marked sts unsewn at back neckline. Sew right shoulder seam in same manner over 7 [8, 9, 10 sts]. With RS tog and matching center of last row of Sleeve to shoulder seam, sew 1 Sleeve into armhole. Rep for other Sleeve. With RS tog, sew Sleeve seams.

COLLAR
Row 1: Hold cardigan with RS facing you; with K hook, join A with sl st in first st on right front neck; ch 1, sc in same st as joining and in rem 3 sc along right front neck; sc in ends of next 3 row along right neck edge, sc in next 10 sc across back neck, sc in ends of next 3 row down left neck edge and in next 4 sc across left front neck, turn. *(24 sc)*

EDGINGS
Body Edging
Sc in first st of collar and in next 11 neckline sc, 2 sc in next sc;

sc in next 11 sc; work 26 [30, 32, 34] sc evenly spaced down right front edge, working in unused lps of beg ch, sc in each lp; working up left front edge, work 26 [30, 32, 34] sc evenly spaced; join in first sc.

Fasten off and weave in ends.

Hold cardigan with RS facing you; with H hook, join C in first st on right back neckline; ch 2 *(counts as a hdc),* 4 hdc in same st; sk next sc; 5 hdc in each rem sc; join in first ch of beg ch-2.

Fasten off and weave in ends.

Sleeve Edging
Hold 1 Sleeve with RS facing you and beg ch at top; with H hook,

join C in first unused lp of beg ch to left of seam; ch 2 *(counts as a hdc),* 4 hdc in same lp; working in rem unused lps, *sk next lp, 5 hdc in next lp; rep from * 6 [6, 7, 7] times; join with a sl st in first ch of beg ch-2.

Fasten off and weave in ends.

Rep on other sleeve.

FINISHING
On WS and with tapestry needle and A, sew hooks on left front edge and eyes directly opposite on right front edge, placing each under a 5-hdc group, beg at neck corner groups and leaving two 5-hdc groups between each closure. 🌿

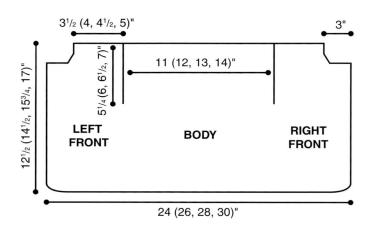

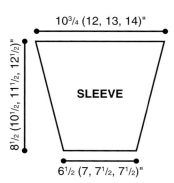

Santa's Boy Tricolor Pullover

DESIGN BY DONNA MAY

SKILL LEVEL
INTERMEDIATE

FINISHED SIZES
Instructions given fit child's size 2; changes for sizes 4, 6 and 8 are in [ ].

FINISHED GARMENT SIZES
Chest: 24 [26½, 29, 31½] inches

MATERIALS
TLC Lustre medium (worsted) weight yarn (5 oz/253 yds/141g per skein):
   1 skein each #5861 navy *(A)*, #5660 light sage *(B)* and #5289 copper *(C)*
Sizes F/5/3.75 and H/8/5mm crochet hooks or sizes needed to obtain gauge
Tapestry needle

GAUGE
With H hook in pattern: 13 sts and 15 rows = 4 inches

PATTERN NOTE
To change color, work last stitch until 2 loops remain on hook; with new color, yarn over and draw through 2 loops on hook. Cut old color.

Instructions

BACK
Note: Back is worked from bottom up. Carry unused colors up side of piece.

RIBBING
Row 1: With F hook and A, ch 8 [8, 8, 9]; sc in 2nd ch from hook and in each rem ch, turn. *(7 [7, 7, 8] sc)*

Row 2: Ch 1, working in **back lps** *(see Stitch Guide)* only, sc in each sc, turn.

Rows 3–38 [3–42, 3–46, 3–50]: Rep row 2.

Row 39 [43, 47, 51]: Rep row 2. At end of last row, do not turn. Change to H hook.

BODY
Row 1 (RS): Ch 1, working in ends of rows across long edge of ribbing, sc in each row, turn. *(39 [43, 47, 51] sc)*

Row 2: Ch 1, sc in each sc, changing to B in last sc, turn.

Row 3: Ch 1, sc in first sc, dc in next sc on 2nd row below, sc in next sc; *dc in next sc on 2nd row below; sc in next sc; rep from * across, turn.

Row 4: Rep row 2, changing to A in last sc, turn.

Rows 5–20 [5–24, 5–28, 5–32]: Rep rows 3 and 4, working 2 rows in each color in following sequence: A, C, A, B, A.

ARMHOLE SHAPING
Note: Continue to work in color pattern as established.

Row 21 [25, 29, 33]: Sl st in first [first 2, first 2, first 2] st(s), ch 1, work in st pattern as established to last [last 2 sts, last 2 sts, last 2] st(s), turn, leaving last st(s) unworked. *(37 [39, 43, 47] sts)*

Row 22 [26, 30, 34]: Ch 1, work in st pattern, turn.

Row 23 [27, 31, 35]: Sl st in first st, ch 1, work in st pattern last st, turn, leaving st unworked. *(35 [37, 41, 45] sts)*

For Sizes 2 & 4 Only
Rows 24–40 [28–44]: Ch 1, work in st pattern, turn.

Continue with Right Back Neck Shaping.

For Size 6 Only
Row 32: Ch 1, work in st pattern, turn.

Row 33: Sl st in first st, ch 1, work in st pattern to last st, turn, leaving last st unworked. *(39 sts)*

Rows 34–50: Rep row 32.

Continue with Right Back Neck Shaping.

For Size 8 Only
Row 36: Ch 1, work in st pattern, turn.

Row 37: Sl st in first st, ch 1, work in st pattern to last st, turn, leaving last st unworked. *(43 sts)*

Rows 38 & 39: Rep rows 36 and 37. *(41 sts at end of row 39)*

Rows 40–58: Rep row 36.

Continue with Right Back Neck Shaping

RIGHT BACK NECK SHAPING
Row 1: Ch 1, work in st pattern in first 10 [11, 12, 12] sts, turn, leaving rem sts unworked. *(10 [11, 12, 12] sts)*

Row 2: Sl st in first [first, first 2, first] st(s), ch 1, work in st pattern next 9 [10, 10, 11] sts, turn. *(9 [10, 10, 11] sts)*

RIGHT BACK SHOULDER SHAPING
Row 1 (RS): Sl st in first 4 [5, 5, 6] sts, ch 1, work in st pattern in next 5 sts, turn.

Row 2: Ch 1, work in st pattern in next 3 sts.

Fasten off and weave in all ends.

LEFT BACK NECK SHAPING
Row 1: Hold piece with RS facing you; sk next 14 [14, 14, 16] sts from Right Back Neck Shaping, join color in sequence in next st; ch 1, work in st pattern in next 10 [11, 12, 12] sts, turn. *(10 [11, 12, 12] sts)*

Row 2: Ch 1, work in st pattern in next 9 [10, 11, 11] sts, turn, leaving rem st unworked. *(9 [10, 11, 11] sts)*

LEFT BACK SHOULDER SHAPING
Row 1 (RS): Ch 1, work in st pattern in first 6 [7, 7, 8] sts, turn, leaving rem 3 [3, 4, 3] sts unworked, turn. *(6 [7, 7, 8] sts)*

Row 2: Sl st in first 3 [4, 4, 5] sts, ch 1, work st pattern in rem 3 sts.

Fasten off and weave in all colors.

FRONT
Work same as for Back through

row 23 [27, 31, 35]. *(35 [37, 41, 45] sts at end of last row)*

Rows 24–34 [28–36, 32–42, 36–48]: Ch 1, work in st pattern, turn.

LEFT FRONT NECK SHAPING
Row 1 (RS): Ch 1, work in st pattern in next 13 [14, 15, 16] sts, turn. *(13 [14, 15, 16] sts)*

Row 2 : Sl st in first st, ch 1, work in st pattern in rem 12 [13, 14, 15] sts, turn. *(12 [13, 14, 15] sts)*

Row 3: Ch 1, work across in st pattern to last st, turn, leaving last st unworked. *(11 [12, 13, 14] sts)*

Row 4: Sl st in first st, ch 1, work in st pattern in rem 10 [11, 12, 13] sts, turn. *(10 [11, 12, 13] sts)*

Row 5: Ch 1, work across in st pattern to last st, turn, leaving last st unworked. *(9 [10, 11, 12] sts)*

For Sizes 2 & 4 Only
Rows 6–40 [6–44]: Ch 1, work in st pattern across, turn.

Continue with Left Front Shoulder Shaping

For Sizes 6 & 8 Only
Row 6: Sl st in first st, ch 1, work in st pattern in rem 10 [11] sts, turn. *(10 [11] sts)*

Rows 7–50 [7–58]: Ch 1, work in st pattern across, turn.

Continue with Left Front Shoulder Shaping.

LEFT FRONT SHOULDER SHAPING
For Sizes 2 & 4 Only
Row 1 (WS): Ch 1, work in st pattern in first 5 sts, turn, leaving last 4 [5] sts unworked. *(5 sts)*

Row 2 (RS): Sl st in first 2 sts, ch 1, work in st pattern in rem 3 sts.

Fasten off and weave in all ends.

Continue with Right Front Neck Shaping.

For Sizes 6 & 8 Only
Row 1 (RS): Sl st in first 5 [6] sts, ch 1, work in st pattern in rem 5 sts, turn. *(5 sts)*

Row 2: Ch 1, work in st pattern in first 3 sts.

Fasten off, leaving last 2 sts unworked. Weave in all ends.

Continue with Right Front Neck Shaping.

RIGHT FRONT NECK SHAPING
Row 1 (RS): Hold piece with RS facing you; sk next 8 sts from Left Front Shoulder Shaping; join color in sequence yarn in next st, ch 1, beg in next st, work in st pattern in next 13 [14, 15, 16] sts, turn. *(13 [14, 15, 16] sts)*

Row 2: Ch 1, work in st pattern to last st, turn; leaving last st unworked. *(12 [13, 14, 15] sts)*

Row 3: Sl st in first st, ch 1, work in st pattern in rem 11 [12, 13, 14] sts, turn. *(11 [12, 13, 14] sts)*

Row 4: Ch 1, work in st pattern in first 10 [11, 12, 13] sts, turn, leaving last st unworked. *(10 [11, 12, 13] sts)*

Row 5: Sl st in first st, ch 1, work in st pattern in rem 9 [10, 11, 12] sts, turn. *(9 [10, 11, 12] sts)*

For Sizes 2 & 4 Only
Rows 6–40 [6–44]: Ch 1, work in st pattern across, turn.

Continue with Right Front Shoulder Shaping

For Sizes 6 & 8 Only
Row 6 (WS): Work in st pattern

across first 10 [11] sts, leave last st unworked; ch 1, turn. *(10 [11] sts)*

Rows 7–50 [7–58]: Ch 1, work in st pattern across, turn.

Continue with Right Front Shoulder Shaping

RIGHT FRONT SHOULDER SHAPING
For Sizes 2 & 4 Only
Row 1 (WS): Sl st in first 4 [5] sts, ch 1, work in st pattern in rem 5 sts, turn. *(5 sts)*

Row 2: Ch 1, work in st pattern in first 3 sts.

Fasten off, leaving last 2 sts unworked. Weave in all ends.

Sizes 6 & 8 Only
Row 1 (RS): Ch 1, work in st pattern in first 5 sts, turn, leaving rem 5 [6] sts unworked. *(5 sts)*

Row 2: Sl st in first 2 sts, ch 1, work in st pattern in rem 3 sts.

Fasten off and weave in ends.

SLEEVE
Make 2.

RIBBING
Row 1 (RS): With F hook and A, ch 6 [6, 6, 7]; working in **back lps** *(see Stitch Guide)*, sc in 2nd ch from hook and in each rem ch, turn. *(5 [5, 5, 6] sc)*

Row 2: Ch 1, working in back lps only, sc in each sc, turn.

Rows 3–25 [3–27, 3–27, 3–29]: Rep row 2. At end of last row, do not turn. Change to H hook.

BODY
Row 1 (RS): Ch 1, working in ends of rows across long edge of ribbing, sc in each row, turn. *(25 [27, 27, 29] sts)*

Row 2: Ch 1, sc in each sc, changing to B in last sc, turn.

Note: Work remainder of Sleeve in same color sequence as Body of pullover.

Rows 3–5 [3–6, 3–6, 3–7]: Ch 1, work in st pattern across, turn.

Row 6 [7, 7, 8]: Continuing with st pattern as established, work 2 sc in first st; work in st pattern to last st; 2 sc in last st, turn. *(27 [29, 29, 31] sts)*

Row 7 [8, 8, 9]: Ch 1, work in st pattern across, turn.

Rows 8–12 [9–13, 9–13, 10–15]: Rep row 7 [8, 8, 9].

Row 13 [14, 14, 16]: Rep row 6 [7, 7, 8]. *(29 [31, 31, 33] sts at end of row)*

Rows 14–19 [15–20, 15–20, 17–23]: Rep row 7 [8, 8, 9].

Row 20 [21, 21, 24]: Rep row 6 [7, 7, 8]. *(31 [33, 33, 35] sts at end of row)*

Rows 21–26 [22–28, 22–28, 25–31]: Rep row 7 [8, 8, 9].

For Sizes 2 & 4 Only
Continue with Cap Shaping.

For Sizes 6 & 8 Only
Row 29 [32]: Rep row 7 [8]. *(35 [37] sts at end of last row)*

Rows 30–36 [33–40]: Ch 1, work in st pattern across, turn.

Continue with Cap Shaping.

CAP SHAPING
*Note: For **sc dec**, draw up lp in 2 sts indicated, yo and draw through all 3 lps on hook.*

Rows 27 & 28 [29 & 30, 37 & 38, 41 & 42]: Ch 1, **sc dec** *(see Note)* in next 2 sts 1 [2, 2, 2] times; work in st pattern across, turn. *(29 [29, 31, 33] sts)*

Rows 29–32 [31–33, 39–41, 43–45]: Ch 1, sc dec in first 2 sts; work in st pattern to last 2 sts; sc dec in last 2 sts, turn. *(21 [23, 25, 27] sts)*

Row 33 [34, 42, 46]: Ch 1, work in st pattern across, turn.

Row 34 [35, 43, 47]: Ch 1, sc dec in first 2 sts, work in st pattern to last 2 sts; sc dec in last 2 sts, turn. *(19 [21, 23, 25] sts)*

Row 35 [36, 44, 48]: Ch 1, work in st pattern across, turn.

Rows 36–38 [37–41, 45–51, 49–57]: Rep rows 33 and 34 [34 and 35, 42 and 43, 46 and 47. *(15 [13, 13, 15] sts at end of last row)*

Rows 39–42 [42–44, 52–54, 58–60]: Rep row 34 [35, 43, 47]. *(7 [9, 9, 9] sts at end of last row)*

Fasten off and weave in all ends.

NECK RIBBING
Row 1: With H hook and A, ch 5; sc in first ch from hook and in each rem ch, turn. *(4 sc)*

Row 2: Ch 1, sc in back lp only

of each sc, turn.

Rows 3–92 [96, 96, 104]: Rep row 2.

Fasten off and weave in ends.

ASSEMBLY
Hold Front and Back with RS tog; sew shoulder seams. With RS tog, match center top of 1 Sleeve to 1 shoulder seam and sew Sleeve to Body. Rep for other Sleeve. Sew Sleeve and side seams.

NECKLINE EDGING
With H hook, join A with a sl st

in first st of right back neckline; ch 1, work 2 sc in end of each row on right back neck, 15 [15, 15, 17] sc across back neck sts, 2 sc in end of each row on left back neck, 9 [10, 10, 11] sc in row ends on left front neck, 9 sc across center front neck and 9 [10, 10, 11] sc in row ends on right front neck.

Fasten off and weave in ends.

FINISHING
Matching every other row end of collar to 1 st of Neckline Edging, sew Collar to Pullover. 🍂

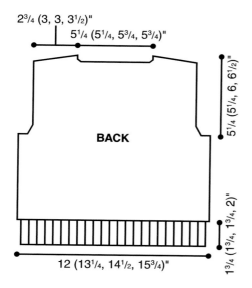

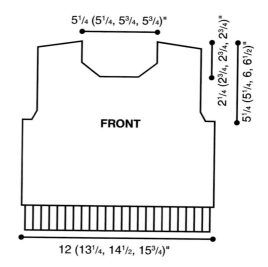

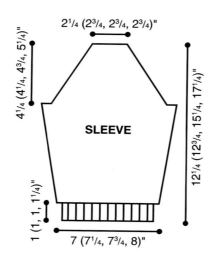

Easy Floral Gift Scarf

DESIGN BY SVETLANA AVRAKH

SKILL LEVEL
EASY

FINISHED SIZE
11 x 65 inches

MATERIALS
Patons Lacette fine
  (baby) weight yarn (1¾ oz/235
  yds/50g per skein):
    2 balls #30415 hint of rose *(A)*
    1 ball #30005 white whisper *(B)*
Sizes E/4/3.5mm and P/15mm
  crochet hooks or sizes needed
  to obtain gauge
Tapestry needle

GAUGE
With P hook: 8 sts = 4 inches

Instructions

SCARF
Row 1 (RS): With P hook and A,
ch 22; sc in 2nd ch from hook
and each rem ch, turn. *(21 sc)*

Row 2: Ch 3 *(counts as a dc on
this and following rows),* dc in
each rem sc, turn.

Row 3: Ch 1, sc in each dc and
in 3rd ch of turning ch-3, turn.

Rep rows 2 and 3 until piece
measures approximately 65
inches, ending with a row 2.

Fasten off and weave in ends.

FLOWER
Make 40.
Rnd 1: With E hook and B, ch 3;
join with a sl st to form a ring; ch

1, 10 sc in ring; join with a sl st in
first sc. Change to A by drawing
lp through; cut B.

Rnd 2: Sk first sc; *in next sc
work (sc, 4 dc, sc); sl st in next
sc; rep from * 4 times; join with a

sl st in first sc.

Fasten off and weave in all ends.

FINISHING
Sew flowers to both ends of Scarf
as desired. 🍂

Snow Maiden Hat & Scarf

DESIGNS BY RUTH G. SHEPARD

SKILL LEVEL ◼◻◻ EASY

FINISHED SIZES
Hat: 20 inches in circumference

Scarf: 5¾ x 56 inches, excluding Fringe

MATERIALS
Patons Divine bulky
(chunky) weight yarn (3½
oz/142 yds/100g per ball):
   1 ball #06006 icicle white *(A)*
Patons Allure super bulky (super
chunky) weight yarn (1¾ oz/47
yds/50g per ball):
   1 ball #04046 platinum *(B)*
Size N/15/10mm crochet hook or
   size needed to obtain gauge
Tapestry needle

GAUGE
2 dc = 1 inch

Instructions

HAT
Row 1 (RS): With A, ch 40; dc in 4th
ch from hook *(beg 3 sk chs count as
a dc)* and in each rem ch. *(39 dc)*

Fasten off.

Row 2: Join B with a sl st in 3rd
ch of beg 3 sk chs of row 1; ch 3,
dc in each rem dc. Fasten off.

Row 3: Join B in 3rd ch of beg
ch-3 of row 2; ch 2, sc in each
rem dc. Fasten off, leaving a 14-
inch end for sewing.

Row 4: Hold piece with RS facing
you and beg ch-40 at top; join A
in first unused lp of beg ch; ch 3,
working in rem unused lps of beg
ch, dc in each lp. Fasten off.

Row 5: Join B in 3rd ch of beg
ch-3 of row 4; ch 3, dc in each
rem dc. Fasten off.

Row 6: Join B in 3rd ch of beg
ch-3 of row 5; ch 3, dc in each
rem dc.

Row 7: Join A in 3rd ch of beg
ch-3 of row 6; ch 2 *(counts as a
sc on this and following row)*, sc
in each rem dc.

Row 8: Join A in 2nd ch of beg
ch-2 of row 7; ch 2, sc in each
rem sc.

Row 9: Join A in 2nd ch of beg
ch-2 of row 8; *ch 1, sl st in next
sc; rep from * across.

Fasten off and weave in ends.

FINISHING
With tapestry needle and
matching yarn, sew ends of rows
tog to form back seam. Weave
14-inch end through sts of row
3. Pull tightly to gather top of Hat
and secure end.

SCARF
Row 1 (RS): With A, ch 114; dc
in 4th ch from hook *(beg 3 sk chs
count as a dc)* and in each rem
ch. *(112 dc)*

Fasten off.

Row 2: Join B with a sl st in 3rd
ch of beg 3 sk chs of row 1; ch 3,
dc in each rem dc. Fasten off.

Row 3: Join A in 3rd ch of beg
ch-3 of row 2; ch 2, sc in each
rem dc. Fasten off.

Row 4: Hold piece with RS facing
you and beg ch-114 at top; join A
in first unused lp of beg ch; ch 3,
working in rem unused lps of beg
ch, dc in each lp. Fasten off.

Row 5: Join B in 3rd ch of beg
ch-3 of row 4; ch 3, dc in each
rem dc. Fasten off.

Row 6: Join A in 3rd ch of beg
ch-3 of row 5; ch 2 *(counts as a
sc)*, sc in each rem dc.

Fasten off and weave in ends.

FRINGE
For Fringe, cut 18-inch lengths of
A and B. For each knot of Fringe,
hold 2 strands of each color tog.
Fold strands in half. With crochet
hook, pull folded end through
end of first row on 1 short end of
scarf. Pull ends through folded
end and tighten knot. Tie knots
across each short end of scarf.
Trim ends even. 🍂

Snowball Hat & Scarf

DESIGNS BY KATHLEEN STUART

SKILL LEVEL ■■□□ EASY

FINISHED SIZES
Hat: 22 inches in circumference

Scarf: 6 x 53 inches

MATERIALS
Lion Brand Homespun bulky (chunky) weight yarn (6 oz/185 yds/170g per skein):
  1 ball each #302 colonial (A) and #309 deco (B)
Size J/10/6mm crochet hook or size needed to obtain gauge
Tapestry needle
Stitch markers

GAUGE
11 sts = 4 inches

SPECIAL STITCHES
Cluster (cl): Keeping last lp of each dc on hook, dc in 4 sts indicated, yo and draw through all 5 lps on hook.

7-double crochet cluster (7-dc cl): Keeping last lp of each dc on hook, dc in 7 sts indicated, yo and draw through all 8 lps on hook.

3-double crochet cluster (3-dc cl): Keeping last lp of each dc on hook, dc in 3 sts indicated, yo and draw through all 4 lps on hook.

Instructions

HAT
Note: Hat is worked in continuous rnds. Do not join unless specified; mark beg of rnds.

Rnd 1: Starting at top of Hat with

A, ch 2; 6 sc in 2nd ch from hook. *(6 sc)*

Rnd 2: In each st work (sc, dc). *(12 sts)*

Rnd 3: [Dc in next st, in next st work (sc, dc)] 6 times. *(18 sts)*

Rnd 4: *Sc in next st, dc in next st, in next st work (sc, dc); rep from * around. *(24 sts)*

Rnd 5: *Dc in next st, sc in next st, dc in next st, in next st work (sc, dc); rep from * around. *(30 sts)*

Rnd 6: *[Sc in next st, dc in next st] twice; in next st work (sc, dc); rep from * around. *(36 sts)*

Rnd 7: *[Dc in next st, sc in next st] twice; dc in next st, in next st work (sc, dc); rep from * around. *(42 sts)*

Rnd 8: *[Sc in next st, dc in next st] 3 times; in next st work (sc, dc); rep from * around. *(48 sts)*

Rnd 9: *[Dc in next st, sc in next st] 3 times; dc in next st, in next st work (sc, dc); rep from * around. *(54 sts)*

Rnd 10: *[Sc in next st, dc in next st] 4 times; in next st work (sc, dc); rep from * around. *(60 sts)*

Rnd 11: *Dc in next st, sc in next st; rep from * around. *(60 sts)*

Rnd 12: *Sc in next st, dc in next st; rep from * around.

Rnds 13–16: [Work rnds 11 and 12] twice.

Rnd 17: Sc in first 2 sts; *sk next 3 sts, 7 dc in next st—*shell made*; sk next 3 sts, sc in next 3 sts; rep from * 4 times; sk next 3 sts, 7 dc in next st; sk next 3 sts, sc in last st; change to B by drawing lp

through; cut A. *(6 shells)*

Rnd 18: Sl st in first sc, ch 2, **cl** *(see Special Stitches)* in first 4 sts; *ch 3, sc in next 3 sts, ch 3, **7-dc cl** *(see Special Stitches)* in next 7 sts; rep from * to last 6 sts; ch 3, sc in next 3 sts, ch 3, **3-dc cl** *(see Special Stitches)* in last 3 sts; join in 2nd ch of beg ch-2.

Rnd 19: Ch 2, 3 dc in next st; *sk next ch-3 sp, sc in next 3 sts, sk next ch-3 sp, 7 dc in next st; rep from * to last 2 ch-3 sps; sk next ch-3 sp, sc in next 3 sts, sk last ch-3 sp, 3 dc in next st; change to A by drawing lp through; cut B.

Rnd 20: Sc in 2nd ch of beg ch-2 and in next st; *ch 3, 7-dc cl in next 7 sts; ch 3, sc in next 3 sts; rep from * to 8 sts; ch 3, 7-dc cl in next 7 sts; ch 3, sc in last st.

Rnd 21: Working in **back lps** *(see Stitch Guide)* only, *sc in next 9 sts, 2 sc in next st; rep from * around. *(66 sc)*

Rnd 22: *[Sc in next st, dc in next st] 5 times; in next st work (sc, dc); rep from * around. *(72 sts)*

Rnd 23: *[Dc in next st, sc in next st] 5 times; dc in next st, in next st work (sc, dc); rep from * around. *(78 sts)*

Rnd 24: *[Sc in next st, dc in next st] 6 times; in next st work (sc, dc); rep from * around. *(84 sts)*

Rnd 25: *Dc in next st, sc in next st; rep from * around.

Rnd 26: *Sc in next st, dc in next st; rep from * around.

Rnd 27: Ch 1, working from left to right, work **reverse sc** *(see Stitch Guide)* in each st.

Fasten off and weave in ends.

SCARF

Row 1: With A, ch 152; sc in 2nd ch from hook; *dc in next ch, sc in next ch; rep from * across, turn. *(151 sts)*

Row 2: Ch 3 *(counts as a dc on this and following rows)*; *sc in next st, dc in next st; rep from * across, turn.

Row 3: Ch 1, sc in first dc; *dc in next st, sc in next st; rep from * across, turn.

Rows 4 & 5: Rep rows 2 and 3.

Row 6: Ch 1, sc in first 2 sts; *sk next 3 sts, 7 dc in next st; sk next 3 sts, sc in next 3 sts; rep from * to last 9 sts; sk next 3 sts, 7 dc in next st; sk next 3 sts, sc in last 2 sts, change to B by drawing lp through; cut A, turn.

Row 7: Ch 2, cl in first 4 sts; *ch 3, sc in next 3 sts, ch 3, 7-dc cl in next 7 sts; rep from * to last 7 sts; ch 3, sc in next 3 sts, ch 3, cl in next 4 sts, turn, leaving turning ch unworked.

Row 8: Ch 2, 4 dc in first st; *sk next ch-3 sp, sc in next 3 sts, sk next ch-3 sp, 7 dc in next st; rep from * to last 2 ch-3 sps; sk next ch-3 sp, sc in next 3 sts, sk last ch-3 sp, 4 dc in next st; change to A by drawing lp through; cut B, turn, leaving turning ch unworked.

Row 9: Ch 1, sc in first 2 sts, *ch 3, 7-dc cl in next 7 sts; ch 3, sc in next 3 sts; rep from * to last 9 sts; ch 3, 7-dc cl in next 7 sts; ch 3, sc in last 2 sts, turn.

Row 10: Rep row 3.

Rows 11–14: [Work rows 2 and 3] twice.

Fasten off and weave in ends. 🦋

Keep Warm Teddy Set

DESIGNS BY KATHLEEN STUART

SKILL LEVEL ■■□□
INTERMEDIATE

FINISHED SIZES
Hat: 18 inches in circumference

Scarf: 4 x 44 inches

Mittens: Child's size

MATERIALS
Lion Brand Wool Ease
  Sport fine (sport) weight yarn
  (5 oz/000 yds/140g per skein):
  2 skeins #232 woods print *(A)*
  small amount of black *(B)*
Size H/8/5mm crochet hook or
  size needed to obtain gauge
Tapestry needle
Stitch markers

GAUGE
18 sc = 4 inches

SPECIAL STITCHES
**Front post double crochet
(fpdc):** Yo, insert hook from front
to back to front around **post**
(see Stitch Guide) of st indicated, draw lp through, [yo, draw
through 2 lps on hook] twice.

**Back post double crochet
(bpdc):** Yo, insert hook from
back to front to back around
post *(see Stitch Guide)* of st indicated, draw lp through, [yo, draw
through 2 lps on hook] twice.

Popcorn (pc): 3 dc in st indicated; drop lp from hook, insert
hook in first dc, draw dropped lp
through st and lp on hook, ch 1.

Instructions

HAT
Rnd 1 (RS): With A, ch 80; join

with a sl st to form ring; ch 3
(counts as a dc), dc in each rem
ch; join with a sl st in 3rd ch of
beg ch-3. *(80 dc)*

Rnd 2: Ch 2 *(counts as a dc on
this and following rnds),* **fpdc**
(see Special Stitches) around
next dc; ***bpdc** *(see Special
Stitches)* around next st, fpdc
around next st; rep from *
around; join with a sl st in 2nd ch
of beg ch-2.

Rnd 2: Ch 2, fpdc around
next st, *bpdc around next st,
fpdc around next st; rep from *
around; join with a sl st in 2nd ch
of beg ch-2.

Rnds 3–6: Rep rnd 2.

Rnd 7: Ch 1, sc in same ch as
joining and in each rem st. Do
not join.

Note: *Remainder of Hat is
worked in continuous rnds. Do
not join unless specified; mark
beg of rnds.*

Rnd 8: *Sc in **front lp** *(see Stitch
Guide)* of next sc, sc in **back lp**
(see Stitch Guide) of next sc; rep
from * around.

Rnds 9–18: Rep rnd 8.

Rnd 19: [Sc in front lp of next
sc, sc in back lp of next st] 18
times; change to B by drawing
lp through; drop A, **pc** *(see
Special Stitches)* in next sc;
change to A; carry B; sc in back
lp of next sc, sc in front lp of
next sc, sc in back lp of next sc;
change B; drop A; pc in next sc;
change to A; cut B; sc in back

lp of next sc; **sc in front lp of
next sc, sc in back lp of next sc;
rep from ** to first sc.

Rnd 20: *Sc in front lp of next st,
sc in back lp of next st; rep from
* around.

Rnds 21–24: Rep rnd 20.

Note: *For **sc dec**, draw up lp
in 2 sts indicated, yo and draw
through all 3 lps on hook.*

Rnd 25: Working in front lp/
back lp pattern as established,
*sc in next 8 sts, **sc dec** *(see
Note)* in next 2 sc; rep from *
around. *(72 sc)*

Rnd 26: Working in pattern as
established, *sc in next 7 sts, sc
dec; rep from * around. *(64 sc)*

Rnds 27–30: Rep rnd 20.

Rnd 31: Working in pattern as
established, *sc in next 6 sts, sc
dec; rep from * around. *(56 sc)*

Rnd 32: Working in pattern as
established, *sc in next 5 sts, sc
dec; rep from * around. *(48 sc)*

Rnd 33: Working in pattern as
established, *sc in next 4 sts, sc
dec; rep from * around. *(40 sc)*

Rnd 34: Working in pattern as
established, *sc in next 3 sts, sc
dec; rep from * around. *(32 sc)*

Rnd 35: Working in pattern as
established, *sc in next 2 sts, sc
dec; rep from * around. *(24 sc)*

Rnd 36: Working in pattern as
established, *sc in next st, sc

Rnd 2: 2 sc in each sc. *(12 sc)*

Rnd 3: [Sc in next sc, 2 sc in next sc] 6 times. *(18 sc)*

Rnd 4: [Sc in next 2 sc, 2 sc in next sc] 6 times. *(24 sc)*

Rnd 5: Sc in each sc.

Rnds 6 & 7: Rep rnd 5.

Fasten off, leaving a 10-inch end for sewing. Weave in other end.

FINISHING

Step 1: On Hat, with tapestry needle, weave long end through sts on rnd 37 and gather to close opening. Secure end.

Step 2: Referring to photo for placement, sew Muzzle to Hat on rnd 19, just below eyes.

Step 3: With tapestry needle and B, embroider nose and mouth on Muzzle using straight sts.

Step 4: Flatten Ears and sew to sides of Hat, having bottom of Ears near rnd 20.

SCARF
Note: *Scarf is worked in continuous rnds. Do not join unless specified; mark beg of rnds.*

Rnd 1: With A, ch 13; 2 sc in 2nd ch from hook; sc in next 10 chs, 4 sc in last ch; working on opposite in unused lps of beg ch, sc in next 10 lps, 2 sc in last lp. *(28 sc)*

Rnd 2: *Sc in front lp of next sc, 2 sc in back lp of next sc; [sc in front lp of next sc, sc in back lp of next sc] 6 times; rep from * once. *(30 sc)*

Rnd 3: *Sc in front lp of next sc, sc in back lp of next sc, 2 sc in back lp of next sc; [sc in front lp of next sc, sc in back lp of next sc] 6 times; rep from * once. *(32 sc)*

dec; rep from * around. *(16 sc)*

Rnd 37: Working in pattern as established, [sc dec] 8 times. *(8 sc)*

Fasten off, leaving 8-inch end for sewing. Weave in other end.

MUZZLE
Note: *Muzzle is worked in continuous rnds. Do not join unless specified; mark beg of rnds.*

Rnd 1: With A, ch 2; 6 sc in 2nd ch from hook.

Rnd 2: 2 sc in each sc. *(12 sc)*

Rnd 3: [Sc in next sc, 2 sc in next

sc] 6 times. *(18 sc)*

Rnd 4: [Sc in next 2 sc, 2 sc in next sc] 6 times. *(24 sc)*

Rnd 5: Sc in each sc.

Rnd 6: Rep rnd 5.

Fasten off, leaving a 10-inch end for sewing.

EAR
Make 2.
Note: *Ear is worked in continuous rnds. Do not join unless specified; mark beg of rnds.*

Rnd 1 (RS): With A, ch 2; 6 sc in 2nd ch from hook.

Rnd 4: *Sc in front lp of next sc, sc in back lp of next sc, sc in front lp of next sc, 2 sc in back lp of next sc; [sc in front lp of next sc, sc in back lp of next sc] 6 times; rep from * once. *(34 sc)*

Rnd 5: *[Sc in front lp of next sc, sc in back lp of next sc] twice; 2 sc in back lp of next sc; [sc in front lp of next sc, sc in back lp of next sc] 6 times; rep from * once. *(36 sc)*

Rnd 6: *[Sc in front lp of next sc, sc in back lp of next sc] twice; sc in front lp of next sc, 2 sc in back lp of next sc; [sc in front lp of next sc, sc in back lp of next sc] 6 times; rep from * once. *(38 sc)*

Rnd 7: [Sc in front lp of next sc, sc in back lp of next sc] 3 times; 2 sc in back lp of next sc; sc in front lp of next sc, sc in back lp of next sc; change to B by drawing lp through; drop A; pc in next sc; change to A; carry B; sc in back lp of next sc, sc in front lp of next sc, sc in back lp of next sc; change to B; drop A; pc in next sc; change to A; cut B; [sc in front lp of next sc, sc in back lp of next sc] 5 times; 2 sc in back lp of next sc; [sc in front lp of next sc, sc in back lp of next sc] 6 times.

Rnd 8: *Sc in front lp of next st, sc in back lp of next st; rep from * around. *(40 sc)*

Rnds 9–138: Rep rnd 8.

Note: *For **sc dec**, draw up lp in 2 sts indicated, yo and draw through all 3 lps on hook.*

Rnd 139: [Sc in front lp of next sc, sc in back lp of next sc] 3 times; **sc dec** *(see Note)* in next 2 sc; sc in front lp of next sc, sc in back lp of next sc; change to B; drop A; pc in next sc; change to A; carry B; sc in

back lp of next sc, sc in front lp of next sc, sc in back lp of next sc; change to B; drop A; pc in next sc; change to A; cut B; [sc in front lp of next sc, sc in back lp of next sc] 5 times; sc dec in next 2 sc; [sc in front lp of next sc, sc in back lp of next sc] 6 times. *(38 sc)*

Rnd 140: *[Sc in front lp of next sc, sc in back lp of next sc] twice; sc in front lp of next sc, sc dec; [sc in front lp of next sc, sc in back lp of next sc] 6 times; rep from * once. *(36 sc)*

Rnd 141: *[Sc in front lp of next sc, sc in back lp of next sc] twice; sc dec; [sc in front lp of

next sc, sc in back lp of next sc] 6 times; rep from * once. *(34 sc)*

Rnd 142: *Sc in front lp of next sc, sc in back lp of next sc, sc in front lp of next sc, sc dec; [sc in front lp of next sc, sc in back lp of next sc] 6 times; rep from * once. *(32 sc)*

Rnd 143: *Sc in front lp of next sc, sc in back lp of next sc, sc dec; [sc in front lp of next sc, sc in back lp of next sc] 6 times; rep from * once. *(30 sc)*

Rnd 144: *Sc in front lp of next sc, sc dec; [sc in front lp of next sc, sc in back lp of next sc] 6 times; rep from * once. *(28 sc)*

Joining row: Flatten rnd 144; working through back lps of sc in front and front lps of sc in back at same time, sl st in each sc.

Fasten off and weave in all ends.

MUZZLE
Make 2.
Note: Muzzle is worked in continuous rnds. Do not join unless specified; mark beg of rnds.

Rnd 1: With A, ch 2; 6 sc in 2nd ch from hook.

Rnd 2: 2 sc in each sc. *(12 sc)*

Rnd 3: [Sc in next sc, 2 sc in next sc] 6 times. *(18 sc)*

Rnd 4: Sc in each sc.

Rnd 5: Rep rnd 4.

Fasten off, leaving a 10-inch end for sewing.

EAR
Make 4.
Rnd 1: With A, ch 2; 6 sc in 2nd ch from hook.

Rnd 2: 2 sc in each sc. *(12 sc)*

Rnd 3: [Sc in next sc, 2 sc in next sc] 6 times. *(18 sc)*

Rnd 4: Sc in each sc.

Rnds 5 & 6: Rep rnd 4.

Fasten off, leaving a 10-inch end for sewing.

FINISHING
Step 1: Referring to photo for placement, sew Muzzles to ends of Scarf, just below eyes.

Step 2: With tapestry needle and B, embroider nose and mouth on each Muzzle using straight sts.

Step 3: Flatten Ears and sew to sides of Scarf at both ends.

MITTENS

RIGHT MITTEN
Rnd 1: With A, ch 30; join with a sl st to form ring; ch 3 *(counts as a dc)*, dc in each rem ch; join with a sl st in 3rd ch of beg ch-3. *(30 dc)*

Rnd 2: Ch 2 *(counts as a dc on this and following rnds)*, fpdc around next dc; *bpdc around next dc, fpdc around next dc; rep from * around; join with a sl st in 2nd ch of beg ch-2.

Rnds 3–5: Rep rnd 2.

Rnd 6: Ch 1, sc in same ch as joining and in next 3 sts, 2 sc in next st; *sc in next 4 sts, 2 sc in next st; rep from * around. Do not join.

Note: Remainder of mitten is worked in continuous rnds. Do not join unless specified; mark beg of rnds.

Rnd 7: *Sc in front lp of next sc, sc in back lp of next sc; rep from * around. *(36 sc)*

Rnds 8–13: Rep rnd 7.

Rnd 14: Ch 6, sk first 10 sc—*thumb opening made*; *sc in front lp of next sc, sc in back lp of next sc; rep from * around.

Rnd 15: Sc in first 6 chs; *sc in front lp of next sc, sc in back lp of next sc; rep from * around. *(32 sc)*

Rnds 16–23: Rep rnd 7.

Rnd 24: [Sc in front lp of next sc, sc in back lp of next sc] 12 times; change to B by drawing lp through; drop A; pc in next sc; change to A; carry B; sc in back lp of next sc sc in front lp of next sc sc in back lp of next sc; change to B; drop A; pc in next sc; change to A; cut B; sc in back lp of next sc, sc in front lp of next sc, sc in back lp of next sc.

Rnds 25–27: Rep rnd 7.

Note: For sc dec, draw up lp in 2 sts indicated, yo and draw through all 3 lps on hook.

Rnd 28: Working in front lp/back lp pattern as established, *sc in next st; *sc in next 3 sts, **sc dec** *(see Note)* in next 2 sc; rep from * to last st; sc in last st. *(26 sc)*

Rnd 29: Working in pattern as established, sc in first sc; *sc in next 2 sc, sc dec; rep from * to last sc; sc in last sc. *(20 sc)*

Rnd 30: Working in pattern as established, sc in first sc; *sc in next sc, sc dec; rep from * to last sc; sc in last sc.

Fasten off, leaving 10-inch end for sewing. Weave in other ends.

THUMB
Note: Thumb is worked in continuous rnds. Do not join unless specified; mark beg of rnds.

Rnd 1: Join A in first sk sc on rnd 13; ch 1, sc in same sc and in next 9 sk sc; working in unused lp on opposite side of beg ch-6 of rnd 14, sc in each lp. *(16 sc)*

Rnd 2: Sc in each sc.

Rnd 3: [Sc in next 6 sc, sc dec] twice. *(14 sc)*

Rnd 4: Sc in each sc.

Rnds 5–10: Rep rnd 4.

Rnd 11: [Sc dec] 7 times.

Fasten off, leaving 10-inch end for sewing.

MUZZLE

Note: *Muzzle is worked in continuous rnds. Do not join unless specified; mark beg of rnds.*

Rnd 1: With A, ch 2; 6 sc in 2nd ch from hook. *(6 sc)*

Rnd 2: 2 sc in each sc. *(12 sc)*

Rnd 3: Sc in each sc.

Rnd 4: Rep rnd 3.

Fasten off, leaving a 10-inch end for sewing. Weave in other end.

EAR
Make 2.
Note: *Ear is worked in continuous rnds. Do not join unless specified; mark beg of rnds.*

Rnd 1 (RS): With A, ch 2; 6 sc in 2nd ch from hook.

Rnd 2: 2 sc in each sc. *(12 sc)*

Rnd 3: Sc in each sc.

Rnd 4: Rep rnd 3.

Fasten off, leaving a 10-inch end for sewing. Weave in other end.

LEFT MITTEN
Rnds 1–23: Work same as rnds 1–23 of Right Mitten.

Rnd 24: [Sc in front lp of next sc, sc in back lp of next sc] 5 times; change to B by drawing lp through; drop A; pc in next sc; change to A; carry B; sc in back lp of next sc sc in front lp of next sc sc in back lp of next sc; change to B; drop A; pc in next sc; change to A; cut B; sc in back lp of next sc; *sc in front lp of next sc, sc in back lp of next sc; rep from * around.

Rnds 25–30: Rep rnds 25–30 of Right Mitten.

THUMB
Work same as Thumb for Right Mitten.

MUZZLE
Work same as Muzzle for Right Mitten.

EAR
Make 2.
Work same as Ear for Right Mitten.

FINISHING
Step 1: On each Mitten, with tapestry needle, weave end left for sewing through sts on rnd 30 and gather to close opening. Secure end. Rep on end of each Thumb.

Step 2: Flatten Ears and sew to sides of mitten near rnds 27–29.

Step 3: With tapestry needle and B, embroider nose and mouth on Muzzle using straight sts. ❦

Stocking Stuffer Scrubbie

DESIGN BY ELAINE BARTLETT

SKILL LEVEL EASY

FINISHED SIZE
7 x 7 inches

MATERIALS
Lily Sugar 'n Cream
  medium (worsted) weight
  cotton yarn (solids: 2½ oz/120
  yds/70g; ombrés: 2 oz/95
  yds/56g per ball):
    1 ball #00095 red *(A)*
    small amount each #00062
      emerald *(B)* and #00001
      white *(C)*
Size H/8/5mm crochet hook or
  size needed to obtain gauge
Tapestry needle
Stitch marker
Purchased dish scrubbie about
  3½ inches in diameter

GAUGE
Gauge is not important for this
project.

Instructions

Rnd 1 (RS): With A make slip
knot on hook and join with sc
through mesh along side of
scrubbie, work 31 more sc evenly
spaced around scrubbie; join
with a sl st in first sc. *(32 sc)*

Rnd 2: Ch 1, sc in same sc and
in next 3 sc; *2 hdc in next sc; 2
dc in next sc; ch 3—*corner sp
made*; 2 dc in next sc, 2 hdc in
next sc; sc in next 4 sc; rep from
* twice; 2 hdc in next sc; 2 dc in
next sc; ch 3—*corner sp made*;
2 dc in next sc, 2 hdc in next sc;

join with a sl st in first sc.

Rnd 3: Ch 3 *(counts as a dc on
this and following rnds),* *dc in
each st to next corner ch-3 sp; in
corner ch-3 sp work (2 dc, ch 3,
2 dc)—*corner made;* rep from * 3
times; dc in each st to beg ch-3;
join in 3rd ch of beg ch-3.

Fasten off.

Rnd 4: Join B in any corner ch-3
sp; ch 3, in same sp work (dc, ch
3, 2 dc); *dc in each dc to next
corner ch-3 sp; in corner ch-3 sp

work corner; rep from * twice; dc
in each dc to beg ch-3; join in 3rd
ch of beg ch-3.

Fasten off.

Rnd 5: With C make slip knot
on hook and join with sc in any
corner ch-3 sp; 3 sc in same sp;
*sc in each dc to next corner ch-
3 sp; 4 sc in corner ch-3 sp; rep
from * twice; sc in each dc to first
sc; join in first sc.

Fasten off and weave in all ends.

Necklaces to Give

FLORAL PENDANT NECKLACE

DESIGN BY
MELODY MACDUFFEE

SKILL LEVEL EASY

FINISHED SIZE
2 inches in diameter

MATERIALS
South Maid size 10 crochet
   cotton (white: 400 yds per ball;
   solids: 350 yds per ball):
      1 ball each #1 white *(A)* and
      #493 French rose *(B)*
Size 7/1.65mm steel crochet hook
   or size needed to obtain gauge
Elite Better Beads Ball Necklace
   (or Omega-style choker of
   choice)
Jump ring

GAUGE
Rnds 1–4 = 1 inch

Instructions

PENDANT
Rnd 1 (RS): With A, ch 4; join
with a sl st to form ring; 12 sc in
ring; join with a sl st in first sc.

Rnd 2: *In next sc work (sc, hdc,
3 dc, hdc, sc)—*petal made*; sl st
in next sc; rep from * 4 times; in
next sc work (sc, hdc, 3 dc, hdc,
sc)—*petal made*; join with a sl st
in joining sl st. *(6 petals)*

Rnd 3: Working in back of petals
made on previous rnd, [ch 2, sl st
in next sl st] 5 times; ch 2; join in
joining sl st.

Rnd 4: *In next ch-2 sp work
(sc, hdc, 5 dc, hdc, sc)—*large*

petal made; sl st in next sl st; rep * 4 times; in next ch-2 sp work (sc, hdc, 5 dc, hdc, sc)—*large petal made*; join in joining sl st. Fasten off.

Rnd 5: Join B in any sl st; working behind petals made on previous rnd, [ch 3, sl st in next sl st] 5 times; ch 3; join in joining sl st.

Rnd 6: *In next ch-3 sp work (4 sc, 2 hdc); hdc in next sl st, 7 dc in next ch- sp; hdc in next sl st, in next ch-3 sp work (2 hdc, 4 sc); rep from * once; join in **back lp** *(see Stitch Guide)* of first sc.

Rnd 7: Ch 1, sc in same lp as joining; working in back lps only, sc in next 2 sts, 2 sc in next st; sc in next 6 sts, 3 sc in next st; sc in next 6 sts, 2 sc in next st; sc in next 6 sts, 3 sc in next st; sc in next 3 sts; join in first sc. Fasten off.

Rnd 8: Join A in first sc of any 3-sc group; ch 1, 2 sc in same sc; sc in next st, 2 sc in next st; sc in next 4 sts, 2 sc in next st; sc in next 12 sts, 2 sc in next st; sc in next 4 sts, 2 sc in next st; sc in next st, 2 sc in next st; sc in next 4 sts, 2 sc in next st; sc in next 12 sts, 2 sc in next st; sc in next 4 sts; join in first sc.

Rnd 9: Ch 1, working over sc of rnd 8 into sts on 2nd row below, sc in each st; join in first sc.

Rnd 10: *Ch 2, sk next sc, sl st in back lp of next sc; rep from * to last sc; ch 2, sk last sc; join in joining sl st.

Rnd 11: In each ch-2 sp work [2 sc, ch 3, sl st in **front lp** *(see Stitch Guide)* of last sc made, sc]; join in first sc.

Fasten off and weave in all ends.

FINISHING
Join jump ring to top center point of pendant and slide over necklace.

TOUCH OF SPARKLE NECKLACE
DESIGN BY NAZANIN FARD

SKILL LEVEL INTERMEDIATE

FINISHED SIZE
18 inches

MATERIALS
DMC Cébélia size 10 crochet cotton (284 yds per ball):
  1 ball #0002 ecru *(A)*
Kreinik Metallic Ombré (100m per spool):
  1 spool #1700 *(B)*
Size 0/2.50mm steel hook or size needed to obtain gauge
Tapestry needle
Create-A-Craft, Plated E Beads, 15g per package #80221-92, 141 beads needed

Darice Jewelry Designer, 11mm spring-ring clasp and ring set
Beading needle with a large enough eye for both fibers to pass through

GAUGE
With 2 strands held tog: 28 sc = 4 inches

Instructions

Note: *Thread beading needle with both fibers. String clasp and 34 beads onto fibers. String on ring.*

Row 1 (RS): Ch 121; sc in 2nd ch from hook, sc in each rem ch, turn.

Row 2: Slide clasp close to work; ch 1, sc in first sc; * slide bead up, sc in next sc; rep from * to last sc; slide ring close to work, sc in last sc, turn.

Row 3: Ch 1, sc in each sc, turn.

Row 4: Ch 1, sc in next 20 sc; *ch 3, slide 3 beads up, sl st in 3rd ch, ch 3, sk next sc, sc in next 2 sc; rep from * to last 20 sc; sc in last 20 sc.

Fasten off and weave in ends.

GOLDEN LEAVES NECKLACE
DESIGN BY NAZANIN FARD

SKILL LEVEL
INTERMEDIATE

FINISHED SIZE
19 inches long

MATERIALS
DMC Cébélia size 10 crochet cotton (284 yds per ball):
   1 ball #0002 ecru *(A)*
Kreinik Metallic Ombré (100m per spool):
   1 spool #1900 *(B)*
Size 0/2.50mm steel hook or size needed to obtain gauge

Tapestry needle
Blue Moon beads G spacer leaves, 40 pieces per package, 34 needed
Darice Jewelry Designer, 11mm lobster-claw clasp and ring set
Beading needle with a large enough eye for both fibers to pass through

GAUGE
With 2 strands held tog: 28 sc = 4 inches

Instructions

Note: *Thread beading needle with both fibers. String clasp and 34 beads onto fibers. String on ring.*

Make slip knot on hook and sl st in ring; *ch 3, [yo, insert hook in first ch made, draw lp through, yo, draw through 2 lps on hook] twice; yo and draw through all 3 lps on hook; slide bead up, ch 3,

bead up; ch 3, [yo, insert hook in first ch made, draw lp through, yo, draw through 2 lps on hook] twice; yo and draw through all 3 lps on hook; slide clasp up; ch 1.

Fasten off and weave in ends.

GIFT OF TIME NECKLACE
DESIGN BY
RUTH G. SHEPARD

SKILL LEVEL ◼◼◻◻
EASY

FINISHED SIZE
18 inches

MATERIALS
Patons Allure super bulky (super chunky) weight yarn (1¾ oz/47 yds/50g per ball):
　　1 ball #04208 turquoise
Size I/9/5.5mm crochet hook or size needed to obtain gauge
Tapestry needle
1 x 1⅞ inches craft watch with slot at each end for attaching watchband.

GAUGE
3 chs = 1 inch

Instructions

NECKLACE
With A, ch 41; sl st in 11th ch from hook; [ch 11, sl st in 11th ch from hook] twice; ch 30. Fasten off.

FINISHING
Hold watch with RS facing you; pull 1 end of piece through slot at bottom of watch; pull end through slot at top of watch, allowing piece to encircle watch. Pull rem end of piece through bottom slot of watch; pull through slot at top of watch, allowing piece to encircle watch. Tie ends of piece tog. 🌿

yo, insert hook in first ch made, draw lp through, yo, draw through 2 lps on hook; slide 2 beads up; rep from * 10 times; ch 3, [yo,

insert hook in first ch made, draw lp through, yo, draw through 2 lps on hook] twice; yo and draw through all 3 lps on hook; slide

Sleepy Bear Huggins

DESIGN BY DEBBIE TABOR

SKILL LEVEL
INTERMEDIATE

FINISHED SIZE
23 inches tall

MATERIALS
Red Heart Symphony
  medium (worsted) weight yarn
  (3½ oz/310 yds/100g
  per skein):
    2 skeins #4904 earth brown *(A)*
TLC Amore medium (worsted)
  weight yarn (6 oz/278 yds/170g
  per skein):
    1 skein each #3823 lake
      blue *(B)*, #3103 vanilla *(C)*,
      #3005 sand *(D)*, #3002
      black *(E)*, #3908
      raspberry *(F)*
Size H/8/5mm crochet hook or
  size needed to obtain gauge
Tapestry needle
Polyester fiberfill
Stitch markers

GAUGE
12 sts = 3 inches

Instructions

HEAD & BODY

NOSE
Note: *Nose is worked in continuous rnds. Do not join unless specified; mark beg of rnds.*

Rnd 1 (RS): With B, ch 4; join with a sl st to form ring; 2 sc in each ch. *(8 sc)*

Rnd 2: 2 sc in each sc. *(16 sc)*

Rnd 3: Sc in each sc.

Rnd 4: Sc in each sc. Change to C by drawing lp through; cut B.

Rnd 5: [Sc in next sc, 2 sc in next sc] 8 times. *(24 sc)*

Rnd 6: Rep rnd 3.

Rnd 7: [Sc in next sc, 2 sc in next sc] 12 times. *(36 sc)*

Rnds 8–11: Rep rnd 3.

Rnd 12: [Sc in next sc, sk next sc, sc in next sc] 12 times. *(24 sc)*

Rnd 13: Rep rnd 3. Change to A; cut C.

Rnd 14: Rep rnd 3.

Rnd 15: Rep rnd 7.

Rnd 16: Rep rnd 3.

Rnd 17: [Sc in next sc, 2 sc in next sc, sc in next sc] 12 times. *(48 sc)*

Rnd 18: Rep rnd 3.

Rnd 19: [Sc in next sc, 2 sc in next sc, sc in next sc] 16 times. *(64 sc)*

Rnds 20–24: Rep rnd 3.

Rnd 25: [Sc in next 2 sc, sk next sc, sc in next sc] 16 times. *(48 sc)*

Rnds 26–28: Rep rnd 3.

Rnd 29: [Sc in next 2 sc, sk next sc, sc in next sc] 12 times. *(36 sc)*

Rnds 30–32: Rep rnd 3.

Rnd 33: [Sc in next 2 sc, sk next sc, sc in next sc] 9 times. *(27 sc)*

Rnds 34–40: Rep rnd 3.

Rnd 41: [Sc in next sc, 2 sc in next sc, sc in next sc] 9 times. *(36 sc)*

Rnd 42: Rep rnd 3.

Rnd 43: [Sc in next sc, 2 sc in next sc, sc in next sc] 12 times. *(48 sc)*

Rnds 44–48: Rep rnd 3.

Rnd 49: [Sc in next sc, 2 sc in next sc, sc in next sc] 16 times. *(64 sc)*

Rnds 50–64: Rep rnd 3.

Rnd 65: [Sc in next 2 sc, sk next sc, sc in next sc] 16 times. *(48 sc)*

Rnds 66–68: Rep rnd 3.

Rnd 69: [Sc in next 2 sc, sk next sc, sc in next sc] 12 times. *(36 sc)*

Rnd 70: Rep rnd 3.

Stuff with fiberfill and continue to stuff as you work rem rnds.

Rnd 71: [Sc in next 2 sc, sk next sc, sc in next sc] 9 times. *(27 sc)*

Rnd 72: [Sc in next sc, sk next sc, sc in next sc] 9 times. *(18 sc)*

Rnd 73: [Sc in next sc, sk next sc, sc in next sc] 6 times. *(12 sc)*

Rnd 74: [Sc in next sc, sk next sc, sc in next sc] 4 times. *(8 sc)*

Rnd 75: [Sc in next sc, sk next sc] 4 times. *(4 sc)*

Rnd 76: [Sl st in next sc, sk next sc] twice.

Fasten off and weave in all ends.

LIP
With A, ch 16; sc in 2nd ch from hook and in each rem ch.

Fasten off and weave in ends.

EAR
Make 2 each with A and C.
Row 1 (RS): Ch 8; sc in 2nd ch from hook and in each rem ch, turn. *(7 sc)*

Row 2: Ch 1, sc in each sc, turn.

Row 3: Rep row 2.

Note: *For **sc dec**, draw up lp in 3 sts indicated, yo and draw through all 4 lps on hook.*

Row 4: Ch 1, sc in next 2 sc, **sc dec** *(see Note)* in next 3 sc; sc in next 2 sc, turn. *(5 sc)*

Note: *For **5-sc dec**, draw up lp in 5 sts indicated, yo and draw through all 4 lps on hook.*

Row 5: Ch 1, **5-sc dec** *(see Note)* in 5 sc.

Fasten off and weave in ends.

FOOT & LEG
Make 2.
Note: *Piece is worked in continuous rnds. Do not join unless specified; mark beg of rnds.*

Rnd 1 (RS): With A, ch 4; join with a sl st to form a ring; 2 sc in each ch. *(8 sc)*

Rnd 2: 2 sc in each sc. *(16 sc)*

Rnd 3: 2 sc in each sc. *(32 sc)*

Rnd 4: Sc in each sc.

Rnds 5–13: Rep rnd 4.

Rnd 14: [Sc in next 2 sc, sk next sc, sc in next sc] 8 times. *(24 sc)*

Rnds 15–38: Rep rnd 4.

Fasten off and weave in ends.

HAND & ARM
Make 2.
Note: *Piece is worked in continuous rnds. Do not join unless specified; mark beg of rnds.*

Rnd 1 (RS): With A, ch 4; join with a sl st to form a ring; 2 sc in each ch. *(8 sc)*

Rnd 2: 2 sc in each sc. *(16 sc)*

Rnd 3: [2 sc in next 2 sc, sc in next sc] 8 times. *(24 sc)*

Rnd 4: Sc in each sc.

Rnds 5–11: Rep rnd 4.

Rnd 12: [Sc in next 2 sc, sk next sc, sc in next sc] 6 times. *(18 sc)*

Rnds 13–25: Rep rnd 4.

Stuff with fiberfill and continue to stuff as you work rem rnds.

Rnd 26: [Sc in next sc, sk next sc, sc in next sc] 6 times. *(12 sc)*

Rnd 27: [Sc in next sc, sk next sc, sc in next sc] 4 times. *(8 sc)*

Rnd 28: [Sc in next sc, sk next sc] 4 times. *(4 sc)*

Rnd 29: [Sl st in next sc, sk next sc] twice.

Fasten off and weave in ends.

TAIL
Note: *Piece is worked in continuous rnds. Do not join unless specified; mark beg of rnds.*

Rnd 1: With A, ch 4; join with a sl st to form ring; 2 sc in each ch. *(8 sc)*

Rnd 2: 2 sc in each sc. *(16 sc)*

Rnd 3: Sc in each sc.

Rnds 4–6: Rep rnd 4.

Fasten off and weave in ends.

TOE PAD
Make 6.
With C, ch 4; join with a sl st to form ring; ch 1, 11 sc in ring; join in first sc.

Fasten off and weave in ends.

HEEL PAD
Make 2.
Rnd 1: With C, ch 4; join with a sl st to form ring; ch 1, 11 sc in ring. Do not join.

Rnd 2: 2 sc in each sc. *(22 sc)*

Fasten off and weave in ends.

TUMMY
Row 1 (RS): With B, ch 4; sc in 2nd ch from hook, 2 sc in next ch; sc in next ch, turn. *(4 sc)*

Row 2: Ch 1, 2 sc in first sc; sc in next 2 sc, 2 sc in last sc, turn. *(6 sc)*

Row 3: Ch 1, [2 sc in next sc, sc in next sc, 2 sc in next sc] twice, turn. *(10 sc)*

Row 4: Ch 1, sc in each sc, turn.

Row 5: Rep row 4.

Row 6: Ch 1, sc in first sc, in next sc work (hdc, dc, hdc); sc in next sc, sl st in next sc, sk next 2 sc, sl st in next sc, sc in next sc, in next sc work (hdc, dc, hdc); sc in last sc.

Fasten off and weave in ends.

FINISHING
Step 1: Referring to photo for placement and with tapestry needle and C, sew Tummy to Body.

Step 2: With tapestry needle and D and E and using straight st, st eyes.

Step 3: Tack Arms to sides of Body.

Step 4: Stuff Foot and Leg pieces with fiberfill. Sew Legs to Body. Tack top of Foot to front of Leg to form ankle. Rep on other Leg.

Step 5: Referring to photo for placement, sew Toe Pads and Heel Pads to bottoms of Feet.

Step 6: With tapestry needle and A, st through Hand and tie to secure to create finger. Rep once more on same Hand to create next finger. Rep on other Hand.

Step 7: With tapestry needle and A, st through Foot between Toe Pads and tie to secure to create toe. Rep once more on same Foot. Rep on other Foot.

Step 8: Sew 1 of each color Ear tog. Rep with 2nd set of Ears. Sew Ears to top of Head.

Step 9: Referring to photo for placement, st single st using E across bottom of Muzzle, and with B and F, st mouth. St Lip around mouth. With A, tack bottom of chin to top of neck to make head lean forward.

Step 10: Stuff Tail with fiberfill and sew to back of Body so that it does not interfere with sitting. 🌿

Floral Apron

DESIGN BY NAZANIN FARD

SKILL LEVEL
INTERMEDIATE

FINISHED SIZE
One size fits most

MATERIALS
J. & P. Coats Royale Fashion
Crochet size 3 crochet cotton
(150 yds per ball):
5 balls #775 warm rose
Size E/4/3.5mm crochet hook or
size needed to obtain gauge
Tapestry needle

GAUGE
22 dc = 4 inches

SPECIAL STITCHES
Beginning cluster (beg cl): Ch
3, keeping last lp of each dc on
hook, 3 dc in st indicated; yo and
draw through all 4 lps on hook.

Cluster (cl): Keeping last lp of
each dc on hook, 4 dc in st indicated; yo and draw through all 5
lps on hook.

Instructions

WAISTBAND
Row 1 (RS): Ch 327; dc in 3rd ch
from hook *(beg 3 sk chs count as
a dc)* and in each rem ch, turn.
(325 dc)

Row 2: Ch 3 *(counts as a dc on
this and following rows)*, dc in
each rem dc and in 3rd ch of beg
3 sk chs, turn.

Row 3: Ch 3, dc in each rem dc
and in 3rd ch of turning ch-3, turn.

Row 4: Ch 3, dc in each rem dc
and in 3rd ch of turning ch-3.
Fasten off.

BIB
First Motif
Rnd 1 (RS): Ch 8, join to form a
ring; ch 1, 16 sc in ring; join with
a sl st in first sc.

Rnd 2: Beg cl *(see Special
Stitches)* in same sc; sk next sc,
ch 3, sk first 139 dc from edge
of waistband, sl st in next dc; ch
3, on motif, sk next sc, **cl** *(see
Special Stitches)* in next sc; ch
2; on band, sl st in 4th dc from
previous sl st, ch 2; on motif,
sk next sc, cl in next sc; ch 3;
on band, sl st in 4th dc from
previous sl st, ch 3; on motif, cl in
next sc; [ch 5, cl in next sc; ch 7,
cl in next sc] twice; ch 5; join in
3rd ch of beg ch-3. Fasten off.

2nd Motif
Rnd 1 (RS): Rep rnd 1 of First
Motif.

Rnd 2: Beg cl in same sc; ch 3;
sl st in corresponding ch-7 sp on
First Motif, ch 3, on working Motif,
sk next sc, cl in next sc; ch 2, sl
st in next ch-5 sp on First Motif,
ch 2, on working Motif, sk next
sc, cl in next sc; ch 3, sl st same
dc on band as last sl st of First
Motif worked, ch 3, on working
Motif, sk next sc, cl in next sc;
ch 2, sl st in 4th dc on band from
last sl st, ch 2, on working Motif,
sk next sc, cl in next sc; ch 3,
on band, sl st in 4th dc from last
sl st, ch 3, on working Motif, sk
next sc, cl in next sc; [ch 5, cl in
next sc; ch 7, cl in next sc] twice;
ch 5; join in 3rd ch of beg ch-3.
Fasten off.

Remaining Motifs
Referrring to diagram for number
and placement, work rem Motifs

in same manner, working joinings
as necessary. Work same as rnd
1 of the First Motif.

SKIRT
Referring to diagram for number
and placement, work Motifs for
Skirt in same manner as for Bib,
skipping first 122 dc on other
side of Waistband for joining of
First Motif.

NECK BAND
Hold piece with RS facing you
and Bib at top; join in 4th ch of
ch-7 sp on upper right-hand
corner of Bib.

Row 1 (RS): Ch 3, sl st in 3rd ch
of next ch-5-sp, ch 3, sl st in 4th
ch of next ch-7-sp, turn.

Row 2: Ch 3 *(count as dc on this
and following row)*, 4 dc in each
of next 2 ch-5 sps; dc in first ch
of beg ch-3, turn.

Row 3: Ch 3, dc in each rem dc
and in 3rd ch of turning ch-3, turn.

Rows 4–46: Rep row 3.

Row 47: Ch 3, sl st in 4th ch of
first ch-7-sp on Motif on opposite
end of Bib, dc in next 4 dc, sl st
in 3rd ch of next ch-5-sp on Motif,
dc next 4 dc, sl st in 4th ch of
next ch-7-sp.

Fasten off and weave in ends.

EDGING
Join in edge dc on inside edge of
first row of Neck Band; ch 1, 2 sc
in same dc and in each rem edge
dc around Neck Band; on Bib, 3
sc in each ch sp to first sc; join in
first sc.

CONTINUED ON PAGE 156

Present a Petite Purse

DESIGN BY NAZANIN FARD

SKILL LEVEL ●□□□
BEGINNER

FINISHED SIZE
7 x 5½ inches

MATERIALS
Caron Glimmer super bulky
   (super chunky) weight yarn
   (1¾ oz/49 yds/50g per ball):
      1 ball #0007 mango
Size K/10½/6.5mm crochet hook
   or size needed to obtain gauge
Decorative button
Tapestry needle
Stitch marker
Prym-Dritz Bag Boutique,
   U-shaped purse handles
7 x 11-inch piece of plastic
   canvas
8 x 12-inch piece of lining fabric
Sewing needle and matching
   thread

GAUGE
12 sc = 4 inches

Instructions

BACK
Row 1 (RS): Ch 22; sc in 2nd ch from hook and in each rem ch, turn.

Row 2: Ch 1, sc in each sc, turn.

Rows 3–38: Rep row 2.

Row 39: Ch 1, sc in next 10 sc, ch 10, sc in next 10 sc.

Fasten off and weave in ends.

FRONT
Rows 1–38: Rep rows 1–38 of Back.

Row 39: Ch 1, sc in each sc.

Fasten off and weave in ends.

SIDE PANEL
Make 2.
Row 1: Ch 5; sc in 2nd ch from hook and in each rem ch, turn.

Row 2: Ch 1, sc in each sc, turn.

Rows 3–10: Rep row 2.

Fasten off and weave in ends.

FINISHING
Step 1: Hold Front and Back with RS tog. With tapestry needle, sew bottom seam.

Step 2: Place plastic canvas piece against WS of pieces. With sewing needle and thread, sew lining fabric to WS of pieces, covering plastic canvas.

Step 3: Sew side panels to Front and Back, leaving 1-inch unsewn on top edges.

Step 4: Referring to photo for placement and with tapestry needle and yarn, sew handles in place.

Step 5: With sewing needle and thread, sew button to Front opposite button lp. ❈

Golden Holiday Jacket CONTINUED FROM PAGE 106

sts; *working over next ch-3 sp, sc in ch-3 on 2nd row below, ch 2, sk next 2 sts, sc in next st, [sc dec] twice; in each of next 9 sts work (dc, ch 1); dc in next st, [sc dec] twice; sc in next st, ch 2, sk next 2 sts; rep from * 5 times; working over next ch-3 sp, sc in ch-3 on 2nd row below, ch 2, sk next 2 sts, [sc dec]

twice; sc in next st, in each of next 9 sts work (dc, ch 1); dc in next st, [sc dec] twice; sc in last st, turn.

Row 5: Ch 1, sc in first 4 sts, [dc in next st, ch 1] 4 times; dc in next st; *in next ch-1 sp work (2 dc, ch 3, sc in 3rd ch from hook, 2 dc); [dc in next st, ch

1] 4 times; dc in next st, sc in next 4 sc, sl st in next sc, [dc in next st, ch 1] 4 times; dc in next st, in next ch-1 sp work (2 dc, ch 3, sc in 3rd ch from hook, 2 dc); [dc in next st, ch 1] 4 times; dc in next st, sc in last 4 sts.

Fasten off and weave in ends. 🍂

Floral Apron CONTINUED FROM PAGE 153

Fasten off and weave in ends.

BORDER
Hold piece with RS facing you; join in top corner of left-hand side of Waistband; ch 1, sc in each dc to Bib; working up side of Bib, 4 sc in each ch sp to Neck Band; working around Neck Band, 2 sc

in each edge st; working down side of Bib, 4 sc in each ch sp; sc in each dc of Waistband; 2 sc in end of each row of Waistband; sc in each unused lp beg ch of Waistband; working down side of Skirt, 4 sc in each ch sp to ch-7 sp in next corner; 9 sc in ch-7-sp; working across bottom of Skirt, 4

sc in each ch sp to next corner ch-7 sp; 9 sc in ch-7 sp; working up side of Skirt, 4 sc in each ch sp; working in unused lps of beg ch of Waistband, sc in each lp; 2 sc in end of each row of Waistband; join in first sc.

Fasten off and weave in ends. 🍂

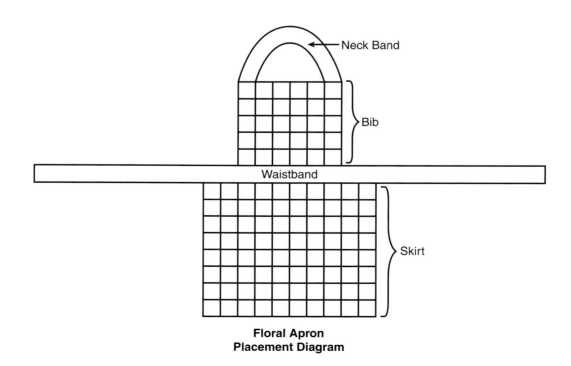

**Floral Apron
Placement Diagram**

Abbreviations & Symbols

beg...beg/beginning
bpdc..back post double crochet
bpsc..back post single crochet
bptr .... back post treble crochet
CC ....contrasting color
ch.. chain stitch
ch-..refers to chain or space previously made (i.e. ch-1 space)
ch sp .... chain space
cl(s)...cluster(s)
cm...centimeter(s)
dc...double crochet
dec............................... decrease/decreases/decreasing
dtr .... double treble crochet
fpdc..front post double crochet
fpsc...front post treble crochet
fptr...front post treble crochet
g..gram(s)
hdc.. half double crochet
inc .... increase/increases/increasing
lp(s)..loop(s)
MC ....main color
mm..millimeter(s)
oz...ounce(s)
pc...popcorn
rem ....remain/remaining
rep ....repeat(s)
rnd(s) ....round(s)
RS...right side
sc... single crochet
sk..skip(ped)

sl st ....slip stitch
sp(s)..space(s)
st(s)..stitch(es)
tog...together
tr ....treble crochet
trtr..triple treble crochet
WS.. wrong side
yd(s).. yard(s)
yo...yarn over

* **An asterisk** is used to mark the beginning of a portion of instructions to be worked more than once; thus, "rep from * twice" means after working the instructions once, repeat the instructions following the asterisk twice more (3 times in all).

[ ] **Brackets** are used to enclose instructions that are to be worked the number of times indicated after the brackets. For example, "[2 dc in next st, sk next st] 5 times" means to follow the instructions within the brackets a total of 5 times.

( ) **Parentheses** are used to enclose a group of stitches that are worked in one space or stitch. For example, "(2 dc, ch 2, 2 dc) in next st" means to work all the stitches within the parentheses in the next space or stitch. Parentheses are also used to enclose special instructions or stitch counts.

Standard Yarn Weight System

Categories of yarn, gauge ranges, and recommended needle and hook sizes

Yarn Weight Symbol & Category Names	1 SUPER FINE	2 FINE	3 LIGHT	4 MEDIUM	5 BULKY	6 SUPER BULKY
Type of Yarns in Category	Sock, Fingering, Baby	Sport, Baby	DK, Light Worsted	Worsted, Afghan, Aran	Chunky, Craft, Rug	Super Chunky, Roving
Crochet Gauge* Ranges in Single Crochet to 4 inch	21–32 sts	16–20 sts	12–17 sts	11–14 sts	8–11 sts	5–9 sts
Recommended Hook in Metric Size Range	2.25–3.5 mm	3.5–4.5 mm	4.5–5.5 mm	5.5–6.5 mm	6.5–9 mm	9 mm and larger
Recommended Hook U.S. Size Range	B-1–E-4	E-4–7	7–I-9	I-9–K-10½	K-10½–M-13	M-13 and larger

* GUIDELINES ONLY: The above reflect the most commonly used gauges and hook sizes for specific yarn categories.

Skill Levels

BEGINNER
Beginner projects for first-time crocheters using basic stitches. Minimal shaping.

EASY
Easy projects using basic stitches, repetitive stitch patterns, simple color changes and simple shaping and finishing.

INTERMEDIATE
Intermediate projects with a variety of stitches, mid-level shaping and finishing.

EXPERIENCED
Experienced projects using advanced techniques and stitches, detailed shaping and refined finishing.

Stitch Guide

CROCHET HOOKS			
Metric	**US**	**Metric**	**US**
.60mm	14	3.00mm	D/3
.75mm	12	3.50mm	E/4
1.00mm	10	4.00mm	F/5
1.50mm	6	4.50mm	G/6
1.75mm	5	5.00mm	H/8
2.00mm	B/1	5.50mm	I/9
2.50mm	C/2	6.00mm	J/10

Chain—ch: Yo, pull through lp on hook.

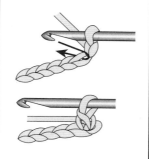

Slip stitch—sl st: Insert hook in st, yo, pull through both lps on hook.

Front loop—front lp
Back loop—back lp

Front Loop   Back Loop

Single crochet—sc: Insert hook in st, yo, pull through st, yo, pull through both lps on hook.

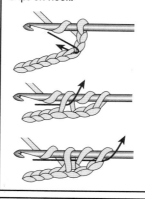

Reverse single crochet—reverse sc: Working from left to right, insert hook in next st, complete as sc.

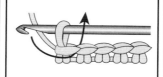

Front post stitch—fp: Back post stitch—bp: When working post st, insert hook from right to left around post st on previous row.

Back   Front

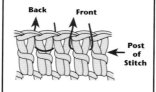

Post of Stitch

Half double crochet—hdc: Yo, insert hook in st, yo, pull through st, yo, pull through all 3 lps on hook.

Double crochet—dc: Yo, insert hook in st, yo, pull through st, [yo, pull through 2 lps] twice.

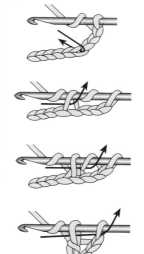

Change colors: Drop first color; with second color, pull through last 2 lps of st.

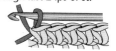

Treble crochet—tr: Yo twice, insert hook in st, yo, pull through st, [yo, pull through 2 lps] 3 times.

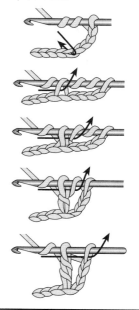

Double treble crochet—dtr: Yo 3 times, insert hook in st, yo, pull through st, [yo, pull through 2 lps] 4 times.

Single crochet decrease (sc dec): (Insert hook, yo, draw up a lp) in each of the sts indicated, yo, draw through all lps on hook.

Example of 2-sc dec

Half double crochet decrease (hdc dec): (Yo, insert hook, yo, draw lp through) in each of the sts indicated, yo, draw through all lps on hook.

Example of 2-hdc dec

Double crochet decrease (dc dec): (Yo, insert hook, yo, draw lp through, yo, draw through 2 lps on hook) in each of the sts indicated, yo, draw through all lps on hook.

Example of 2-dc dec

US		UK
sl st (slip stitch)	=	sc (single crochet)
sc (single crochet)	=	dc (double crochet)
hdc (half double crochet)	=	htr (half treble crochet)
dc (double crochet)	=	tr (treble crochet)
tr (treble crochet)	=	dtr (double treble crochet)
dtr (double treble crochet)	=	ttr (triple treble crochet)
skip	=	miss

Special Thanks

We would like to thank the talented crochet designers whose work is featured in this collection.

Cindy Adams
Festive Shell Bath Set, 95
Golden-Glow Throw, 88

Svetlana Avrakh
Blue Christmas Throw, 85
Easy Floral Gift Scarf, 130

Elaine Bartlett
Stocking Stuffer Scrubbie, 142

Donna Collinsworth
Colorful Garland, 17

Nazanin Fard
Bright & Easy Bolero, 99
Christmas Tree Greeting Card, 71
Floral Apron, 152
Golden Leaves Necklace, 147
Poinsettia Greeting Card, 71
Present a Petite Purse, 154
Snowflake Greeting Card, 71
Snowman Greeting Card, 71
Touch of Sparkle Necklace, 146

Mary Ann Frits
Christmas Wreath, 25

Ellen Gormley
Be Merry Bottle Cover, 77

Karen Hay
Christmas Tree Table Topper, 44

Tammy Hildebrand
Golden Holiday Jacket, 103

Jennine Korejko
Elf Shelf Sitter, 26
Gingerbread Man Shelf Sitter, 26
Perky Penguins, 7
Snowman Shelf Sitter, 26

Melody MacDuffee
Colorful Ornaments, 17
Floral Pendant Necklace, 144
Lacy Snowballs Table Set, 62
Stained Glass Flowers Afghan, 81

Donna May
Santa's Boy Tricolor Pullover, 125
Santa's Girl Floral Cardigan, 121

Joyce Nordstrom
Favorite Colors Gift Afghan, 92
Sending Warm Wishes Afghan, 91

Sue Penrod
Beads & Holly Beverage Tags, 60
Candy Candy Beverage Tags, 60
Christmas Ornament Trims, 14
Peppermint Candy Ornaments, 19
Peppermint Wreath Coaster &
   Napkin Ring, 55

Laura Polley
Holiday Stripe Jacket, 107
Holiday Walk Dog Coat, 112
Lustrous Centerpiece, 57
Lustrous Table Runner, 57

Delsie Rhoades
Elegant Edging, 67
Glistening Tassel Cover, 52
Holiday Party Trims, 68
Last-Minute Gift Trim, 79

Ruth Shepard
Gift of Time Necklace, 148
Snow Maiden Hat & Scarf, 132

Darla Sims
Plush Warmers
   for Mother & Child, 116

Kathleen Stuart
Keep Warm Teddy Set, 136
Light Bulb Hot Pads, 96
Santa Tree Skirt, 22
Snowball Hat & Scarf, 134
Snowman Trio, 47

Debbie Tabor
Sleepy Bear Huggins, 149
Whimsical Santa & Snowman
   Ornaments, 41

Kathy Wesley
Noel Stocking, 34
Snowman Stocking, 34